Translation and Literature

VOLUME 3

TRANSLATION AND LITERATURE

Translation and Literature is an annual serial published by Edinburgh University Press. It may be ordered through any bookshop or direct from the Press using the form included at the back of this volume.

Intending contributors should refer to the notes on the final page of this issue.

General Editor: Dr Stuart Gillespie, Department of English Literature, The University, Glasgow G12 8QQ, UK.

American Editor: Prof. Greg Clingham, Department of English, Bucknell University, Lewisburg, PA 17837, USA.

Review Editor: Mr R. M. Cummings, Department of English Literature, The University, Glasgow G12 8QQ, UK.

Translation and Literature

VOLUME 3

EDINBURGH UNIVERSITY PRESS

© Edinburgh University Press Ltd 1994
22 George Square, Edinburgh

Typeset in Linotron Ehrhardt
by Koinonia Ltd, Bury, and
printed and bound in Great Britain by
Hartnolls Ltd, Bodmin

A CIP record for this book is
available from the British Library

ISBN 0 7486 0426 X (limp)

The Editors and Publisher gratefully acknowledge
support from a British Academy Learned Journals
Award, 1993-4.

This journal is a member of the
Council of Editors of Learned Journals.

Contents

REVIEWS

Articles

Ovid, Golding, and The Tempest

Sarah Annes Brown[1]

Although the importance of Ovid for Shakespeare has always been recognized, attention has focused until recently on the influence of the *Metamorphoses* upon early works such as *Venus and Adonis*.[2] Within the last few years, however, the strong Ovidian presence in Shakespeare's Late Plays, in which overt allusions to Ovidian stories give way to a more subtle engagement with the *Metamorphoses*, has been increasingly acknowledged.[3] David Armitage suggests that by this point in Shakespeare's career, 'myth has become more integral to the poetic fabric of the plays, developing from decorative spangling in the early work to concealed fertile allusion'.[4] It may be, indeed, that our thinking needs to be done in a vocabulary quite different from the conventional lexis of 'allusions' and 'sources': Marion Trousdale has argued in a more general context that both classical and contemporary works

> served the Elizabethans less as source in our sense than as model in which pattern was both copied and concealed. It was not a case of the goods of one container being selectively put into a different container with a little extra added . . . Rather the sense of pattern suggests a tracing, or to use the word which Thomas Elyot uses when he defines *idea* in his *Dictionary* of 1538, a print.[5]

Certainly the use of the term 'Ovidian' to describe an English writer's work may imply many different things, not least because any meaning attached to such a vague (but useful) epithet is bound to shift in accordance with changing perceptions of Ovid's chief characteristics. *Venus and Adonis* may be described as 'Ovidian' by virtue of its mythological subject-matter, its interest in wordplay and paradox, and its preoccupation with sexuality, particularly non-standard sexuality. But the aspects of Ovid's work which are most relevant for *The Tempest* are his fondness for calling attention to the fictive nature of his writing; his manipulation of readers' expectations; the identifications he makes between himself and the 'creators' in the *Metamorphoses*, whether gods or artists; and the blurring

of boundaries between what is real and unreal, nature, art, or artifice.[6] It
is also significant that, in a more diffuse and less easily characterized way,
Ovid's attitude towards the characters depicted in the *Metamorphoses* is,
or appears to be, comparatively dispassionate and disengaged.

In studying the Shakespeare–Ovid relationship one is also dealing with
the phenomenon of literary translation in the strict sense of the term.
Although Shakespeare appears to have been familiar with at least some
parts of the *Metamorphoses* in the Latin, it can be assumed that his use of
Arthur Golding's translation of 1565–7 was a vital influence on his
reception of Ovid (I shall provide some of the supporting evidence on this
point for *The Tempest* shortly). One of Golding's modern admirers, Ezra
Pound, wondered in his 'Notes on Elizabethan Classicists':

> Can we, for our part, know our Ovid until we find him in Golding?
> Is there one of us so good at his Latin, and so ready in imagination that
> Golding will not throw upon his mind shades and glamours inherent
> in the original text which had for all that escaped him? Is any foreign
> speech ever our own, ever so full of beauty as our *lingua materna*
> (whatever *lingua materna* that may be)? Or is not a new beauty created,
> an old beauty doubled when the overcharge is well done?[7]

Golding's vigorous colloquial style, I propose, would have given Shakespeare a more direct and uncluttered vision of Ovid's world simply
because it would have been freed of all the hindrance and obfuscation
attendant upon reading any work not in one's native tongue.

$$* \quad * \quad *$$

The Tempest is in many respects a curious work. 'The play', writes
Raymond Powell, 'is an enigma, seeming both to contain Meaning, of a
kind conceivably more significant than that of Shakespeare's previous
plays, and yet refusing to disclose what that meaning is.'[8] Its action
progresses in a way that suggests it will culminate either in revenge or
forgiveness. The latter course is indicated by the apparent turning-point
when Ariel says that, were he human, he would feel pity for Prospero's
enemies, and Prospero replies:

> Hast thou, which art but air, a touch, a feeling
> Of their afflictions, and shall not myself,
> One of their kind, that relish all as sharply,
> Passion as they, be kindlier mov'd than thou art?
>   (V.i.21–4)[9]

Yet although Prospero forgives all his enemies, the only one to repent is Alonso, whose fault was perhaps the most venial. Sebastian and Antonio maintain a truculent silence, an absence of reaction rather than positive defiance, until the arrival of Stephano and Trinculo prompts them to make a few characteristically sarcastic quips. Whereas an Edmund or a Iachimo will end in fulsome repentance, the chief villains in this play, so often described in terms of its supposed engagement with ideas of reconciliation and forgiveness, remain defiant. Thus one may say that there is an immediate slippage in David Armitage's account of the play's Ovidian background when he writes:

> Ovid's outlook, as well as his subject matter, is metamorphic. He emphasizes regeneration and transfiguration; achieved possibility and relieved suffering; capricious gods and indistinct causality. Like Shakespeare in his late plays, Ovid goes beyond irredeemable tragedy to romance, which is always provisional in its catastrophes and promises reunion after division, life after death, and joy after disaster.[10]

Throughout *The Tempest*, a curious impression that something is escaping us is created, an elusive sense that what we are seeing or reading is taking place somehow outside the main action. The play raises expectations in its audience, based on previous experience of fiction and narrative, only to defeat them. For example, despite Prospero's approval of the love which develops between Ferdinand and Miranda, he decides to test the prince's worth by affecting anger. The audience might expect to witness a touching scene where Prospero reveals his motives for making Ferdinand carry logs and gives the couple his blessing. In fact, not for the only time in this play, we seem to arrive just too late. Prospero's words at the beginning of Act IV, 'If I have too austerely punish'd you, / Your compensation makes amends', would seem to be spoken immediately after this pleasant revelation. If we look at scenes II.i and III.iii, further evidence may be found to suggest that we are missing all the action, almost as if we were continually being shown the wrong part of the island. Alonso and Gonzalo have only just woken up at the end of II.i, yet when we next see them in III.iii they want to go to sleep again. Gonzalo's words 'here's a maze trod, indeed, / Through forth-rights and meanders!' (III.iii.2–3) seem an appropriate comment on the action of the play. Admittedly, both occasions when they sleep serve as opportunities for the murderous ambitions of Sebastian and Antonio; yet even they seem infected by a kind of *vis inertiae*. We might expect a playwright to manipulate his material in order to allow the hero to thwart the plans of the villains, but we do not expect the villains to create their own completely gratuitous delays if the hero – in this case Ariel – appears to be detained.

The desultory action of *The Tempest* lacks the sense of purpose and motivation which we expect from a narrative. As soon as Prospero has everyone in his power, he decides not to exact vengeance: his portentous machinations suddenly seem like the actions of a novice chess player who can devise an apparently subtle strategy which disintegrates after a few moves because he has failed to take into account either his opponent's response or long-term developments. His strategy, which has hitherto appeared so complicated, becomes useless, for Alonso resigns his right to tribute voluntarily, and Sebastian and Antonio remain unmoved. Under-lying all these other problems, as so many critical accounts of the play find, is the question of the nature and extent of Prospero's powers. At times he seems a beneficent, almost godlike figure, at others a cantankerous and forgetful old man; and, although more than natural forces seem to be at work in the play, it is not always clear whether they stem from Prospero, the island itself, or some mysterious external agency.

One passage which touches on some of these problems is the following speech, the most direct borrowing from Ovid in the play, and perhaps in Shakespeare's work as a whole. Although at first Prospero seems to be giving us a thorough account of his powers and their provenance, the internal contradictions within the speech, and the apparent disparities between its contents and the events in the play, raise rather than resolve questions.

> Ye elves of hills, brooks, standing lakes, and groves;
> And ye that on the sands with printless foot
> Do chase the ebbing Neptune, and do fly him
> When he comes back; you demi-puppets that
> By moonshine do the green sour ringlets make,
> Whereof the ewe not bites; and you whose pastime
> Is to make midnight mushrooms, that rejoice
> To hear the solemn curfew; by whose aid –
> Weak masters though ye be – I have bedimm'd
> The noontide sun, call'd forth the mutinous winds,
> And 'twixt the green sea and the azur'd vault
> Set roaring war. To the dread rattling thunder
> Have I given fire, and rifted Jove's stout oak
> With his own bolt; the strong-bas'd promontory
> Have I made shake, and by the spurs pluck'd up
> The pine and cedar; graves at my command

Have wak'd their sleepers, op'd, and let 'em forth,
By my so potent art. But this rough magic
I here abjure; and, when I have requir'd
Some heavenly music – which even now I do –
To work mine end upon their senses that
This airy charm is for, I'll break my staff,
Bury it certain fadoms in the earth,
And deeper than did ever plummet sound
I'll drown my book.

(V.i.33–57)

The following passage from the *Metamorphoses*, given in Golding's translation as well as the original Latin Shakespeare is thought to have used, has long been recognized as the source of Prospero's invocation:

auraeque et venti montesque amnesque lacusque,
dique omnes nemorum, dique omnes noctis adeste,
quorum ope, cum volui, ripis mirantibus amnes
in fontes rediere suos, concussaque sisto,
stantia concutio cantu freta, nubila pello
nubilaque induco, ventos abigoque vocoque,
vipereas rumpo verbis et carmine fauces,
vivaque saxa sua convulsaque robora terra
et silvas moveo iubeoque tremescere montis
et mugire solum manesque exire sepulcris!
te quoque, Luna, traho, quamvis Temesaea labores
aera tuos minuant; currus quoque carmine nostro
pallet avi, pallet nostris Aurora venenis!

(VII, 197–209)[11]

Ye Ayres and windes: ye Elves of Hilles, of Brookes, of Woods alone,
Of standing Lakes, and of the Night approche ye everychone.
Through helpe of whom (the crooked bankes much wondring at the thing)
I have compelled streames to run cleane backward to their spring.
By charmes I make the calme Seas rough, and make ye rough Seas plaine
And cover all the Skie with Cloudes, and chase them thence againe.
By charmes I rayse and lay the windes, and burst the Vipers jaw,
And from the bowels of the Earth both stones and trees doe drawe.
Whole woods and Forestes I remove: I make the Mountaines shake,
And even the Earth it selfe to grone and fearfully to quake.
I call up dead men from their graves: and thee O lightsome Moone

I darken oft, though beaten brasse abate thy perill soone
Our Sorcerie dimmes the Morning faire, and darkes ye Sun at Noone.

(VII, 265–77)[12]

The speech comes from Book VII of the *Metamorphoses*, and is spoken by Medea, the Colchian witch who helped Jason steal the Golden Fleece from her father. After they are married, Jason begs Medea to prolong the life of his own father, Aeson. The invocation which is drawn on so heavily by Shakespeare is spoken just before she cuts up Aeson and places him in a cauldron full of magic potion from which he emerges as a youth. This feat enables her to trick the daughters of Jason's enemy Pelias into cutting their father's throat in the hope that the same miracle will be performed on him. This time the potion is neutral, and Pelias remains dead.

Because Prospero's speech is familiar in its own right, it is easy to overlook its curious qualities (exactly what is he claiming he can do? Do his claims conform with the actions which we have already seen him perform?), and because it is also familiar as a supreme example of Shakespeare's use of Ovid, it is not always remembered how strange it is that Shakespeare should lift a speech almost verbatim from so apparently inappropriate a context. Although Leonard Barkan, in his study of Ovid's Renaissance *Nachleben*, acknowledges the change of context, he does not see this anomaly as in any way problematic:[13]

> So Prospero enters upon his final celebration of magic, a retrospective upon all the metamorphoses of art and life: protean powers, the changes of nature, miraculous transformations, and by extension the arts of the theater. It is also the closest Shakespeare ever comes to an extended quotation from Ovid . . . As so often, Shakespeare plays with reversal: Prospero is a white magician and not an evil sorcerer like Medea; he is a father renewing the lives of his children rather than a child rejuvenating the father.[13]

But the importance of Medea's speech as a gauge of Shakespeare's debt to Ovid need not be limited to the fact that it is such a close imitation of a passage of his *Metamorphoses*. The Martindales' analysis seems unnecessarily reductive:

> In this instance it should be plain that the use Shakespeare is making of Ovid is imitative, not allusive; educated members of the audience would recognise the presence of Ovid, but there is no question of any such complex interplay between the divergent meanings of the

two texts as our more ingenious critics so often suppose. Our concern should rather be with style, where a comparison can highlight what is distinctive in Prospero's speech.[14]

One may begin to assess the nature of the 'interplay' between the two texts by noting that Shakespeare has retained Golding's 'elves' as a translation of Ovid's *di* (VII, 198; the very inaccuracy of the translation makes it unlikely that he would have chosen this particular word independently of Golding). The diminution in solemnity which this choice of word had already brought about in Golding's translation is compounded by Shakespeare. Golding, like Ovid, begins the invocation with an appeal to the power of the elements before introducing the more bathetic reference to mere elves, 'Ye Ayres and windes: ye Elves of Hilles, of Brookes, of Woods alone'. Prospero never simply addresses the elements, only the elves, and omits all mention of the winds, only retaining those natural features of landscape traditionally associated with minor English rural deities: 'Ye elves of hills, brooks, standing lakes, and groves'. The 'di . . . noctis' which Golding translates as 'Elves . . . of the Night' have disappeared from Shakespeare's speech. The slight diminution of Medea's sonorous dignity continues in Shakespeare's adaptation of Ovid's evocation of to-and-fro movement. In the *Metamorphoses*, Medea is enabled, through the intervention of the gods, to bring about violently unnatural and contradictory movements in the seas and clouds. Prospero's diminished deities are also associated with a change of direction in the movement of the sea. But here it is no more than the natural ebb and flow of the tides, and, far from causing this motion, the 'demi-puppets' frolic on the beaches in a way that suggests complete ignorance of the reason for the phenomenon. They run 'on the sands with printless foot', which evokes their ethereal qualities, but also implies that they do not even make as much impression on their environment as a human being – and neither do they seem inclined to affect it in any supernatural way. The activities with which the elves are associated are within the province of traditional English fairies, making magic rings and mushrooms. But these are natural phenomena, not the violent alterations of nature which Medea claims to have the power to carry out. The beginning of this speech, then, perhaps sounds more impressive than its content warrants. The sonorous invocation, with its portentous repetition of 'ye', the stately metonymy of 'Neptune', and the ponderous word-order of 'whereof the ewe not bites', might be considered inappropriate in the light of the actual triviality of the phenomena Prospero is describing and the elves' apparent lack of power over their surroundings.

This preponderance of effect over content might be said to characterize *The Tempest* as a whole, as one can begin to show from the remainder of Prospero's speech. He goes on to mention two actions which he claims to have carried out with the help of the 'weak masters' and which at first appear impressive: he has caused the tempest and raised people from the dead. The second assertion would seem to be the more problematic of the two – we have after all 'seen' the tempest occur at the opening of the play, whereas not only have we not seen anyone rise from the dead, but the very act seems inappropriately sinister and necromantic. Similar references to ghosts rising from their graves in *Julius Caesar* and *Hamlet* are described as terrifying portents. But, within the context of *The Tempest*, some of Medea's claims, in the mouth of Prospero, seem to have as much to do with the artistry of the playwright Shakespeare as with Prospero's magic powers. (This suggestion of self-reference is in itself very Ovidian – the *Metamorphoses* is a supremely self-conscious work – and I shall return to this area in what follows.) As for the tempest, Prospero evokes it in this speech in far more literary terms than either Golding or Ovid – he has, he says, "twixt the green sea and the azur'd vault / Set roaring war'.

An analogue for the artifice which characterizes the presentation of this tempest may be found in the story of Ceyx and Alcyone from Book XI of the *Metamorphoses*.[15] When King Ceyx is forced to make a sea voyage, his wife Alcyone, worried by the dangers, is only placated when he promises faithfully to return to her. He is drowned in a tempest, and the goddess Juno, tired of the futile prayers for his safety made by Alcyone, sends Iris to Somnus, god of sleep, to order him to send a spirit in the shape of Ceyx to Alcyone telling her of his death.[16] When this has been done, Alcyone wanders in grief to the spot where her husband took leave of her and sees his corpse floating on the water. She jumps into the sea, but both she and Ceyx are turned into halcyons, birds associated with calm weather. Alycone is the daughter of Aeolus, god of the winds, and after the metamorphosis he ensures that the waters remain calm while the halcyons are nesting.

Prospero, because of his apparent control over the tempest, resembles Aeolus, and seems rather more in control than Alcyone's father, who was apparently unable to save his son-in-law. Prospero's authority, however, both actual and moral, becomes more open to question as the events of the play unfold. If Miranda is like Alcyone, it is not as the mature queen grieving for her husband, but as the wide-eyed child marvelling at her father's powers. Alcyone recalls this earlier self when warning Ceyx of the dangers of the sea, and the recollection is rendered very vividly by Golding: 'right well I know theyr powre, / And saw them oft a little wench within my father's bowre' (Golding, XI, 502–3). Miranda shares Alcyone's fear:

> If by your Art, my dearest father, you have
> Put the wild waters in this roar, allay them.
>
> (I.ii.1–2)

> aequora me terrent et ponti tristis imago:
> et laceras nuper tabulas in litore vidi
> et saepe in tumulis sine corpore nomina legi.
>
> (XI, 427–9)

Imago is a favourite word of Ovid's; he frequently uses it to connect natural phenomena, and particularly the objects which result from metamorphoses, with works of art.[17] The phrase *ponti tristis imago* might be accurately translated 'the stern visage of the deep', as it is in the Loeb edition, or else as 'the sad image/picture of the deep'. Its use in this passage distances Alcyone (and the reader) from the terrors of the sea. The idea of reading, as applied to the funeral monuments 'sine corpore', is perhaps extended back to the previous line as well, bringing out the alternative meaning of the word *tabula* which can mean a writing tablet as well as a plank, and possibly even suggesting such literary near-homophones of 'litore' as 'littera'.[18] If the reader is led to think of this meaning of *tabulas*, then he may also abstract the word 'ceras' from 'laceras', because wax was the standard material for writing tablets. Under the dictionary entry for *cera*, we find Livy's phrase 'ex illis tabulis cerave recitata', which demonstrates that the two words would often be found together.[19] Placing the dangers of the sea within the context of a literary composition is perfectly apposite, as the long description of the storm is such an obvious set piece, begging comparison with similar passages in Virgil.[20] Again, Alcyone's exclamation later in the tale, when she has seen the image of her dead husband, 'tamen iunget nos littera' (XI, 706), once more suggests that Ovid is reminding us that we are reading a literary fiction (the Loeb translation, 'at least the lettered stone shall join us', narrows the possible interpretations). In the immediate context, Alcyone is referring to an inscription on a memorial tablet, but she also seems to be anticipating the way her name will be joined with Ceyx in literature, including of course the *Metamorphoses* itself.

Miranda's use of the word 'Art' is perfectly appropriate simply as a synonym for magic, and on one level this is clearly what it is. But if we follow the lead given by the hint of artifice attached to Alcyone's evocation of storms, then the implications of the word 'art' may be extended. Despite its vivid presentation in the first scene, the tempest takes on an air of unreality after it has died away. No one has been harmed and there is not even any damage to the sailors' clothes. The violent effects of the storms

which Prospero claims to have raised in his rendition of the Medea speech
are by no means in evidence. The storm in Ovid is comparable to a work
of art only because of the literary ingenuity with which he describes it:
its results could not be more devastatingly destructive. Shakespeare's
tempest, on the other hand, is evoked with vivid simplicity, and the idea
of its connection with artifice only emerges after it is over. In *The Tempest*
the link is made more unforcedly than it is in Ovid, because Prospero's
storm does no harm. This is not the case in the *Metamorphoses*, where, as
so often in Ovid, violence is treated with an aesthetic detachment which
is sometimes disconcerting, and gravity mingles with wit.[21] The account
of the drowning Ceyx repeating his wife's name over and over again is
touching, yet there is a certain amount of hyperbole in Ovid's assertion
that he carries on naming her even when the waves have closed over his
lips. This slight lack of decorum comes over strongly in Dryden's lively
translation:

> dum natat, absentem, quotiens sinit hiscere fluctus,
> nominat Alcyonen ipsisque inmurmurat undis.
>
> (IV, 566–7)

> As oft as he can catch a gulp of Air,
> And peep above the Seas, he names the Fair,
> And, ev'n when plung'd beneath, on her he raves,
> Murmuring Alcyone below the Waves.[22]

The words with which Prospero describes the storm also shift it beyond
the realms of concrete reality into the province of illusion:

> The direful spectacle of the wreck, which touch'd
> The very virtue of compassion in thee,
> I have with such provision in mine art
> So safely ordered, that there is no soul –
> No, not so much perdition as an hair
> Betid to any creature in the vessel
> Which thou heard'st cry, which thou saw'st sink.
>
> (I.ii.26–32)

The word 'spectacle' suggests that the storm was only a chimera, a pageant
with no substance, and indeed has connotations of dramatic representa-
tions which become problematic in the context of a play and recall the
connections that have been made between Prospero and Shakespeare
himself. A spectator might initially be surprised to learn that the storm

was not a reality, only to reflect that the special effects which made it seem real were themselves an illusion which had never really deceived him. Artificial rolls of thunder, for example, could be perceived, not as the stage manager's attempt to convince an audience that the storm is real, but as Prospero using his magic to persuade Miranda of the same thing. By emphasizing Miranda's cognizance of the storm through her faculties of sight and hearing, Prospero seems to be suggesting that this is the only sense in which the storm was a reality and that it had no existence outside Miranda's (and implicitly the audience's) perceptions.

Whereas Ovid is in the position of narrator and can remind the reader that he is reading fiction, no single person or scene in *The Tempest* has this kind of authority.[23] Thus our perception of the storm in the very first scene of the play, and the subsequent events which give an impression of its unreality, undercut each other in a shifting interplay resulting in no definitive version of events. Whereas in the *Metamorphoses* Ovid continually contrives to remind the reader wittily that there is no 'true' version of events because the poem is no more than a literary construct, Shakespeare makes his audience unclear what version to believe. The characters themselves are undecided about the nature of their situation and disagree as to whether the island is bleak or fertile, and, most significantly in the context of a storm whose reality is questioned, whether their clothes are wet or dry. And these ambiguities may be seen as part of the 'metatheatrical' dimension of this part of the play. Deaths by drowning are in literature the usual result of a storm at sea. In *The Tempest*, such deaths are not simply omitted: strong suggestions are given that people may have died which are then reassuringly contradicted. In this sense only can people be said to have been raised from the dead in this drama. Prospero's claim to have raised the dead, at first so portentous and alarming, may, like his claim to have raised a storm, be reduced to a matter of audience manipulation.

Against all this it might be argued that Shakespeare, in view of his close adherence to the *Metamorphoses*, may have been led by his relish of Golding to allow the one discordant element in Medea's speech, the only feat that Prospero, as a white magician rather than a necromancer, presumably could not perform, to be slipped in amongst all the others. (Admittedly, it is difficult to establish exactly where the parameters of either Prospero's powers or 'goodness' are situated.) But Shakespeare was not copying Golding blindly. We have already seen that he omitted the reference to 'Elves of Night', and Medea's sinister claim that she has brought the moon down from the sky is also elided. Again, critical emphasis on the theme of rebirth and renewal in the Romances might incline the reader to interpret Prospero's words metaphorically and infer that spiritual rather than physical renewal is the miracle Prospero has carried out. This would have the effect of making Shakespeare's choice of Medea's speech seem the outcome of more than the verbal and atmospheric felicities of this passage, since Medea's invocation is a prelude to her rejuvenation of Aeson – a spectacular display of the very magic powers which Prospero vows to abjure at the end of his version of the speech. Despite the apparent unsuitability of the context of Shakespeare's Ovidian source, the critic eager to emphasize the supposed reconciliation at the end of the play might plead that, because the element of miraculous physical resurrection in Medea's story is so happily consistent with the spiritual regeneration with which *The Tempest* concludes, Medea's speech becomes far from incongruous. But if Shakespeare did indeed have the context of Medea's speech in mind, and was not merely appropriating a dramatic set piece, it is unlikely that he would have overlooked so completely the narrative sequel, the murder of Jason's new wife and children, only fleetingly mentioned by Ovid but nevertheless notorious.[24]

I would therefore suggest a somewhat different reading, offering the possibility that Prospero's 'false' (but according to the argument outlined above, metaphorically 'true') claim to have raised the dead to life is not so different from his 'true' claim to have raised a tempest. The physical reality of the one and the spiritual reality of the other may be equally illusory. Prospero cites his 'so potent Art' as having enabled him to perform the feat of raising the dead to life, and, although 'magic' would seem to be the understood qualifier of 'art', certain elements in *The Tempest* suggest that the only way the dead are raised to life is by literary art. At the beginning of the play, Prospero's 'art' is cited as the cause of the tempest, and, as is appropriate considering the popular identification between Prospero the magician and Shakespeare the playwright, seems to have as much to do with literary technique as with magic. Prospero might also be termed a stage manager because when he describes his ability to summon up music he includes a little interjection which makes him appear to be giving his tardy technicians a cue: 'and, when I have requir'd / Some heavenly music – which even now I do – / To work mine end upon their senses' (V.i.51–3). Prospero's claim to have raised the dead to life may thus be accorded the same status as his claim to have raised a tempest. Once again, the play at first gives the impression that deaths have taken place, an impression eventually contradicted. There is a subtle distinction between Prospero's claim and that of Ovid's (and Golding's) Medea. Medea does not claim that she can raise the dead to life, but only 'manes . . . exire sepulcris' (VII, 206; 'call up dead men from their graves'). By using the metaphor of waking sleepers, Prospero both suggests that he is restoring the dead to their original state, i.e. life, and, even though the

metaphor of sleep for death is well-worn, hints that the dead were not
really dead.

An evocation of a death which does not happen is contained in Ariel's
song in which he seems to be telling Ferdinand that his father has
drowned. Although Prospero has already assured Miranda that the storm
has harmed no-one, Ferdinand does not know this and responds to the
song by saying 'This ditty does remember my drown'd father' (I.ii.405).
It is not simply death that Ariel suggests Alonso has undergone, but
metamorphosis:

> Full fadom five thy father lies;
>   Of his bones are coral made;
> Those are pearls that were his eyes;
>   Nothing of him that doth fade
> But doth suffer a sea-change
> Into something rich and strange.
> Sea-nymphs hourly ring his knell:
>   (I.ii.396–402)

Any perceived contradiction in Prospero's 'demi-puppets' helping him
raise people from the dead is explained if we accept that this apparent
necromancy consists of no more than the conjunction of a haunting song,
an impressionable young man, and an audience which is open to
suggestion.

The song illustrates one common strand in Ovidian metamorphosis.
Those who undergo transformation frequently retain many of their
features after they have been metamorphosed, but these are modified to
conform with their new identity. An obvious example is the metamorphosis of Daphne into a laurel:

> mollia cinguntur tenui praecordia libro,
> in frondem crines, in ramos bracchia crescunt,
> pes modo tam velox pigris radicibus haeret,
> ora cacumen habet: remanet nitor unus in illa.
>   (I, 549–52)

And therwithall about hir breast did grow a tender barke.
Hir haire was turned into leaves, hir armes in boughes did growe,
Hir feete that were ere while so swift, now rooted were as slowe.
Hir crowne became the toppe, and thus of that she earst had beene,
Remayned nothing in the worlde, but beautie fresh and greene.
                            (I, 672–6)

But the two passages create quite different effects. Daphne's changes are presented as part of a consistent process, signalled in particular by the symmetry of Ovid's line 550. This ordered clarity does not distinguish Ariel's song, the dreamy imprecision of which leads to copulative indeterminacy. Shakespeare's lines 397–8 illustrate the divergence of his methods from Ovid's. The line 'Of his bones are coral made' is syntactically elusive; we are not sure whether Ariel is describing a completed or an ongoing process. In the next line, in comparison to the symmetry of line 550 of the Daphne passage, the order of the transformed feature and the thing it has become is reversed, and whereas 397 suggests the metamorphic process is ongoing, the transformation of the eyes into pearls is mysterious and absolute. The overall impression is one of disintegration rather than the strange logical integrity of Daphne's metamorphosis.

One specific incident in the *Metamorphoses* which this song brings to mind is the transformation of seaweed into coral, caused by the petrifying powers of Medusa's head:

> for both the leafe and bough
> Full straungely at the touch thereof became both hard and tough.
> The Seanymphes tride this wondrous fact in divers other roddes
> And were full glad to see the chaunge, bicause there was no oddes
> Of leaves or twigs or of the seedes new shaken from the coddes.
>
> (IV, 913–17)

The words 'chaunge', 'straungely', and 'Seanymphes', and the detached Ariel-like curiosity of these nereids, might even suggest that Shakespeare had this passage in mind. The primary meaning of the Latin word *medulla*, which Ovid uses to describe the pith of the twigs, is 'bone marrow'. The image of water as a transforming medium, which comes over so mysteriously in *The Tempest*, is also apparent in Ovid's conclusion to this episode, although it is characterized by the matter-of-fact empiricism of natural history rather than wonder:

> For still like nature ever since is in our Corall founde:
> That looke how soone it toucheth Ayre it waxeth hard and sounde,
> And that which under water was a sticke, above is stone.
>
> (IV, 918–20)

A more general analogue to the idea of human bodies becoming like precious substances when they make contact with water is the description of Hermaphroditus as he swims in Salmacis' pool, which

Shakespeare borrowed for *Venus and Adonis*. Ovid straightforwardly describes the way people's appearance changes when seen under water, and no attempt is made to suggest that an actual metamorphosis is taking place even though the pool is about to acquire metamorphic properties: 'As if a man an Ivorie Image or a Lillie white / Should overlay or close with glasse that were most pure and bright' (Golding, IV, 438-9).[25] Ariel's song, on the other hand, appears to assert that Alonso has been metamorphosed by the sea.

The song may be described as Ovidian for more than one reason. The most obvious is the use of metamorphic imagery. But the generation of uncertainty surrounding an assertion is also typical of Ovid, as two similar incidents in the *Metamorphoses* illustrate. Ovid suggests that Ceyx may have lifted his head from the water to meet Alcyone's kiss: 'Folk dowt if Ceyx feeling it too rayse his head did strayne / Or whither that the waves did lift it up' (XI, 851-2). Ovid similarly implies that another apparently drowned man, Orpheus, may still be alive 'as his head floats along the Hebrus and 'his livelesse toong did make / A certeine lamentable noyse as though it still yit spake' (XI, 55-6). Although we rationally know that Alonso is still alive, it is impossible to forget Ariel's strange evocation of his metamorphic decay, just as, at the end of *The Winter's Tale*, it is the arresting image of a statue apparently coming to life, rather than Paulina's rational explanation for this marvel, which has most impact upon a spectator's imagination.

Even though we know that Alonso is safe, the song is still a powerful evocation of the strangeness of the isle, and it is rendered more unsettling by the fact that we have only *heard* of Alonso's safety from Prospero – we do not actually see him again until Act II. The association of Alonso with metamorphosis might be taken as a portent of the regenerative moral change he apparently undergoes. Yet it is eloquent of the haphazard presence of such regeneration in this play that Alonso's metamorphosis is presented as the result neither of Prospero's grace, nor his own will, but simply of the disinterested forces of a morally neutral environment.

Even the cynical Antonio speaks in a way which suggests he has some feeling for the miraculous nature of their escape. But rather than suggesting a spiritual dimension to his experience, the passivity of his involvement is emphasized. The continued laconic truculence of Antonio and Sebastian, even at the very end of the play, contributes to the difficulties in interpreting this play as a simple drama of forgiveness. Antonio also uses the language of the theatre, and this, like the way Prospero's art is described, adds to the effect of Ovidian unreality, comparable to that evoked by Alcyone's description of the storm:

> she that from whom
> We all were sea-swallow'd, though some cast again,
> And by that destiny, to perform an act
> Whereof what's past is prologue, what to come
> In yours and my discharge.
>
> (II.i.241–5)

Ariel echoes Antonio's words when he appears to them 'like a harpy':

> You are three men of sin, whom Destiny,
> That hath to instrument this lower world
> And what is in't, the never-surfeited sea
> Hath caus'd to belch up you;
>
> (III.iii.53–6)[26]

These portentous lines and his assertion that 'I and my fellows / Are ministers of Fate' (III.iii.60–1) are certainly impressive, but their authority is undermined by Prospero's commendation of Ariel's skill in playing his part so well:

> Bravely the figure of this harpy hast thou
> Perform'd, my Ariel; a grace it had, devouring.
> Of my instruction hast thou nothing bated
> In what thou hadst to say:
>
> (III.iii.85–8)

The impact and moral authority of Ariel's speech are thus called into question, not by any denial of his assertions, but by our knowledge that he was acting a part dictated to him by Prospero. This, in turn, draws our attention to the fictional nature of the whole play. An explanation for events in *The Tempest* is prevented by the lack of reliable authority. Prospero talks vaguely of 'bountiful Fortune' (I.ii.178), but whereas a harpy might well be the mouthpiece for such a destiny, the 'harpy' in *The Tempest* has been given his words by Prospero, and we are left with no better authority than he. Ariel is only Prospero's agent – and even his power and control over the situation seem shaky. He claims triumphantly:

> My high charms work
> And these mine enemies are all knit up
> In their distractions. They now are in my pow'r;
> And in these fits I leave them
>
> (III.iii.90–3)

before dashing back to see how Ferdinand and Miranda are progressing. But, far from being subdued by this display, Antonio and Sebastian appear quite unaffected by Prospero's magic and exit the scene with the expressed intent of doing battle with the 'fiends' of the island (III.iii.103–5).

There are similar contradictions in the presentation of the masque. On one level it seems to be wholly nugatory, and this is the impression given by Prospero himself when he describes the spectacle he is about to call up:

> Go bring the rabble,
> O'er whom I give thee pow'r, here to this place.
> Incite them to quick motion; for I must
> Bestow upon the eyes of this young couple
> Some vanity of mine art;
>
> (IV.i.37–41)

On the other hand, the apparent attendance of three goddesses and the convincing majesty of their speeches undercuts Prospero's disclaimer. These conflicting impressions serve to make the masque in some way mysteriously ineffable, neither a simple case of *deus ex machina*, nor yet a flimsy and delusive conjuring trick. This elusiveness is the hallmark of Shakespeare's Ovidianism throughout the Late Plays; the explanations for such strange events as Hermione's descent from the pedestal and Thaisa's return to life are neither wholly rational nor decidedly magical. As with the storm, whose special effects can be attributed to either stage machinery or Prospero's magic, the masque becomes problematic in its theatrical context. The goddesses speak with regal grandeur and the actors who portrayed them would presumably be dressed in all the sumptuous finery that the theatre's budget would permit. An audience might therefore be surprised that Prospero refers to them as a 'rabble'. Yet, fully aware of the reality of the theatre, even though he may have temporarily suspended his disbelief, a spectator might recall that the boys (now women) who are representing the goddesses are at least as far from being divine as Prospero's airy minions. The contradiction of impressive effects which turn out to have only flimsy substance distinguishes both Ariel's appearance as a harpy and the masque. The same mixture characterized the opening lines of Prospero's Medea speech, whose style is more impressive than its content, as well as the two specific claims as to phenomena which appear to be awesome and supernatural but may be reduced to mere theatrical devices.

It is the disruptive Caliban who makes it necessary for Prospero to dismiss his 'rabble'. Next to Prospero himself, it is this strange compound of barbarity and sensitivity who has attracted most comment in the play; and Shakespeare's conception of his character may also derive from the *Metamorphoses*. One phase of the *Metamorphoses* seems to have particular affinities with *The Tempest*, the sequence which describes Aeneas' progress from Troy to Italy, and which comprises roughly the second half of Book XIII and the first half of Book XIV.[27] Interspersed with details of Aeneas' voyage are accounts of legends concerning minor ocean deities, and here, more than at any other time in Ovid's poem, we are aware of the sea and its denizens. Some of these stories have interesting points of contact with the narrative of *The Tempest*, and many of the different places mentioned by Ovid seem to have lent something to Shakespeare's conception of Prospero's isle.

The stories of Acis and Galatea, and Glaucus and Scylla, seem in Golding's translation to be 'sea pastorals'; the homely yet dreamily idyllic qualities that we see in Polyphemus' song and Glaucus' account of his mysterious metamorphosis set these stories apart from other Ovidian tales, such as those of Arethusa and Perimele, which also deal with water nymphs but whose narratives are more classically austere. Because they contain features for which Shakespeare's contemporaries felt an affinity, Golding, through the mere act of translating the stories, seems to have transformed them into English creations. It seems probable that Shakespeare was at some level using both these tales as models for his evocation of the magical seascape which constitutes the setting of *The Tempest*.

Miranda, like Galatea, has two rivals for her love. We learn of Caliban's attempted rape, which caused him to be banished from Prospero's favour, and watch the progress of Ferdinand's more gallant courtship. Galatea is also troubled by the unwelcome attentions of a brutish lover, Polyphemus; no more successful than Caliban, he seems temporarily to have thwarted the designs of her more favoured suitor, Acis, by killing him with a rock, only to see his rival being metamorphosed into an immortal river god through the intervention of Galatea.

Polyphemus is an interesting mixture of contrarieties whose unrequited love for Galatea has a touching quality for all his grotesqueness and violent jealousy of Acis. Similar contrarieties, more problematically presented, inhere in the character of Caliban. In the Vaughans' recent book on Caliban, a connection is made between Homer's Polyphemus and Caliban, also between Ovid and *The Tempest*;[28] yet Ovid's Polyphemus is not acknowledged as a source, even though Ovid's presentation of the Cyclops within a context which is more erotic and more pastoral than that of Book IX of the *Odyssey* makes this a more probable source than

Chapman's Homer. The analysis of Caliban's place within the tradition
of the archetypal 'wild man' may accommodate a link between him and
Ovid's Polyphemus, since the Cyclops, particularly as Englished by
Golding, himself forms part of such a tradition. Both live in caves and both
have a particular affinity with the natural world, an attribute which is
treated ambiguously by both Shakespeare and Ovid and which determines
both their positive and their negative aspects, emerging in their use of
images taken from their surroundings, and in the proprietorial pride they
take in their environment. This latter quality is partly dictated by the fact
that they both live on islands to which they feel they have a special claim.
An important aspect of the Cyclops' wooing is his promise to share all the
delights of his island home with Galatea:

> The Quarry is my bowre
> Heawen out of whole mayne stone. No Sun in sommer there can swelt,
> No nipping cold in wintertyme within the same is felt.
> Gay Apples weying downe the boughes have I, and Grapes like gold,
> And purple Grapes on spreaded Vynes as many as can hold,
> Bothe which I doo reserve for thee. Thyself shalt with thy hand
> The soft sweete strawbryes gather, which in wooddy shadowe stand.
> The Cornell berryes also from the tree thy self shalt pull,
> And pleasant plommes, sum yellow lyke new wax, sum blew, sum full
> Of ruddy jewce. Of Chestnuts eeke (if my wyfe thou wilt bee)
> Thou shalt have store: and frutes all sortes: All trees shall serve for thee.
>   (XIII, 953–63)

Golding's translation brings out the naive enthusiasm which Polyphemus
feels for his treasures, the ingenuous glee with which he catalogues his
possessions and takes care to point out even the different varieties of a
particular fruit. Caliban is a subtler creature than the Cyclops, but he
demonstrates a similar literal-minded naivety and pride in his familiarity
with 'his' island when he berates Prospero for his change in manner
towards him:

> When thou cam'st first,
> Thou strok'st me and made much of me, wouldst give me
> Water with berries in't; and teach me how
> To name the bigger light, and how the less,
> That burn by day and night; and then I lov'd thee,
> And show'd thee all the qualities o' th' isle,
> The fresh springs, brine-pits, barren place and fertile.
>   (I.ii.332–8)

Caliban's naive way of talking about the sun makes it clear that he derived
even his most basic knowledge from Miranda. Polyphemus is similarly
indebted to humans for his information ('for you men / Report one Jove
too reigne, of whom I passe not for too ken', Golding, XIII, 990–1). Both
pupils speak of what they have learnt ('one Jove', 'the greater light') with
an imprecision which suggests they have not entirely mastered their
lessons.

In his assiduity to please his mistress, Polyphemus displays a trusting
eagerness paralleled in Caliban's promises to Stephano and Trinculo.
Although he is dismissed by Galatea as an 'owgly Giant' (896) whose
attempts to beautify himself only serve to accentuate his grotesqueness,
Polyphemus' lengthy love complaint has its own plangent charm despite
its rustic lack of sophistication. Because we hear of his pipe, we might
suppose that Polyphemus' declaration of love is meant to be a song. The
repetitions in Golding's translation, as the following short extract
demonstrates, make it easy to imagine this passage being set to music:

> More whyght thou art than Primrose leaf my Lady Galatee,
> More fresh than meade, more tall and streyght than lofty Aldertree,
> More bright than glasse, more wanton than the tender kid forsooth,
> Than Cockleshelles continually with water worne, more smoothe,
> More cheerefull than the winters Sun, or Sommers shadowe cold,
> More seemely and more comly than the Planetree too behold,
> Of valew more than Apples bee although they were of gold.
>
> (XIII, 929–35)

It is significant that Polyphemus is associated with music, because the one
passage always cited to support Caliban's status as a complex and sensitive
character is the following famous speech:

> Be not afeard. The isle is full of noises,
> Sounds and sweet airs, that give delight, and hurt not.
> Sometimes a thousand twangling instruments
> Will hum about mine ears; and sometime voices,
> That, if I then had wak'd after long sleep,
> Will make me sleep again; and then, in dreaming,
> The clouds methought would open and show riches
> Ready to drop upon me, that, when I wak'd,
> I cried to dream again.
>
> (III.ii.130–8)

The beauty of this speech is accentuated by Stephano's crass rejoinder, 'This will prove a brave kingdom to me, where I shall have my music for nothing' (III.ii.142–3). But one should not overemphasize Caliban's spirituality. Although he is able to respond to music, the one image which it summons up for him is of boundless riches, even though he does express this vision of wealth in terms of a Danaën epiphany which prevents it from seeming too overtly materialistic. Concern with material possessions is also a characteristic of Polyphemus, who expects Galatea to be impressed by the details of his livestock (Golding, XIII, 964–8).

Partly because Ferdinand is not a particularly engaging or forceful hero, it is tempting to feel that Miranda should have chosen Caliban, if only because he has all the best lines – significantly, he speaks verse whereas his companions, Stephano and Trinculo, speak prose. Polyphemus' speech is also memorable, but both characters are irredeemably marred by their essential violence and brutishness. The Cyclops' hatred for Acis is as strong as his love for Galatea:

And if I catch him he shall feele that in my body is
The force that should bee. I shall paunch him quicke. Those limbs of his
I will in peeces teare, and strew them in the feeldes, and in
Thy waters, if he doo thee haunt.

(XIII, 1015–18)

Caliban expresses his willingness for Prospero to be killed in an equally savage way:

there thou mayst brain him,
Having first seiz'd his books; or with a log
Batter his skull, or paunch him with a stake,
Or cut his wezand with thy knife.

(III.ii.84–7)

and it is highly significant that the same unusual word *paunch*, meaning 'disembowel', is used by both Golding and Shakespeare, and that this is the only example of the verb in the Shakespearean corpus.[29]

*   *   *

Caliban's inhumanity leads one on to yet another preoccupation which is common to both *The Tempest* and the *Metamorphoses*. It is possible to identify points within this section of Ovid's poem which show a particular focus on this issue. Two episodes, the account of the Cercopes (Golding, XIV, 100–20) and Achemenides' relation of Circe's encounter with the Greeks (XIV, 280–350), are particularly relevant to an analysis of the theme of humanity versus bestiality in *The Tempest*.

The Cercopes were turned into apes as a fitting punishment for their 'leawdnesse' and 'wilfull perjurye' (XIV, 108). Aeneas is diverted towards their island through 'His Pilot by a stroke / Of tempest being drownd in sea' (XIV, 103–4). The foul behaviour of these beasts resembles that of Caliban. We learn that Jove 'did transforme them everychone / Intoo an evillfavored kynd of beast' and that 'he did bereeve them of the use of speeche and toong, / Which they too cursed perjurye did use bothe old and yoong. / Too chatter hoarcely, and too shreeke, too jabber, and too squeake' (109–10, 116–18). This is an unusual metamorphosis because it is portrayed as a punishment for the abuse of a specifically human faculty, speech. Caliban, as Miranda disgustedly informs us, treats this privilege in equally cavalier fashion (I.ii.353–60). Caliban's reply to her speech at this point –

> You taught me language, and my profit on't
> Is, I know how to curse. The red plague rid you
> For learning me your language!
>
> (I.ii.363–5)

– provides another link with Ovid's apes, for their fault is also 'cursed perjurye' (117). Also interesting is Caliban's worry that he, Stephano, and Trinculo shall be 'turn'd to barnacles, or to apes / With foreheads villainous low' (IV.i.247–8).

The physical appearance of the Cercopes does not recall Caliban, whose appearance Shakespeare does not describe very precisely, as much as the strange 'shapes' who bring the banquet to Alonso and his companions:

> He knit in lesser space
> Theyr members, and he beate mee flat theyr noses too theyr face,
> The which he filled furrowlike with wrinckles every where.
> He clad theyr bodyes over all with fallow colourd heare,
> And put them intoo this same Ile too dwell for ever there . . .
> He hath them left, and for too moppe and mowe, but not too speake.
>
> (XIV, 111–15, 119)

Gonzalo describes in amazement the strange beings who have just appeared:

> For certes these are people of the island,
> Who though they are of monstrous shape yet, note,
> Their manners are more gentle-kind than of
> Our human generation you shall find
> Many, nay, almost, any
>
> (III.iii.30–4)

and Alonso adds, 'I cannot too much muse / Such shapes, such gesture, and such sound, expressing, / Although they want the use of tongue, a kind / Of excellent dumb discourse' (III.iii.36–9). Gonzalo begins to ruminate on other travellers' tales about strange beasts which, because they are grotesque, also recall the Cercopes:

> When we were boys,
> Who would believe that there were mountaineers
> Dewlapp'd like bulls, whose throats had hanging at 'em
> Wallets of flesh? Or that there were such men
> Whose heads stood in their breasts?
>
> (III.iii.43–7)

One obvious disparity between the 'shapes' and the Cercopes is the former's alleged gentle demeanour. Both may appear bizarre, but there is a great difference between the senseless jabbering of the Cercopes and the islanders' 'excellent dumb discourse'. In manner at least, the shapes have more in common with the men whom Circe has transformed into beasts, whose apparent ferocity belies their gentle nature:

> A thousand Lyons woolves and beares did put us in a feare
> By meeting us. But none of them was too bee feared there.
> For none of them could doo us harme: but with a gentle looke
> And following us with fawning feete theyr wanton tayles they shooke.
>
> (XIV, 294–7)

Returning to Golding's account of the Cercopes, we can find yet stronger evidence that Shakespeare had been influenced by this passage when he wrote his play, for we encounter a direct verbal echo of the phrase 'moppe and mowe' which Golding used in his description of these creatures – 'He hath them left, and for too moppe and mowe, but not too speake' (XIV, 119) – on two separate occasions in *The Tempest*. The first occurrence is particularly significant because it is used to describe the actions of the shapes: 'Enter the Shapes again, and dance, with mocks and mows, and carrying out the table' (III.iii, SD). Theobald emended 'mocks' to 'mops' to achieve consistency with the second occasion where the phrase is used, this time by Ariel when he announces that the masque is about to begin:

> Before you can say, 'come', and 'go',
> And breathe twice, and cry, 'so, so',
> Each one, tripping on his toe,
> Will be here with mop and mow.
> (IV.i.44–7)

Even though both 'mop and mow' and 'mock and mow' were common doublets at this time, within the context of a framework of correspondences between Ovid and Shakespeare the repetition of Golding's phrase seems to be more than mere coincidence.

*   *   *

Such small but telling similarities of language are the visible tip of a veritable iceberg of Ovidianism in Shakespeare's later work, more massive, if less self-evident, than the more superficial Ovidianism of the early plays and poems. Connecting, say, *Venus and Adonis* with the *Metamorphoses*, inevitably quoting the 'Ovidian' lines, 'Narcissus so himself forsook, / And died to kiss his shadow in the brook' (*Venus and Adonis*, 161–2), is a perfectly legitimate way of acknowledging an incontrovertible relationship; but it makes no significant difference to the way in which we read either Ovid or Shakespeare. Making a claim for an equally strong, more submerged, yet more nuanced Ovidian presence in the Late Plays is a more challenging position to take up, not only because Ovid is less in evidence in these plays, but also because, if his influence is accepted, we may be forced to renegotiate our perception of these two poets individually as well as the way they interconnect.

University of St Andrews

NOTES

1. I would like to thank Dr T. A. Mason of Bristol University for his help in preparing this article.
2. A well-known early example is Francis Meres's comment, 'the sweete wittie soul of Ovid lies in mellifluous honey-tongued Shakespeare, witness his Venus and Adonis, his Lucrece, his sugred sonnets among his private friends, &c.' (Meres, *Palladis Tamia* (London, 1973), p. 282).
3. See for very recent examples Anthony Brian Taylor, 'Shakespeare and

Golding', *N&Q*, 36 (1991), 492–9, and Jonathan Bate, *Shakespeare and Ovid* (Oxford, 1993).

4. David Armitage, 'The Dismemberment of Orpheus: Mythic Elements in Shakespeare's Romances', *Shakespeare Survey*, 39 (1987), 122–33 (p. 125).

5. Marion Trousdale, 'Recurrence and Renaissance: Rhetorical Imitation in Ascham and Sturm', *ELR*, 6 (1976), 156–79 (p. 158).

6. A discussion of these characteristics can be found in J. B. Solodow, *The World of Ovid's Metamorphoses* (Durham, N.C., 1988).

7. *Literary Essays of Ezra Pound*, edited by T. S. Eliot (London, 1954), p. 235. The importance of Sandys's translation of the *Metamorphoses* for that formidable Latinist, Milton, might be adduced to support Pound's assertion.

8. Raymond Powell, *Shakespeare and the Critics' Debate* (London, 1980), p. 73.

9. This and all subsequent quotations from Shakespeare are taken from *William Shakespeare: The Complete Works*, edited by Peter Alexander (London, 1951).

10. Armitage, p. 126.

11. This and all subsequent quotations from Ovid are taken from the Loeb *Metamorphoses*, translated by Frank Justus Miller, 2 vols (London, 1984).

12. This and all subsequent quotations from Golding are taken from *Arthur Golding's Translation of the Metamorphoses*, edited by W. H. D. Rouse (London, 1961).

13. Leonard Barkan, *The Gods Made Flesh: Metamorphosis and the Pursuit of Paganism* (New Haven, 1986), pp. 287–8.

14. Charles and Michelle Martindale, *Shakespeare and the Uses of Antiquity* (London, 1990), p. 25. Marion Trousdale also focuses on Shakespeare's imitative use of the Ovidian speech, notably its form: 'But although the circumstances, occasion, actors, and language differ, the image or idea in both passages, that of invoking magical powers, is the same . . . The sense of imitation as a process is attached, not to particulars, but to that which can be abstracted as perceptible intellectual form' (Trousdale (n. 5), p. 174).

15. This tale may have been familiar to Shakespeare through the retellings by Chaucer in *The Book of the Duchess* and Gower in the *Confessio Amantis* as well as through the *Metamorphoses* itself. My forthcoming PhD thesis, 'Some Aspects of the Poetic Reception of Ovid's *Metamorphoses*' (University of Bristol), includes an account of the influence of the tale of Ceyx and Alcyone on *Cymbeline*. David Armitage aligns the storm in this tale with similar evocations in *Venus and Adonis*, *Pericles*, *The Winter's Tale*, and *The Tempest* (Armitage, p. 128).

16. We might compare the way Golding describes Alcyone searching for Ceyx after she has woken up, 'With that shee lookes if any print appeere / Of footing where as he did stand upon the floore behynd' (XI, 798–9), with Prospero's description of the light-footed elves.

17. See Solodow (n. 6), pp. 208–9.

18. Frederick Ahl, *Metaformations: Soundplay and Wordplay in Ovid and Other Classical Poets* (Ithaca, 1985), pp. 55–6, notes that Latin poets happily associate syllables with long and short versions of the same vowel.

19. C. T. Lewis, *Elementary Latin Dictionary* (Oxford, 1891), *s.v.* 'cera'.

20. See particularly *Aeneid*, I, 81–91.

21. Dryden remarked on this feature of Ovid's writing in the Dedication to

Examen Poeticum: 'He is often luxuriant, both in his fancy and Expressions; and as it has lately been observ'd, not always Natural. If Wit be pleasantry, he has it to excess: but if it be propriety, Lucretius, Horace, and above all Virgil are his superiors' (*The Poems of John Dryden*, edited by James Kinsley, 4 vols (Oxford, 1958), II, 795).

22. *Ceyx and Alcyone*, 222–5, quoted from Dryden, *Poems*, IV. David Hopkins makes the following comment on Dryden's translation of these lines: 'Here the diction ("peep", "gulp"), the pat antitheses which (among other things) seem almost to mimic the bobbing motion of a body in water, and the near-comic potential . . . ensure that the reader's reaction to the events is far removed from that of Shakespeare's Miranda in similar circumstances' (*Ovid Renewed: Ovidian Influences on Literature and Art from the Middle Ages to the Twentieth Century*, edited by Charles Martindale (Cambridge, 1988), p. 186).

23. An example of Ovid playing with the idea of his own unreliability is his comment on Scylla: 'virginis ora gerens, et, si non omnia vates / ficta reliquerunt, aliquo quoque tempore virgo' (XIII, 733–4). If the stories we are told by other poets are to be regarded so dubiously, what does this say about the *Metamorphoses* itself?

24. See, however, William C. Carroll's rather different reading:

    Prospero is required to become Medea temporarily so that he can fully experience in her the extremity of his own desires and the dream she represents . . . When he claims later the Medean power to have made graves open, we can recognize the translation of his own powers into the more sinister terms of his demonic opposite. Prospero is not Medea or Sycorax, but he can confirm himself only by first becoming them willingly, by releasing his self in order to reclaim it.

    (*The Metamorphoses of Shakespearean Comedy* (Princeton, N.J., 1985), pp. 240–1).

25. Shakespeare uses similar imagery several times in *Venus and Adonis*, a poem which owes much to the tale of Salmacis and Hermaphroditus:

    Full gently now she takes him by the hand,
    A lily prison'd in a gaol of snow,
    Of ivory in an alabaster band;
    So white a friend engirts so white a foe.
    (361–4)

    But hers [Venus' eyes] which through the crystal tears gave light
    Shone like the moon in water seen by night.
    (500–1)

    Whereat her tears began to turn their tide
    Being prison'd in her eye like pearls in glass.
    (979–80)

    This debt is remarked on by, among others, Charles Martindale, *John Milton and the Transformation of Ancient Epic* (London, 1986), p. 166.

26. However, the fatalistic, psalm-like quality of both speeches quoted here is perhaps more reminiscent of Jonah than Ceyx. The verb 'belch', in particular, might recall the whale (Jonah 2.5–10).

27. For another account of these similarities, see Bate (n. 3), pp. 246–8.
28. Alden T. Vaughan and Virginia Mason Vaughan, *Shakespeare's Caliban: A Cultural History* (Cambridge, 1991), pp. 56–85.
29. The episode of Acis and Galatea also offers certain parallels between the figures of Acis and Ferdinand. One should note in particular the connection/ comparison of hair with reeds at I.ii.213 of *The Tempest* and at XIII, 1044– 9 of Golding.

Four Eighteenth-Century Modernizations of *The Shipman's Tale* as Audiovisual Performance

Betsy Bowden

> Ye knowe ek that in forme of speche is chaunge
> Withinnne a thousand yeer[1]

It would not have surprised Geoffrey Chaucer to learn that in 1700, after three centuries of language change, John Dryden would publish several Canterbury tales that he had modernized – translated, that is, within the same language. During the subsequent century Alexander Pope, and other writers both known and anonymous, produced thirty-four modernized Canterbury tales, plus tale links and adaptations of each other's Chauceriana.[2] Like Dryden, they sought the middle ground of 'paraphrase' rather than word-for-word translation ('metaphrase') or loose imitation, such that each modernizer conveys his own sense of the Middle English poetry in forms meant to appeal to contemporary readers. During the eighteenth century two writers modernized the *Wife of Bath's Prologue*, three the *Miller's Tale*, three the Reeve's, and four the Shipman's; other tales were modernized once apiece or not at all. Translators converged, that is to say, upon Chaucer's bawdy –

> and yet thei spake hem so,
> And spedde as wel in love as men now do;
> Ek for to wynnen love in sondry ages,
> In sondry londes, sondry ben usages.
> (*Troilus and Criseyde*, II, 25–8)

Neither would Chaucer have wondered at the wide variety of responses from eighteenth-century readers to passages that touch upon love. In *The Shipman's Tale*, for example, consider the scene in the garden just before the merchant's wife calls him to dinner. In Chaucer's poem the wife and the monk, her husband's friend, here reach an agreement to have sex in exchange for a hundred franks, which the monk, unbeknown to her, will borrow from the husband. In a modernization of 1721, a jovial monk hugs the wife warmly before turning to the topic uppermost in his mind, dinner.

In 1731, the two exchange a discreet kiss. In 1750, a leering monk plies the wife's milky bosom with one hand and with the other grasps her euphemism, while their conjoining lips glow with greedy kisses throughout ten full-fraught lines replacing three simple ones of Middle English.

This article will not attempt to posit causes behind such dramatically different effects: my argument is based on evidence available rather than anticipated. Virgin texts stand ready to meet techniques of performance analysis currently being developed by musicologists, folklorists, rhetoricians, and others. I will show that the four eighteenth-century modernizers of *The Shipman's Tale* create different effects not only by translating Chaucer's language, but also by translating discourse and imagery on paper into four implied audiovisual performances.

From time immemorial, of course, actors and actresses have been translating text into performance. Story-tellers, parents, English professors, and others do likewise, though no doubt sometimes less consciously. Only since the invention of sound recording and motion picture film, however, have scholars had any audiovisual evidence for analytical purposes. Very recently, just during the past two decades, recording technology has become widely available and affordable enough for specialized data collection. Beginning in 1979, accordingly, I tested a hypothesis that literary critics' differing interpretations of a given passage relate to the imagined performance that each individual 'hears' and 'sees' while reading silently. Thanks to thirty-odd Chaucerians who read aloud key passages onto cassette tape, I showed how many critical debates hinge upon imagined performance: here a sincere or hypocritical Pardoner, there a vulgar, or jolly, or pathetic, or dangerously seductive Wife of Bath. The present article elicits evidence from four readers from the past who, like today's Chaucerians, translate text into performance in their minds' eyes and ears.

The four translators are John Markland (younger brother of the classical scholar Jeremiah), 1721; Henry Travers (a clergyman), 1731; Andrew Jackson (a bookseller), 1750; and William Lipscomb (another clergyman), 1795.[3] No external evidence documents books known to the authors, except for Lipscomb's mentioning that he discovered Dryden's *Nun's Priest's Tale* only after modernizing it himself. Their modernizations are so dissimilar, however, that each probably worked without awareness of the others. For present purposes, each version is considered to be an independent response to Chaucer's text, uninfluenced by the other three modernizations. In contrast, twentieth-century critics respond to one another's commentary, and, to an extent unattainable by eighteenth-century writers, also take into consideration the literary and social conventions of the late fourteenth century. Despite these and other distinctions between the two contexts, interpretation then and now involves translation into imagined performance. We will observe ways in which the modernizers specify characters' vocal intonations, facial expessions, movements, gestures, and physical appearances in co-ordination with visual imagery. Similarly, standard twentieth-century criticism often urges that the silent reader of a printed passage see and hear a particular staging of it. Close analysis often highlights a text's interwoven patterns of visual imagery, as well as describing (or prescribing) vocal tones for characters and narrator. In an article here chosen as representa-tive, dating from 1975, John C. McGalliard explains how 'functional dialogue' contributes to characterization in *The Shipman's Tale*. Usually he describes only his own preferred performance:

> We first hear [the wife] speak in the scene in the garden with Daun John; she goes through a succession of complaints, confidences, and nervous entreaty . . . she was on the defensive; she had to wheedle, to plead, to beg.[4]

In understandable psychological reaction, McGalliard continues, the wife hurries to the counting house to 'bully and browbeat her husband'. She addresses him with 'exasperation' at line 214, followed by 'eight lines [in which] she scolds him without restraint' plus one 'peremptorily summon-ing him to mass and dinner'.

As critics occasionally do, McGalliard then describes an alternative possible performance in order to reject it:

> To be sure, the lines [214–23] could have been spoken in a tone of affectionate cajolery; but the exclamation, "The devel have part on alle swiche rekenynges!" and the merchant's serious though mild reply probably indicates that such was not the case.[5]

Might such have been the case, though, for any modernizer of the scene? Do any of the four eighteenth-century wives cajole affectionately? Do any husbands reply in tones other than serious, mild ones? Chaucer provides the script, but no stage directions except the word 'boldely':

> Up to hir housbonde is this wyf ygon,
> And knokketh at his countour boldely.
>   "*Quy la?*" quod he. "Peter! it am I,"
> Quod she; "What, sire, how longe wol ye faste?
> How longe tyme wol ye rekene and caste
> Youre sommes, and youre bookes, and youre thynges?

The devel have part on alle swiche rekenynges!
Ye have ynough, pardee, of Goddes sonde;
Com doun to-day, and lat youre bagges stonde.
Ne be ye nat ashamed that daun John
Shal fasting al this day alenge goon?
What, lat us heere a messe, and go we dyne."
        "Wyf," quod this man, "litel kanstow devyne
The curious bisynesse that we have."

                                                        (212–25)

As we shall see, two of our modernizers retain 'boldly' for the wife's
knocking; Lipscomb hears 'sounding blows'; Markland replaces knocks
with 'haste'. Sound effects are secondary, though. It is, rather, the
possibilities inherent in two human voices which produce such differing
interpretations of the marital dynamics in Chaucer's scene. Lipscomb,
Markland, and Jackson project the wife's voice in tones similar to those
described by McGalliard, albeit with distinct degrees of boldness and
irritability. All five husbands differ, as will be heard – heard by seeing
print, of course.

In the scene as staged by the latest modernizer, Lipscomb, the wife's
terse, abrupt sentences imply unconcealed impatience. To McGalliard in
1975 the husband's reply is 'serious though mild'. To Lipscomb, likewise
reading silently, it instead sounds 'meek and soothing':

        at his door she knocks with sounding blows.
    "Wherefore," she says, "thus endless do you pore
"O'er musty books, and dead, and useless store?
"Think you Dan John the live-long day can fast?
"Come down and dine; the hour's already past."
        "Wife," he replied, in meek and soothing tone,
"Little to you a merchant's cares are known."
                                                        (156–62)[6]

Markland also abbreviates the wife's speech, though not so drastically. He
nonetheless doubles her direct accusation of shame, and neatly combines
Chaucer's images of God and the devil:

Up to the Compting-house she goes in haste,
Why *Peter, Peter,* will you all Day fast?
Come down for shame, and let your Money stand;
Sure you have got enough of *Satan's* Sand.
You ought to be asham'd, that Cousin *John*

> With empty Stomach all this Day has gone.
> Come, let us hear a Mass, and then go dine.
> Wife, said the Man, you little can divine.
> The dang'rous Bus'ness that we Merchants have.
>
> (205–13)

With unrestrained scolding, this hypocritical wife casts double shame on her husband for unchristian and inhospitable behaviour, having just arranged that one of God's servants will pay with Satan's sand[7] for a night of her own unchristian hospitality. Markland's merchant, notwithstanding, replies with the most self-possession of the five. Although his words look firm and blunt partly because of a misplaced period after 'divine', the implied tone comes more surely from his terming a merchant's work 'dang'rous Bus'ness'. Especially in comparison with the self-pitying 'cares' that beset Lipscomb's merchant, and the pompous 'difficulties' to be propounded by Jackson's, Markland's phrase evokes the merchant/ adventurer figure popular in early eighteenth-century writings.

The wife in Jackson's version surpasses Markland's in hypocrisy. She scolds the merchant for spending too much time on accounts while she and his friend have supposedly done nothing more than pass a tedious morning. In fact, though, it is Jackson's monk and wife whose conjoined lips have long been glowing greedily with devoured kisses. Even taking into account Jackson's tendency towards polysyllabic utterances by all characters and narrator, his merchant's reply projects stuffy self-involvement. This husband claims unassailable intellectual superiority to the female at his side: in Jackson's staging, the wife

> Knocks boldly at his Door, which made him cry
> Who's there? O, *Peter,* answer'd she, 'tis I;
> Why (went she on) must we for ever fast?
> In how long Time will your Accounts be cast?
> Your Gold, Books, Bonds, Receipts and other Things,
> The Devil o'erspread 'em with his brooding Wings.
> You've Bags enough of Heav'n's admired Sand;
> Come down to Day, let them in quiet stand;
> For Shame make haste, what know ye not, Dan *John*
> Has, all this tedious Morning, fasting gone.
>   Wife, he reply'd, thou scarcely canst conceive
> The Difficulties that we Merchants have.
>
> (215–26)

It remains for Travers to create the alternative tone of affectionate cajolery rejected by McGalliard. In the 1731 rendering, indeed, the wife addresses her mate as 'my Love' rather than swearing by St Peter the doorkeeper. She substitutes 'Duce' for 'devil'; she remarks that merchants in general, not just he as an individual, spend too much time accounting; and she notes that such a good provider deserves a rest. In response, a doting husband addresses her innocent ignorance rather than his own problems. She cajoles, and he replies as if to a child:

> [She] knock'd full boldly at her Husband's Door.
> *Qui la?* quoth he. 'Tis I am here, my Love,
> What mean you thus to sit and starve above?
> Lord! when will all this long Account be made?
> The Duce confound these tedious Folks of Trade.
> Thy Wealth has prosper'd to a large Degree,
> And *Mammon* is a bounteous God to thee;
> Then let thy Bags in Peace a while remain,
> And plod no longer on these Works of Gain.
> For is it not a most unfriendly Crime
> That poor Sir *John* goes fasting all this Time?
> 'Tis highly shameful he should starve and pine,
> Then prithee come, let's go to Mass, and dine.
>   Dame, quoth the Merchant, thou'rt a simple Wife,
> And unexperienc'd in a Tradesman's Life.
>
>   (196–210)

In four of these five dialogues, the wife's voice stays quite consistent, with only Travers dissenting: she scolds. How would a husband respond, though, to a wife's rebuke that he spends too much time earning money that she will spend on fancy clothes? The five authors differ strikingly. For McGalliard, the merchant replies in a 'serious though mild' voice; for Lipscomb, he is 'meek and soothing'; for Markland, bluntly defensive; for Jackson, pompous and complacent; for Travers, fond and belittling. Alluring questions arise about a discrepancy that appears sex-determinant – questions that beckon towards the no-man's-lands of authorial intent, biographical speculation, and Gender Studies. Might four out of five women readers instead stereotype the husband in this passage, while creating more variety in their five calls to dinner by wives contemplating cuckoldry? I hereby issue a call for any concrete data on the matter, synchronic and/or diachronic. In the meantime, let us attend to the next item of existing evidence: the dialogue between wife and husband after his cuckolding.

Just back from Paris at tale's end, the merchant is out of debt and eager

to pay the marriage debt, all night long in bed. He is fully contented –
except that he had almost embarrassed himself by requesting his hundred
franks that the monk had already repaid to the wife. Five husbands raise
the issue in five distinct tones of voice. Just as variously, five wives respond
that Daun John had mentioned no debt, and that such a gift – already spent
on clothes 'for youre honour' – had seemed appropriate reimbursement
for frequent 'beele cheere' at their table (*ShipT* 421, 409).

Chaucer provides plenty of action following the night of wedded mirth,
but, as before, only the term 'boldely' as stage direction. Applied directly
to the wife's voice here, rather than to her fist on wood, the ambiguous
adverb's potential for flexibility in performance allows her reply to sound
indignant for McGalliard, stone-faced for Markland, quick and fearless
for Lipscomb, raving for Travers, and loud or screeching for Jackson.
Wives thus answer husbands' respective tones of mild reproach, stern
accusation, humble prayer, pretended anger, and affectionate post-coital
teasing. Chaucer supplies the versatile script:

> Whan it was day, this marchant gan embrace
> His wyf al newe, and kiste hire on hir face,
> And up he gooth and maketh it ful tough.
>   "Namoore," quod she, "by God, ye have ynough!"
> And wantownly agayn with hym she pleyde
> Til atte laste thus this marchant seyde:
> "By God," quod he, "I am a litel wrooth
> With yow, my wyf, although it be me looth.
> And woot ye why? By God, as that I gesse
> That ye han maad a manere straungenesse
> Bitwixen me and my cosyn daun John . . .
> Telle me alwey, er that I fro thee go,
> If any dettour hath in myn absence
> Ypayed thee, lest thurgh thy necligence
> I myghte hym axe a thing that he hath payed."
>   This wyf was nat afered nor affrayed,
> But boldely she seyde, and that anon,
> "Marie, I deffie the false monk, daun John!"
>   (377–87, 396–402)

In McGalliard's staging of this scene, the husband 'gently' gives his wife
a 'mild reproach'. Deciding quickly that 'the best defense was a strong
offense', she expresses 'indignation against Daun John', which will slide
'smoothly and plausibly' into her lie. In arguing for consistency of
characterization, McGalliard thus has the husband speak mildly and the

wife peremptorily both here and in the previous dialogue (pp. 9, 2).

Each modernizer likewise keeps consistent his own interpretation of the two characters' voices. In the counting house of Markland's 1721 version, the wife spoke blatant hypocrisy without visible qualms. Now in bed, she has full control of facial muscles and vocal tone both. Markland's merchant, who sternly informed her earlier of 'dang'rous Bus'ness', here assuredly does not murmur the 'mild reproach' of McGalliard's. Even with force and strength at low ebb, he accuses his wife directly of the 'negligence' that has disgraced him. He emphatically orders her to reform:

> At Morning he renew'd his *warm Embrace*,
> And kiss'd her Lips, and sooth'd a *better Place*.
> When making ready for th' Encounter tough,
> No *more (said she)* in truth *you've had enough*.
> Then wantonly she play'd, and *egg'd him on*,
> Till all his *Force* was lost, and *Strength* was gone.
>   At length, he said, altho' this is no Place,
> Nor fitting Time to mention my Disgrace:
> Yet I must tell you, I'm a *little griev'd*,
> That you ne'er told me *what you had receiv'd* . . .
> Therefore I prithee *ne'er do so again*,
> But when my Debtors *pay thee, tell me plain*.
> Lest through thy Negligence, I lose my Trade,
> By wrong Demanding what's already Paid.
>   His Words no change of Countenance could make,
> But steady and unmov'd, she boldly spake;
> Marry, that Traytor *Monk* do I defy.
>   (362–71, 380–6)

In Lipscomb's 1795 version, a Walter Mitty figure stands in stark contrast to Markland's passionate adventurer come home. He stands literally as well, for the scene has shifted from bedroom to front gate. In the counting house before his journey, he soothed his wife meekly. Re-entering his own yard now, consistent in character, he pleads and whines. His implied vocal tone is conveyed by the term 'humbly', by auxiliary verbs of uncertainty, and by syntax – especially in the triplet, where short phrases interrupt his prayer that she please consider his proffered suggestion. The wife's quick reply, following hard on his hesitancy, fearlessly defies husband as well as monk:

> Yet he forgot not in her ear to tell
> The words that from Dan John at Paris fell:

"In truth, sweet wife," he said, "thou'rt much to blame,
"And might'st have caus'd me undeserved shame;
"For it would sorely much my soul have griev'd,
"To have ask'd a payment, once before receiv'd:
"Ne'er then in future fail, I humbly pray,
"To tell me, if by chance, while I'm away,
"To thee a debtor should his portion pay."
Fearless return'd the dame with quick reply,
"The false, th' audacious traitor I defy."

(275–85)

Lipscomb has kept the couple on their feet; Travers lets them converse while discreetly horizontal. Travers specifies a fatherly merchant's precise tactics: he will pretend to be angry in order to impress his supposedly ingenuous child-wife. Although he is careful to chide her for friends' hurt feelings and wronged hearts, de-emphasizing the financial aspect, anger begets feigned anger. The raving wife in this 1731 production would assume a facial expression very unlike that of her cool-headed counterpart directed by Travers, who like Markland matriculated at Cambridge in 1719 and otherwise shared a social and interpretive context:

So when they'd box'd about the Good Old Cause,
And weary Mirth at last requir'd a Pause;
The Merchant thus bespoke his am'rous Dame,
And seem'd to kindle with an angry Flame.
    I thought you'd been a more ingenuous Wife
Than thus to raise me such a hateful Strife;
To make my Cousin's friendly Love decline,
And set his Heart at Variance so with mine . . .
Then tell me, Dear, if any One there be
Who in my Absence pays his Debts to thee;
Lest I perhaps assert a dang'rous Claim,
And wrong my Friend by some injurious Aim.
    She heard with Anger, and began to rave,
I tell thee, Dear, Sir *John*'s a scoundrel Knave.

(353–60, 365–70)

In 1750, at rest after repeated acts of vigorous conjugality on Jackson's risqué stage, the husband raises the topic of anger in teasing terms of endearment: 'My Love . . . . / . . .You're naughty, dear'. His pompous, affectionate voice would sound sexually satiated, rather than masked in make-believe scolding as in Travers's imagined performance. In reply, a bold wife raises her voice – in pitch? in volume? in both? 'Accent rais'd' certainly refers to vocal tone, but Jackson has interpreted Chaucer's ambiguous 'boldely' with a phrase that itself retains ambiguity. In addition, Jackson enhances the sex act with visual stimuli featuring food and animals:

> When Day peept forth, his lovely Wife he clips,
> And feasted on the Honey of her Lips;
> Stroak'd the dear Pad, and bounding toughly rode:
> Enough, said she, enough, you've cool'd your Blood;
> And wantonly with him again she play'd;
> At length to her, this worthy Merchant said.
>
> My Love, I have a Crow to pluck with you,
> You're naughty, dear, and I am angry now;
> The social Frankness is estrang'd by thee,
> Which was between my Coz, Dan *John*, and me . . .
> Then prithee, Wife, of such Neglects take heed;
> To pay, and still be dun'd, is hard indeed.
>
> This Wife was neither daunted nor amaz'd,
> But boldly thus reply'd, with Accent rais'd;
> Dan *John*, that treacherous Monk, to Hell may go.
>
> (375–84, 393–7)

The wife thus curses the man with whom she once played as zestfully as she does here with her husband.

How do the four modernizers treat that previous night of lovemaking, the one enjoyed by monk and wife while husband is away? Because Chaucer's brief, businesslike scene supplies no speech until the morning after, its potential impact is more visual than aural:

> This faire wyf acorded with daun John
> That for thise hundred frankes he sholde al nyght
> Have hire in his armes bolt upright;
> And this acord parfourned was in dede.
> In myrthe al nyght a bisy lyf they lede
> Til it was day, that daun John wente his way,
> And bad the meynee 'Farewel, have good day!'
>
> (314–20)

Lipscomb in 1795, in one bland couplet, whisks past as if on fast-forward:

> There for the hundred franks she yields her charms,
> Th' expected payment, to his longing arms.
>
> (221–2)

Travers, though far from explicit, makes the act seem more like fun. Infusing the scene with a golden glow that deflects attention from finances, he replaces Chaucer's 'bisy' with his own favourite word 'buxom', used here in an eighteenth-century sense rather than a Middle English one.[8] Travers adds the term to several other passages that, like this one, acquire vaguely pleasant atmospheres of good-natured generosity:

> 'Twas order'd so that by a crafty Game
> This golden Sum was paid the Merchant's Dame,
> Sir *John* regal'd it with this lovely Wife,
> And both my Cousins led a buxom Life;
> 'Till he in Prudence saw his Hour to start,
> And so took leave as usual to depart.
>
> (299–304)

In contrast to Lipscomb and Travers, who veil the proceedings, Markland and Jackson eagerly seize upon metaphorical possibilities already embedded in Chaucer's own image-patterns of sex, money, food, and animals.[9] Earlier in the tale, the monk tells his friend that he needs the hundred franks to buy 'certein beestes' for his abbey's food supplies (*ShipT* 272). So guided by Chaucer, Markland brings edible animals to the business of adultery:

> The *Monk* and Wife a hasty Bargain wrought,
> That for these hundred Crowns so duely brought,
> He should enjoy her Company in Bed.
> This they perform'd, a busy Life they led,
> And *stock'd the Cattle on the Merchant's Head.*
> No sooner had the Sun put forth his Face,
> And warn'd the Lovers of their last Embrace,
> When up from Bed the *Monk* well-sated starts,
> And taking leave of all, in haste departs.
>
> (299–307)

Markland adds one food image, 'well-sated', plus mercantile terms: 'Bargain', 'duely brought', 'Company', 'stock'd'. The last two words are meticulously chosen, for 'company' is sexual in context with commercial overtones, while 'stock' in 1721 can refer to business supplies, animals raised for food, and procreative sexuality (*OED*, *s.v.* 'company'; 'stock'). In developing Chaucer's own imagery, Markland also adds to the coital scene the remarkably persistent animal image for adultery: horns. As the monk and the lady make the beast with two backs, this bovine attribute grows on her mate.

Jackson, like Markland, modernizes the scene with commercial terms that make near-punning reference to sexual intercourse: after the money is 'to her paid down', then 'this Agreement Action ratify'd'. But Jackson adds animal imagery that differs from Markland's. Both authors specify cattle for the Middle English 'beestes'. The beasts that clamber into bed with Jackson's monk, however, do so not with moos but exuberant neighs:

> This virtuous Wife with this good Monk agreed,
> That for these hundred Crowns, to her paid down,
> All Night he might divert himself with *Roan*;
> Gallop, or amble, all her Paces try,
> For Gold inchanted her inchanting Eye:
> And this Agreement Action ratify'd;
> That Night he rode, as Monks devoutly ride.
> The Leagues he journey'd, or how oft he baited,
> I do not find by Lady *Fame* related;
> But with the rising Day Dan *John* arose,
> And bidding all farewel, away he goes.
>
> (310–20)

And indeed, Jackson has transported to the Shipman's story the hard-riding, gold-wearing, virile pilgrim Monk of Chaucer's *General Prologue*, who is also evoked by both Markland and Jackson in the final passage to be discussed. Both modernizers are attuned to resonances between Daun John in *The Shipman's Tale* and the pilgrim Monk, in whose portrait are intertwined images of sex, food, animals, and wealth (*GP* 165–207). Both Markland and Jackson observe also that a pilgrim Merchant, with marital problems of his own, is listening to *The Shipman's Tale* (*GP* 270–84; *MchT* 1213–44).

Nearly two centuries later, G. L. Kittredge would describe the potential for roadside drama in the Shipman's account of a virile monk and a cuckolded merchant.[10] Although so many Chaucerians this century have responded to dramatization issues first raised by Kittredge, few have followed through the rich *Shipman's Tale* possibilities – largely on account of five first-person plural pronouns referring to wives, within eight early lines of the tale. The narrator opens by declaring that extravagant wives bring woe to 'hym that payen moot for al'; a remark follows that niggardly husbands run the risk that we wives may find 'another [to] payen for oure cost' (*ShipT* 10, 18). For scholars, *The Shipman's Tale* is problematic owing to cheerful amorality. So is the Wife of Bath, the only pilgrim who could use first-person plural for wives. Perhaps too eagerly, Chaucerians came to regard *The Shipman's Tale* as not quite relevant to *The Canterbury Tales* as a whole.[11] By assigning *The Shipman's Tale* to an incipient Wife of Bath and largely avoiding it, scholars have ignored the sensible solution proposed in 1934 by Frederick Tupper:

> Years ago the Riverside (Cambridge, Massachusetts, 1878) and the Globe (London, 1899) editions of Chaucer met the difficulty by putting the first person passage in quotation marks . . . . In this way the passage becomes a conscious artistic touch, not an oversight. A recitation of the opening section, with due regard of the voice for the sudden transition in the quoted lines from a man's stern criticism of "revelous" women to his clever mimicry of a gaily bedecked wife's taunting chant of triumph over the purse of husband or lover makes delighted assurance doubly sure. I have read it so for forty years. Indeed, how else can one read the text as it stands?[12]

Tupper's observation stands near the start of an unfortunate half-century interlude, now ending, during which students of Chaucer's poetry sometimes respected editorial punctuation as if it were part of the Middle English text. Line-end punctuation was rare in editions of Chaucer before the eighteenth century; quotation marks were not added to the *Canterbury Tales* until 1835, along with other pedagogical aids in the first school edition. Earlier, all four modernizers noticed the pronouns' incongruity and simply changed lines 12–19 of *The Shipman's Tale* to third-person warnings.[13]

Tupper also states clearly that explication of poetry is related to oral delivery of it, whether in the classroom or in one's educated imagination. Subsequent scholars began to blur distinctions. Instead of describing the 'staging' that he or she would recommend, based on superior knowledge of the subject, a scholar doing close analysis might slide toward claims that certain vocal tones really are there in the black marks on the paper. Heightened awareness of imagined performances, which are continually being created by silent readers including oneself, act as reminders that texts themselves have no voices. Voices come from throats, not from ink on paper. Furthermore, modernizations and other pre-twentieth-century Chauceriana can keep academic readers alert to the false experience of a 'text' neatly arranged on paper and introduced to every scholar, at some point in the past, in a particular printed edition.

For the final passage to be discussed here, two main alternatives presented themselves to the eighteenth-century modernizers. We have seen how Markland and Jackson both propagate Chaucer's animal imagery to enliven the businesslike sex act. So, too, both bring images of food to enrich the sexual commerce during negotiations for that act, in the garden just before the wife leaves to scold or cajole her husband. Chaucer provides the potential by juxtaposing hugs and kisses with the monk's invocation of dinnertime. He concludes his pledge:

> "For I wol brynge yow an hundred frankes."
> And with that word he caughte hire by the flankes,
> And hire embraceth harde, and kiste hire ofte.
> "Gooth now youre wey," quod he, "al stille and softe,
> And lat us dyne as soone as that ye may;
> For by my chilyndre it is pryme of day.
> Gooth now, and beeth as trewe as I shal be."
>   "Now elles God forbede, sire," quod she;
> And forth she gooth as jolif as a pye,
> And bad the cookes that they sholde hem hye,
> So that men myghte dyne, and that anon.
>
>   (201–11)

Lipscomb's truncated scene has no body contact and no figurative language. The wife herself will cook single-entendre food:

> "Doubt not the franks I'll bring, the debt to pay:
> "Now go," he said, "and let us quickly dine;
> "Be to your promise true, as I to mine."
>   "That will I do," she says, with joyous air,
> Then homeward hastens, dinner to prepare.
>
>   (150–4)

Travers allows one quick peck, for his monk keeps talking while kissing. Perhaps the two are cautious because of the 'mayde child' watching them. Now often explained as a servant, in 1731 she readily becomes the wife's 'infant Daughter waddling by her Side' (84; compare *ShipT* 95). The toddler's mother then smiles and scampers away, in Travers's mind's eye:

> Be sure that you our mutual Oath uphold,
> And take this Kiss in Earnest of my Gold;
> Go, order Dinner to be ready soon,
> For by my Dial 'tis the Hour of Noon.

> Away she scamper'd with a smiling Look,
> And issu'd forth her Orders to the Cook.
>
> (189–94)

In contrast to Lipscomb and Travers, Markland and Jackson both elaborate the scene's visual metaphors. Both develop the stereotype of ever-hungry visiting clergy, subtle here but overt elsewhere (in, for example, *The Summoner's Tale*). Each could also observe that Chaucer portrays the pilgrim Monk of *The General Prologue* with foods both literal and metaphorical, and implies sexual attraction with a phrase like 'manly man' (*GP* 167). At this tale's juncture of actual dinnertime and overt monastic eroticism, however, the two modernizers tilt the imagery in opposite directions: Markland towards food, Jackson towards sex.

Each author's rendering of *ShipT* 201–11 is consistent with characterization elsewhere in his poem. As the tale opens, for example, Chaucer uses two ambiguous adjectives to term the monk 'a fair man and a boold' (*ShipT* 25). Expanding 'boold' into an oxymoron implying flirtatiousness, Jackson also adds an adjective that recalls the pilgrim Monk's well-anointed face: 'An oily Monk, demurely bold and fair' (26; compare *GP* 199). Three decades earlier, Markland instead puts foremost the cheery face and ample tummy of 'A jovial *Monk*, a portly Man, and bold' (32). Accordingly, in rewriting lines 201–11 of *The Shipman's Tale*, Markland portrays Daun John as a hearty eater, not a greasy lover, and as a self-effacing charmer who jokes about clerical appetites:

> For I will bring you soon an hundred Franks,
> And therewithal he caught her by the Flanks;
> And kiss'd her often, and embrac'd her hard,
> Go now, said he, let Dinner be prepar'd,
> And let us get our Meat, I pray you, soon,
> For a *Priest's Stomach always points to Noon.*
> Away she goes with Pleasure in her Looks,
> And diligently hastens on the Cooks:
> Bids them bestir themselves and bring away,
> The *Monk* was hungry, and must Dinner stay.
>
> (195–204)

Jackson's monk has an appetite too, but dinner will have to wait. Speaking 'with a luscious Leer' (193), he disclaims all else that gold can buy, for the sake of extravagant feasting on this female face and body. He has clearly learned his techniques from hende Nicholas in *The Miller's Tale*:

Had I a Realm, and all the Gold therein,
That and myself shou'd hail thee sov'reign Queen.
This, this, I value more than Crowns or Reigning!
And with that Word he caught her by the *Meaning;*
Which found the quick Sensation it convey'd,
As Trees are nourish'd with the Streams they shade:
His other Hand her milky Bosom plies,
Whilst on her Face he feasts his greedy Eyes;
Till their conjoining Lips with Kisses glow,
Devoured fast. —— At length he let her go,
To see that Dinner was provided soon,
For by his Calendar he found it Noon.
And when they'd plighted each their Faith anew,
As pert as any Pye, away she flew;
Gave Orders that the Cooks no Time shou'd lose.

(199–213)

'And with that Word he caught her by the . . .' Perhaps literary scholars can agree on this one. Other meanings of texts are, and should be, less easily grasped.

From various directions – reception aesthetics, reader response theory, and of course Translation Studies – scholars are asking valid questions about readers' comprehension and indeed re-creation of the texts that they read. Modernizations of Chaucer can show how readers have translated into implied performances this one example from the corpus of Middle English narrative poetry. Future studies of other passages, other works, other authors may test and refine this method of approach: materials are in plentiful supply, and sadly neglected.

Rutgers University, Camden

NOTES

1. *Troilus and Criseyde*, II, 22–3; quoted from *The Riverside Chaucer*, edited by Larry D. Benson (third edition, Boston, 1987). Subsequent quotations from Chaucer are taken from this edition and adopt its line-numbering. I would like to thank Kimberly Adams for her thorough suggestions on this article.
2. On Pope's acknowledged and unacknowledged modernizations, see my *Chaucer Aloud: The Varieties of Textual Interpretation* (Philadelphia, 1987), pp. 207–53. For texts of other eighteenth-century modernizations, with background and bibliography, see my *Eighteenth-Century Modernizations from The Canterbury Tales* (Woodbridge, 1991).

3. For further information on these four figures, see *Eighteenth-Century Modernizations*, pp. 55, 64, 151, 177.
4. John C. McGalliard, 'Characterization in Chaucer's *Shipman's Tale*', *PQ*, 54 (1975), 1–18 (pp. 5, 8).
5. McGalliard, p. 8.
6. This and subsequent line references to the eighteenth-century versions are cited from *Eighteenth-Century Modernizations* (n. 2).
7. Markland here makes metaphorical sense of the Middle English phrase meaning 'what God has sent' (*ShipT* 219). The only glossary then available, in Thomas Speght's edition of Chaucer (1598, 1602, 1687), confuses the issue.
8. *OED*, *s.v.* 'buxom'. Travers seems not to be displaying ignorance but playing with the word's shift in meaning from 'obedience' to 'geniality'. In Speght's seventeenth-century glossaries, he could have found '*buxumnes*, lowlines', and he retains the Middle English meaning elsewhere in his modernization of *The Shipman's Tale*: see ll. 159–62.
9. Criticism, including studies of these four patterns, is summarized in *The Riverside Chaucer* (n. 1), pp. 910–11. One thorough discussion is that by Janette Richardson, *Blameth Nat Me: A Study of Imagery in Chaucer's Fabliaux* (The Hague, 1970), who argues that the 'amoral' imagery patterns must stand in ironic contrast to a moral ideal that is never stated. Her conclusion is representative of one trend in twentieth-century criticism, whereby she 'hears' a tone of sarcasm or disapproval in passages that on paper are potentially neutral.
10. George Lyman Kittredge, *Chaucer and His Poetry* (Cambridge, Mass., 1915), pp. 170–4.
11. For the idea that *The Shipman's Tale* was originally meant for the Wife of Bath, see the summary of criticism in *The Riverside Chaucer* (n. 1), p. 910.
12. Frederick Tupper, 'The Bearings of the Shipman's Prologue', *JEGP*, 33 (1934), 352–72 (pp. 357–8).
13. Markland 16–25, Travers 13–22, Jackson 13–22, Lipscomb 33–40. Charles Cowden Clarke, in *The Riches of Chaucer* (2 vols, London, 1835), was the first to add quotation marks. Chaucerians have recently confronted the problem in 'Modern Punctuation as an Impediment to Understanding Chaucer' (Chair: Emerson Brown, Jr), New Chaucer Society, Canterbury, August 1990. See also Howell Chickering, 'Unpunctuating Chaucer', *Chaucer Review*, 25 (1990–1), 96–109, and my *Chaucer Aloud* (n. 2), pp. 179–84. For assignment of *The Shipman's Tale* to the Shipman, independent of punctuation issues, see Murray Copland, '*The Shipman's Tale*: Chaucer and Boccaccio', *Medium Aevum*, 35 (1966), 11–28.

The Genesis of Byron's
Hints from Horace

Jane Stabler

'Horace', observed Ezra Pound, 'would seem to confer no boons upon his translators.'[1] We could go further, and say that the invocation of Horace's name has been a mortification for the many writers who felt bound to fulfil the 'utile dulci' ideal of the *Ars poetica*. This Horatian ideal was notorious enough for Byron to joke about the expectation it raised in his readers in *Don Juan* (XIII, 81). But Byron's readers did not, in his lifetime, have an opportunity to see the text of his verse translation of the *Ars poetica*, first published in a complete form posthumously, in 1831. Even today, Byron's version, known as *Hints from Horace*, is seldom read and less often discussed. This essay will examine the relationship between Horace's poem and Byron's. I shall consider the contexts of Byron's work on the *Hints* in two distinct periods of his life, showing how the changed circumstances of his later career inflected his revision of the text, and explore the ways in which Byron's version both reaffirms his allegiance to classical aesthetics and subverts an ideal of cultural refinement that had become synonymous with Horace's name.

Horace's literary criticism had been accepted in England as the standard guide to the civilizing effect of poetry from the Renaissance onwards. Several major scholarly editions of the *Ars poetica* were produced in England during the eighteenth century, although it was the content rather than the form of the poem that was cited as commendable.[2] George Colman's 1783 translation of the *Ars poetica* was prefaced by a dedicatory letter describing the poem as one which

> has been almost universally considered . . . as a loose, vague, and desultory composition; a mass of shining materials; like pearls unstrung, valuable indeed, but not displayed to advantage.[3]

Nevertheless, the *Ars poetica* was a source of authoritative maxims and instruction. Essays in the *Spectator* and *Tatler* often drew mottos from it. Edmund Burke invoked Horace in his 'Essay on Taste' and in his *Reflections on the Revolution in France*:

The precept given by a wise man, as well as a great critic, for the construction of poems, is equally true as to states. '*Non satis est pulchra esse poemata, dulcia sunto.*' There ought to be a system of manners in every nation which a well-formed mind would be disposed to relish.[4]

Burke's emphasis on the disposition of the 'well-formed' individual is instructive, creating as it does a unity of aesthetic excellence and social harmony. And the concept of art as unity has, in fact, remained in close association with Horace's name into the twentieth century. Mikhail Bakhtin links Horace with Aristotle and Boileau as the main advocates of what Bakhtin terms 'organic poetics'. These figures, Bakhtin argues, were

> permeated with a deep sense of the wholeness of literature and of the harmonious interaction of all genres contained within this whole. It is as if they literally hear this harmony of the genres.[5]

Although elsewhere Bakhtin characterizes Horatian satirical and epistolary genres as 'novelistic' discourse, his echoing in this passage of the image of the harmony of the spheres suggests the construction of a universal, sacrosanct authority, almost an iconography, in Horace's name.

During the eighteenth century the paradigm of Horatian unity was invoked to criticize formally or generically 'disruptive' works such as *Tristram Shandy*. The *Journal Enclycopédique* referred to this novel as 'Horace's monster',[6] and Sterne wrote to an early reader of the manuscript of Volumes I and II:

> I like Your Caution of the Ambitiosa recidet ornamenta – as I revise My book, I will shrive My conscience upon that sin.[7]

Byron's writing was also criticized for its digressiveness and for straying away from neo-classical aesthetic propriety. It is interesting, therefore, that one of the principal phases of Byron's interest in Horatian aesthetics came whilst he was working on the fifth canto of *Don Juan*, the work he called his 'poetical *Tristram Shandy*'.[8]

Byron's complex attitude to Horatian critical orthodoxy is demonstrated in a letter to Thomas Moore of 1 June 1818. Responding to Moore's criticism of the enjambement between stanzas in Canto IV of *Childe Harold's Pilgrimage*, Byron claimed:

> The fact is, that the terza rima of the Italians, which always *runs* on and in, may have led me into experiments, and carelessness into

conceit – or conceit into carelessness – in either of which events failure will be probable, and my fair woman, "superne", end in a fish; so that Childe Harold will be like the mermaid, my family crest, with the Fourth Canto for a tail thereunto.

(BLJ, VI, 46)

As Leslie Marchand pointed out, 'superne' is an allusion to the image of artistic failure at the beginning of the *Ars poetica*: 'desinat in piscem mulier formosa superne'.[9] The *Ars poetica* might have been in Byron's mind in 1818 because he was to draw from it the early 'domestica facta' epigraph for *Don Juan*, which was commenced later that summer. But this is not the only point in this letter for which Byron invoked the *Ars poetica*. Byron's fascination with his own waywardness was not extended to the vagaries of Leigh Hunt, and he goes on to complain of the excesses of Hunt's *Foliage*:

When I saw "Rimini" in MSS., I told him that I deemed it good poetry at bottom, disfigured only by a strange style. His answer was, that his style was a system, or *upon system*, or some such cant; and, when a man talks of system, his case is hopeless [. . .] he sent out his "Foliage" by Percy Shelley ***, and, of all the ineffable Centaurs that were ever begotten by Selflove upon a Night-mare, I think this monstrous Sagittary the most prodigious.

(BLJ, VI, 46–7)

Marchand picks up the echo of *Troilus and Cressida* ('The dreadful Saggitary appals our numbers', V.v.14–15), but does not note the continued allusion to Horace's monsters from the beginning of the *Ars poetica* as translated by Byron:

> till Nature with a blush
> Saw cits grow centaurs underneath his brush? . . .
> Believe me, Moschus, like that picture seems
> The book, which, sillier than a sick man's dreams,
> Displays a crowd of figures incomplete,
> Poetic night-mares, without head or feet.[10]

The difference between the two echoes of Horace is that whereas Byron saw *Childe Harold* as having 'tailed-off' into a 'failure' both rich and strange, he presented Hunt's art as the product of 'Selflove'.[11]

The self-sufficiency of Hunt's 'system' was one of the things that Byron also objected to in the poetry of the 'Lake School'. Troubled images of the narcissistic or self-begotten work of art (with its sexual correlatives of masturbation and incest) appear in Byron's writing throughout his career, most famously in connection with Keats. For example, Byron referred to his *Vision of Judgement* as 'my nightmare to balance the incubus of [Southey]'s impudent anticipation of the Apotheosis of George the Third' (*BLJ*, VIII, 236). By calling Southey's work an 'incubus', Byron was extending the image of poetic self-sufficiency to the domain of political sycophancy and nepotism. The 'nightmare' of his own response indicates Byron's awareness that he was contributing to the same economy of writing that sustained Southey.

In the letter to Moore of 1 June 1818, Byron played with an image of a grotesque compound which was aesthetically disturbing (in Hunt's case), but also as distinctive as the 'family crest'. I want now to show how Byron's version of the *Ars poetica* experiments with the contrary energies of monstrosity and restraint, exemplifying his oscillation between 'classical' and 'romantic' schools of poetry.

The first version of *Hints from Horace*, to which I refer in what follows, dates from 1811, when Byron was staying in the Capuchin convent in Athens where he found a copy of Horace.[12] Byron thought of his version, or more specifically, as he referred to it at this date, 'imitation',[13] as a sequel to *English Bards and Scotch Reviewers*, and addressed it to Hobhouse, who was to 'fill the same part that the "Pisones" do in Horace' (*BLJ*, II, 43).[14] Before he returned to England, Byron found himself pleased with the closeness of his imitation, but he also spoke of deviation, adaptation, variation, subjunction, and difference with respect to Horace's poem.[15] In the preface Byron claimed:

> The Latin text is printed with the Imitation, not only to show where I have left Horace, but where Horace has left me.
>
> (McGann, p. 428)

Michael Worton and Judith Still have discussed the way in which all translations and imitations may be read as performative acts of criticism and interpretation, or in a Lacanian reading as 'textual modalities of recognition and transgression of the Law'.[16] I would like to suggest, though, that Byron's 'varying' of this particular configuration of the Law displays more considerable fractures of voice and authority than other translations of the *Ars poetica*. Byron's digressions from the Horatian source-text in prose and verse are shaped by surges of Popean and Juvenalian satire, which collide with the Horatian tone. A juxtaposition of satirical tones is an identifiable Popean characteristic, but, unlike Pope's satires, *Hints from Horace* is disrupted by a shifting attitude to Horatian orthodoxy. Byron's illustrative contemporary examples, the 'intertexts' of the poem, acquire an autonomous energy which threatens the ideal unity of the Horatian cultural icon.

A good example of the way Byron digresses from Horace comes in the requiem for Samuel Foote:

> Farce followed Comedy, and reached her prime
> In ever-laughing Foote's fantastic time,
> Mad Wag! who pardoned none, nor spared the best,
> And turned some very serious things to jest.
>
> (327–30)

If the *Ars poetica* were printed as a parallel text as Byron desired, we would see that Horace is at this point warning against the disruptive effects of sudden turns, transitions, and alterations. A parallel text of the *Hints* with Horace's Latin was set up in print in 1811, but it is incomplete and the Foote lines are not included in the extant portion (McGann, p. 425). In Moore's 1831 edition of *The Works of Lord Byron*, an edited version of the Latin is appended beneath relevant sections of Byron's text. No parallel text is provided for the lines on Foote, so to appreciate Byron's remodelling the reader has to possess some knowledge of the absent Horatian instruction. E. H. Coleridge's edition of 1898 does not subjoin the Latin, and the 1904 Oxford University Press edition by Frederick Page, corrected by John Jump in 1970, merely redistributes Moore's selection of the *Ars poetica*: there is still no Horatian original to set beside these lines, or those immediately following:

> Nor Church nor State escaped his public sneers,
> Arms nor the Gown, Priests, Lawyers, Volunteers:
> 'Alas, poor Yorick!' now forever mute!
> Whoever loves a laugh must sigh for Foote!
>
> (331–4)

At this point, the reader who is aware of Byron's departure from Horatian precept can contrast:

> uerum ita risores, ita commendare dicaces
> conueniet Satyros, ita uertere seria ludo,
> ne quicumque deus, quicumque adhibetitur heros,
> regali conspectus in auro nuper et ostro,

migret in obscuras humili sermone tabernas,
aut, dum uitat humum, nubes et inania captet.

(225–30)

(But it will be fitting so to seek favour for your laughing, bantering
Satyrs, so to pass from grave to gay, that no god, no hero, who shall
be brought upon the stage, and whom we have just beheld in royal
gold and purple, shall shift with vulgar speech into dingy hovels,
or, while shunning the ground, catch at clouds and emptiness.)[17]

Byron's digression from Horace is transgressive in its effect because it
rewrites the very generic law Horace is expounding: Byron commemorates
Foote's ability to undermine Horatian precept by translating figures of
authority into low comedy.

The voice of cultural authority that the *Ars poetica* offered through
school exercises, epigraphs, and continuous exemplary citation was (and
to some extent still is) unified, oracular, and largely unaltered by the
passage of time.[18] In the 1811 version of the *Hints from Horace*, however,
Byron roams away from the discussion of aesthetic principles to extend
his illustrative contemporary examples. In the proofs of the poem that
were set up at this time, the Latin text is printed *en face*, making it possible
to see how far Byron's version overruns the Latin in spatial terms.[19]
Eighteenth-century English translations of the *Ars poetica* generally
extended to over one hundred lines more than the original. Out of fourteen
translations published during the eighteenth century, however, only two
are longer than Byron's 1811 version.[20]

Byron's expansive treatment can be illustrated from this passage of the
Latin:

imberbis iuuenis, tandem custode remoto,
gaudet equis canibusque et aprici gramine campi,
cereus in uitium flecti, monitoribus asper,
utilium tardis prouisor, prodigus aeris,
sublimis cupidusque et amata relinquere pernix.

(161–5)

(The beardless youth, freed at last from his tutor, finds joy in horses
and hounds and the grass of the sunny Campus, soft as wax for
moulding to evil, peevish with his counsellors, slow to make needful
provision, lavish of money, spirited, of strong desires, but swift to
change his fancies.)

The layout of the 1811 proofs offers graphic evidence of Byron's latitude in translation: for five lines of Latin, Byron's version supplies eighteen lines of English verse and several prose notes. This process of accretion is lost in the McGann text, although it is still possible to enjoy the pace of an example running wild:

> Behold him freshman! forced no more to groan
> O'er Virgil's devilish verses, and – his own;
> Prayers are too tedious, lectures too abstruse,
> He flies from T[a]v[e]ll's frown to 'Fordham's Mews';
> (Unlucky T[a]v[e]ll! doom'd to daily cares,
> By pugilistic pupils and by bears!)
> Fines, tutors, tasks, conventions threat in vain,
> Before hounds, hunters, and Newmarket plain.
> Rough with his elders, with his equals rash,
> Civil to sharpers, prodigal of cash,
> Constant to nought – save hazard and a whore,
> Yet cursing both, for both have made him sore:
> Unread (unless, since books beguile disease,
> The p[o]x becomes his passage to degrees);
> Fool'd, pillaged, dunn'd, he wastes his terms away,
> And unexpell'd, *perhaps*, retires M.A.
> Master of Arts! as *hells* and *clubs* proclaim,
> Where scarce a blackleg bears a brighter name!
>
> (223–40)

The verse is interrupted by parentheses which remind the reader firstly of Byron's career (Tavell was a Fellow of Trinity who presumably objected to Byron's keeping a bear in college), and secondly of an unsavoury connection between the consumption of books and the consumption of the body. A prose note to line 227 also draws the reader's attention to allusive minutiae:

> *Infandum, regina, jubes renovare dolorem.* I dare say Mr. T[a]v[e]ll (to whom I mean no affront) will understand me; and it is no matter whether any one else does or no. – To the above events, 'quaeque ipse miserrima vidi, et quorum pars magna fui', all times and terms bear testimony.
>
> (McGann, p. 435)

The note itself, in turn, is fragmented by quotation from Virgil (*Aeneid*, II, 3), a tongue-in-cheek aside, and a pun on the source of friction between college authority and Byron. The personal tone of the note shows how

Byron's translation imported the appendages of satire to complicate the aesthetic treatise: notes to previous English translations of Horace's poem had, of course, tended to discuss interpretative points rather than extending the satirical incursions of the work.

Another example of Byron's pull towards monstrosity in the 1811 *Hints* appears in the lines on the solitary Druid:

> Up to his den Sir Scribbler hies, and soon
> The gather'd gall is voided in lampoon.
> Perhaps at some pert speech you've dared to frown,
> Perhaps, your poem may have pleased the town!
> If so, alas! 'tis nature in the man:
> May Heav'n forgive you, for he never can!
> Then be it so, and may his withering bays
> Bloom fresh in satire! though they fade in praise;
> While his lost songs no more shall steep and stink,
> The dullest, fattest weeds on Lethe's brink;
> But springing upward from the sluggish mould,
> Be (what they never were before) be – sold!
>
> (707–18)

There is no source in the Latin for this portrait: the satire is generated by Byron's use of Popean idiom. But the lines are also *self*-generating, in the sense that they are produced by the progress they describe. The satire of *English Bards and Scotch Reviewers* (1809) led to a resurgence of Byron's reputation after his lyrics had flopped. In this passage we can trace the grotesquely fertile workings of the satiric imagination.

Contrasting with the celebration of splenetic excess, the *Hints* of 1811 also supplies a defence of the laissez-faire pacifist:

> Who takes our Laws, and Worship, as they are,
> Nor roars reform for Senate, Church, and Bar,
> In practice rather than loud precept wise,
> Bids not his tongue, but heart – philosophize.
>
> (497–500)

Again, there is little basis for this in Horace's text, which at this point focuses on the poet's delineation of public figures:

> quod sit conscripti, quod iudicis officium, quae
> partes in bellum missi ducis, ille profecto
> reddere personae scit conuenientia cuique.
>
> (324–6)

(He who has learned . . . what is imposed on senator and judge, what is the function of a general sent to war, he surely knows how to give each character his fitting part.)

But Byron was prepared to 'roar reform' at other points in the poem:

> Repeal that act! – again let Humour roam
> Wild o'er the stage! – we've time for tears at home
> (357–8)

> Our Church, our State, our Courts and Camps concede
> Reward to very moderate heads indeed!
> (579–80)

The advocacy of a reverential attitude to British institutions can thus be seen as a deviation from Horace's sense and a contradiction of the speaker's sentiments elsewhere in the poem. The 1811 *Hints* may be said to question not only its Horatian source, but also its own protocols.[21]

Mary Rebecca Thayer has observed that Byron's verse interpolations in the *Hints*

> constitute a large part of the poem, and make it rather a piece of bitter satirical verse than an epistle about literature, with only an incidental element of mild satire, as is the original. The *Hints from Horace*, therefore, so far from being really Horatian in tone, rather serves to accentuate Byron's lack of sympathy with Horace.[22]

It is true that the tone of the speaker sometimes departs from the measured, conversational progress of the *Ars poetica*:

> Arise, my Jeffrey! or my inkless pen
> Shall never blunt its edge on meaner men;
> Till thee or thine mine evil eye discerns,
> 'Alas! I cannot strike at wretched kernes.'[23]

The thirty–eight–line challenge to Jeffrey was added to *Hints from Horace* when Byron returned to England in 1811.[24] It has no basis in the *Ars poetica* and, indeed, contravenes the Horatian precept regarding correction:

> Your friend's 'a Johnson', not to leave a word,
> However trifling, which may seem absurd;
> Such erring trifles lead to serious ills,
> And furnish food for critics, or their quills.
>
> (761-4)

But we should qualify Thayer's conclusion as to the un-Horatian tone of the *Hints*. The discontinuity of any one voice in Byron's 1811 version makes it a much more unstable epistle than even that elastic genre allowed. The presence of a defence of criticism and an *ad hominem* attack on a critic within the same work almost allows *Hints from Horace* to be read as a carnivalesque text after the models of Mikhail Bakhtin and Julia Kristeva, in which prohibition and transgression coexist and enter into dialogue.[25]

The attack on Jeffrey is described by McGann as 'the only passage which recalls the severer style' of *English Bards and Scotch Reviewers*' (p. 427). In the prose notes, however, it is much easier to see the vigorous, vituperative blows of eighteenth-century Juvenalian satire. The idiom of the prose notes also emphasizes the shift from the oral culture of Horace (who warns of relentless mediocre recitation) to the printed culture of Pope (whose *Dunciad*, for example, warns against relentless mediocre publication). The satirical link between *corpus* and corpse is not available in the *Ars poetica*, but plays a significant role in the 1811 *Hints from Horace*, where the repetition of human behaviour (the rake's progress through college, for example) parallels the endless reproduction of texts. The prose note on the patronage of artisan poets (a late addition to the 1811 printer's copy) is a case in point:

> What does it signify whether a poor dear dead dunce is to be stuck up in a Surgeons' or in a Stationers' Hall? Is it so bad to unearth his bones as his blunders? Is it not better to gibbet his body on a heath, than his soul in an octavo?
>
> (p. 441)

Such shifts away from Horace's text were augmented as Byron revised the poem back in England.[26]

*   *   *

Byron's interest in *Hints from Horace* revived in 1820. On 28 March of that year he added the following postscript to a letter to John Murray:

> P.S. – I have some thoughts of publishing the "hints from Horace"

written ten years ago – if Hobhouse can rummage them out of my
papers left at his father's – with some omissions and alterations
previously to be made – when I see the proofs.

(*BLJ*, VII, 60)

Byron's correspondence at this time supplies the context for his
reappraisal of *Hints from Horace*, and gives some indication of the way that
a re-encounter with an old work may effect a revolution of perspective.
On the following day, 29 March 1820, Byron sent Murray a note on Pope
which was to be attached to the prose 'Observations on an Article in
Blackwood's Edinburgh Magazine'. This was a response to an attack on
Don Juan, Cantos I and II. Here, Byron attacked the 'Age of the Decline
of English Poetry' led by the Lake School coterie,[27] and his accompanying
letter announced a battle to uphold taste in English writing:

I have at last lost all patience with the atrocious cant and nonsense
about Pope, with which our present blackguards are overflowing,
and am determined to make such head against it, as an Individual
can by prose or verse – and I will at least do it with good will. —
— There is no bearing it any longer, and if it goes on, it will destroy
what little good writing or taste remains amongst us. — — I hope
there are still a few men of taste to second me, but if not, I'll battle
it alone – convinced that it is in the best cause of English literature
[. . .] You have given me a screed of Metaphor and what not about
Pulci – & manners, "and going *without clothes*" [. . .] I differ from
you about the "refinement" which has banished the comedies of
Congreve – are not the Comedies of *Sheridan* acted to the thinnest
houses? [. . .] But last and most to the purpose – Pulci is *not* an
indecent writer – at least in his first Canto as you will have perceived
by this time. — — You talk of *refinement*, are you all *more* moral?
are you *so* moral? – No such thing, – *I* know what the World is in
England by my own proper experience.

(*BLJ*, VII, 61)

Byron was at this point determined to publish his prose response to
Blackwood's, but in June he changed his mind in deferential response to
a letter from Hobhouse. Byron now first sees the possibility of linking his
critical writing on the Lake School with the text of the *Hints*:

My dear Hobhouse – You are right – the *prose* must not be published
– at least the merely *personal part*; – and how the portion on Pope
may be divided I do not know. – I wish you would ferret out at

Whitton – the "Hints from Horace". I think it (the Pope part) might
be appended to that Popean poem – for publication or no – as you
decide. I care not a damn.

(*BLJ*, VII, 114)

In September 1820, Hobhouse had finally recovered the *Hints from Horace*
and wrote:

> I have looked out your hints from Horace – very good, [. . .] but
> you will not like to attack friends who are hitched into the rhymes
> there.[28]

Byron responded:

> The "Hints &c." are good are they? As to the friends we can change
> their names unless they rhyme well – in that case they must stand.
> Except Scott and Jeffrey and Moore – Sir B. Burgess and a few more
> I know no friends who need be left out of a good poem.

(*BLJ*, VII, 178)

The reappearance of *Hints from Horace*, then, is to be connected with
Byron's determination to champion Pope against the Lakers. As McGann
notes, Byron's new interest in the poem occurred 'in the context of his
prose defences of Pope . . . and also at the time he was seriously renewing
his attack upon contemporary English social and literary culture' (p. 427).
Byron requested that 'all that regards *Pope*' in the prose letter to
Blackwood's should be put 'as a note under the name of *Pope*' where it
occurs first in the *Hints* (*BLJ*, VIII, 61). But Byron's desire to make an
impact on the English literary scene was frustrated by a series of diversions
and delays. On 11 January 1821, Byron's journal entry records that he had
corrected a set of proofs of *Hints from Horace*. This set was, however,
incomplete, and Byron protested vehemently to Murray against 'cutting
and slashing':

> I [. . .] have made the few corrections I shall make in what I have
> seen at least. – I will omit nothing and alter little; – the fact is (as
> I perceive) – that I wrote a good deal better in 1811 – than I have
> ever done since. – I care not a sixpence whether the work is popular
> or not.

(*BLJ*, VIII, 60)

On 1 March 1821, Byron wrote to Murray to acknowledge receipt of another proof. This was still without the Latin and without the 'note under the name of *Pope*', but it included the satiric passage on Jeffrey that Byron had instructed Murray to remove.[29] A year later, *Hints from Horace* remained unpublished. Byron's letter to Moore of 4 March 1822 described the *Hints* as 'written in 1811, but a great deal, *since*, to be omitted' (*BLJ*, IX, 118). A complete text of *Hints from Horace* was finally published in 1831, but even the most recent edition of Byron's poems, edited by McGann, which uses as much of the 1821 proof as has survived, excludes the note on Pope which was the polemic behind Byron's revision of his work.

What was the effect of all these aspirations and negotiations on the revised text of Byron's version? The difficulty Byron experienced in recovering the *Hints* from his friend and publisher, and his failure in winning them over to the publication of both the *Hints* and *Don Juan*, became part of the fabric of these poems. The urgency of Byron's commitment to Pope led him to recast Pope's role in the *Hints*: the emendations resulting from this constitute the main difference between the 1821 and the 1811 versions of the *Hints from Horace*. For example, Byron cancelled the couplet:

> Satiric rhyme first sprang from selfish spleen.
> You doubt – see Dryden, Pope, St. Patrick's dean.
>
> (114a–b)

The accompanying prose note was also removed for the obvious reason that it detracted from the wholly positive view of Pope that Byron was attempting to uphold. This trimming of the *Hints* might be thought to distance the text still further from Horace's *Ars poetica* – especially if we bear in mind that the new note on Pope would have been over 400 lines long.[30] But Byron's reworking of his text has the effect of reinstating a discussion of aesthetic principles. In 1811, I would argue, Byron was mainly concerned with using Horace as an occasion for contemporary satire, whereas in 1821 Byron's aim was to move towards a fusion of Horace and Pope. To this end, many of the discursive prose notes of 1811 were removed. According to McGann (pp. 439–40), the very long and very funny satirical note on Southey and the 'Edinburgh Annual Register' was cut from forty-eight lines to fifteen words. Reduction on this scale would have allowed the prose note on Pope to stand out as the main site of debate about contemporary aesthetics. This note presents Pope as a very different figure from the 1811 fount of 'selfish spleen'. In 1821 the poetry of Pope is 'the Christianity of English Poetry' (Nicholson, p. 106). For example, in the 1811 Preface Byron advertised his Popean couplets as a vehicle for satire:

I have here rhymed the theme of Magazines, the anti-hero of a novel,
the mark of anonymous letters, and Slander of every description in
various periodical publications.

(p. 430)

In 1821 this Preface was discarded, and in the new note on Pope Byron
defended Popean rhyme, not for its ability to yoke together heterogeneous
elements, but for its formal 'faultlessness'. The *Ars poetica* in 1811 was a
means of continuing *English Bards and Scotch Reviewers*; in 1821 it was the
model to uphold Byron's defence of 'the Poetry of Art'.[31] This new
emphasis may be seen in the 1821 emendation of the opening couplet.
Byron revised to:

> Who would not laugh, if Lawrence, skilled to grace
> His classic canvass with each flatter'd face

instead of:

> Who would not laugh, if Lawrence, hired to grace
> His costly canvass with each flatter'd face
>
> (1–2)

This change removes the mercenary element in portraiture and supplants
it with the ideal of craftsmanship.

Byron emphasized the nine-year gap between the original composition
of the *Hints* and its intended presentation to the world. The appeal of the
nine years was that it coincided with Horace's dictum '*nonumque prematur
in annum*' (388), but the time-span haunted Byron in other ways too:

> 'Where is the world,' cries Young, 'at *eighty*? Where
>   The world in which a man was born?' Alas!
> Where is the world of *eight* years past? '*Twas there* –
>   I look for it – 'tis gone, a Globe of Glass!
> Cracked, shivered, vanished, scarcely gazed on, ere
>   A silent change dissolves the glittering mass.
> Statesmen, chiefs, orators, queens, patriots, kings,
> And dandies, all are gone on the wind's wings.
>
> (*Don Juan*, XI, 76)

This stanza dates from 1822, and I would argue that it expresses the
'silent change' which Byron experienced when he received his proof of
the *Hints*. The stanza immediately preceding this one carries a

compressed version of the rake's progress which is found in *Hints from Horace*.[32] In 1821, Byron's re-reading of the *Hints from Horace* yielded an ironized version of that poem: not only did Byron find that some of his specific names had to be changed ('written in 1811, but a good deal *since* to be omitted'), but his relationship with the English reading public had gone as well.

The 1811 *Hints* relied on a shared community of cultural reference to make its satirical points. Whether the poet addressed 'Moschus', a wider English audience, or a poetic adversary, references to 'our island', 'Our life and language', 'our Bens or Beaumonts', 'our Shakespeare', 'our days in each Aegean clime', 'our plays', even 'our Pope' (86, 104, 121, 131, 343, 354, 386) all served to recall a sense of shared tradition. In 1821 all these references remain, but are implicitly ironized by the context of Byron's alienation from 'the general voice of his countrymen', as John Gibson Lockhart depicted Byron's exile in *Blackwood's Edinburgh Magazine* (Nicholson, p. 362). Byron rejected the shared pronoun of English identity in his 'Letter to John Murray Esqre' (1821) when he claimed:

> if any great national or natural Convulsion could or should overwhelm your Country in any such sort as to sweep Great Britain from the kingdoms of the Earth . . . the surviving World would snatch Pope from the Wreck – and let the rest sink with the People.
> (Nicholson, p. 150)

And it would have been difficult for Byron to re-read the lines on the poet, 'fasting and forgot', whose mediocre achievements include '[daubing] a shipwreck like an alehouse sign' (32–4), without recalling the public outcry which had greeted his depiction of the shipwreck in Canto II of *Don Juan*: 'the whole circle of poetry does not contain a more striking contrast of beauty and deformity', observed a review in the *Investigator*.[33] Similarly, the lines in *Hints*, 1811, on dramatic decorum –

> At least, we moderns – wisely 'tis confest
> Curtail, or silence, the lascivious jest!
> (445–6)

– acquire a heightened ironic tone in the context of the contemporary response to *Don Juan*'s gamut of *double entendre*.

The discussion of the poetry of the day which Byron undertook in the 1821 version of *Hints* drew both Horace and Pope into the defence of a poem that defied canons of correctness. *Don Juan* was, unquestionably, one of Horace's monsters, but whilst reviewers criticized the poem for immoral and tasteless desecration of art, the poem criticized its readers for an artful construction of taste and morality:

> Or (to the point with Horace and with Pulci)
> *'Omne tulit punctum, quae miscuit utile dulci'.*
> (XIII, 81)

This allusion invites the reader to recognize what nineteenth-century society has made of the *Ars poetica*. Byron wrote scathingly of the cultural ideals of 'this immaculate period, this Moral Millennium of expurgated editions in books, manners' (Nicholson, p. 170). The prose note on Pope which was to accompany the 1821 version of *Hints from Horace* identifies the new canons being established by Byron's ex-readership:

> Pope little expected that the "Art of Sinking in Poetry" would become an object of serious Study – and supersede not only his own but all that Horace – Vida – Boileau – and Aristotle had left to Posterity, of precept, – and the greatest poets in all nations – of example.
>
> (Nicholson, p. 116)

The second *Hints from Horace* and *Don Juan* are attempts to make the reader resist the 'laudable delicacy' and 'crying-out elegance of the day' (Nicholson, p. 170), and to reconstruct an aesthetic decorum with a moral gloss. In 1811, Byronic digression turned Horatian aesthetics to satire, but in 1821 the text suggests that it is the audience which has digressed. *Hints from Horace* in 1821 presents three names who are no longer in favour with 'the taste of the times' (Nicholson, p. 149): Horace, Pope, Byron. By aligning them with the cultural icon of the *Ars poetica*, Byron suggests that his contemporary readership has erred. The onus of interpretation lies not only with the translator. As the title of the *Hints* intimates, the crucial translation is the one made by the reader. Writing to Peacock in 1819, Shelley remarked that he 'had rather err with Plato than be right with Horace'.[34] Byron's versions of the *Ars poetica* counter the dualism behind Shelley's argument, demonstrating one of the possible ways both to err and be right with Horace.

University of Glasgow

NOTES

1. *Literary Essays of Ezra Pound*, edited by T. S. Eliot (London, 1954), p. 241.
2. See, for example, the editions by Richard Bentley (1711), Richard Hurd

(1757), and Gilbert Wakefield (1794). For this and other information on the eighteenth-century *Ars poetica* I am indebted to C. O. Brink, *Horace on Poetry: The Ars Poetica* (Cambridge, 1971). All subsequent quotations from the Latin are taken from this edition.

3. *Q. Horatii Flacci Epistola ad Pisones, De Arte Poetica . . . Translated from Horace* (London, 1783), p. ii.
4. Edmund Burke, *Reflections on the Revolution in France and on the Proceedings in Certain Societies in London Relative to that Event*, edited by Conor Cruise O'Brien (Harmondsworth, 1983), p. 172.
5. *The Dialogic Imagination: Four Essays by M. M. Bakhtin*, edited by Michael Holquist, translated by Caryl Emerson and Michael Holquist (Austin, 1981), p. 5.
6. See *Sterne: The Critical Heritage*, edited by Alan B. Howes (London, 1974), p. 382.
7. *Sterne: The Critical Heritage*, p. 40. 'Ambitiosa . . . ornamenta': 'lop off ostentatious ornaments', *Ars poetica*, 447–8.
8. Letter to Douglas Kinnaird, 14 April 1823, in *Byron's Letters and Journals*, edited by Leslie A. Marchand, 12 vols (London, 1976; hereafter '*BLJ*'), X, 150: 'You must not mind occasional rambling I mean it for a poetical T[ristram] Shandy – or Montaigne's Essays with a story for a hinge'. Montaigne invoked Horace's example of artistic 'failure' to account for the digressive progress of the *Essays*: see *The Complete Essays*, edited by M. A. Screech (Harmondsworth, 1987), p. 206.
9. *BLJ*, VI, 46; *Ars poetica*, 4.
10. Lines 3–4, 11–14; Byron, *The Complete Poetical Works*, edited by Jerome J. McGann, 7 vols (Oxford, 1980–93), I, 289. All subsequent quotations of the preface, text, and notes to the *Hints from Horace* are taken from this volume, and citations of 'McGann' refer to it. Quotations from *Childe Harold's Pilgrimage* and *Don Juan* are also taken from this edition.
11. Byron made the connection between Hunt's *Rimini* and the aesthetic criticism of the *Ars poetica* in a letter to Hunt of 22 October 1815: '"difficile est proprie communia dicere" seems at times to have met with in you a literal translator' (*BLJ*, IV, 320). Another comparison between the Lake School and the 'bad poet' of the *Ars poetica* is implied in *Don Juan*, III, 98: 'We learn from Horace, Homer sometimes sleeps; / We feel without him: Wordsworth sometimes wakes'.
12. I have not been able to ascertain which edition of Horace Byron used at the monastery. Authorities agree, however, that there are few textual variants in the recent history of the *Ars poetica*, and it seems safe to assume that Byron's edition would not have differed substantially from what is available to us today. See *Texts and Transmissions: A Survey of the Latin Classics*, edited by L. D. Reynolds (Oxford, 1983), pp. 182–6.
13. See McGann, p. 288. Byron described the final version of his text in 1821 as an 'Allusion in English Verse' (McGann, p. 427). Given the ubiquity of the term for English versions of the classics in the preceding century and beyond, it is very doubtful whether, as McGann claims, this later subtitle is 'borrowed from Rochester's similar Horatian exercise, "An Allusion to Horace, the Tenth Satire of the First Book"'. But the modification to the subtitle does

suggest that Byron gradually reduced the proximity between his poem and Horace's. I shall argue later, however, that this description would be a simplification of the relationship.

14. By a strange coincidence, Hobhouse also attempted a 'litteral [sic] verse rhyme translation of the same poem with learned notes' in the same year whilst he too was abroad. See *Byron's Bulldog: The Letters of John Cam Hobhouse to Lord Byron*, edited by Peter W. Graham (Ohio, 1984), pp. 66–7. This version, like Byron's, went unpublished.

15. These comments on *Hints from Horace* are drawn from Byron's letters in 1811. See *BLJ*, II, 42–5, 112.

16. *Intertextuality: Theories and Practices*, edited by Michael Worton and Judith Still (Manchester, 1990), p. 9.

17. Quoted from the Loeb translation by H. Rushton Fairclough in *Horace: Satires, Epistles and Ars Poetica* (London, 1926), p. 469. Subsequent prose translations of the *Ars poetica* are quoted from this volume.

18. A discussion of the importance of Horace in schools and eighteenth-century culture more generally can be found in R. M. Ogilvie, *Latin and Greek: The History of the Influence of the Classics on English Life from 1600 to 1918* (London, 1964), pp. 34–73. Byron immortalized his early difficulties with Horace in *Childe Harold's Pilgrimage*, IV, 77: 'Then farewell Horace; whom I hated so, / Not for thy faults, but mine'. Byron's relation to Horace has been reconsidered by E. Kegel-Brinkgreve, 'Byron and Horace', *ES*, 57 (1976), 128–38.

19. I acknowledge with thanks the permission of the Earl of Lytton to view the proofs of Byron's *Hints from Horace* which form part of the Lovelace Papers deposited in the Bodleian Library.

20. See Allen R. Benham, 'Horace and his *Ars Poetica* in English: A Bibliography', *Classical Weekly*, 49 (1955), 1–5.

21. See also Frederick L. Beaty, *Byron the Satirist* (Illinois, 1985), pp. 54–9, for further discussion of Byron's difficulty in imposing a unifying progression of thought on his Horatian material in the *Hints*.

22. Mary Rebecca Thayer, *The Influence of Horace on the Chief English Poets of the Nineteenth Century* (New Haven, 1916), p. 39.

23. Lines 11–14 of the text printed by McGann, pp. 318–19, as 'Lines Associated with *Hints from Horace*'. The quotation from *Macbeth* (V.vii.7) is noted by McGann (p. 444). 'Kernes': foot-soldiers, here as opposed to commanders.

24. McGann, pp. 318–9, 425–7, 443–4.

25. See Bakhtin, *The Dialogic Imagination* (n. 5); Julia Kristeva, *Desire in Language: A Semiotic Approach to Literature and Art*, translated by Leon S. Roudiez (Oxford, 1980).

26. Byron described the progress of the *Hints* to Francis Hodgson on 13 October 1811. The most recent additions to the poem were 'some savage lines on Methodism, and ferocious notes on the vanity of the triple Editory of the Edin. Annual Register' (*BLJ*, II, 112). This gives some indication of the accretive process involved in the composition of the *Hints*.

27. Byron, *The Complete Miscellaneous Prose*, edited by Andrew Nicholson (Oxford, 1991; hereafter 'Nicholson'), p. 104.

28. Graham (n. 14), p. 299.

29. Byron acted to prevent the publication of the anti-Jeffrey passage before he left England in 1816. See the note by Robin Breyen, '"Hints from Horace": An Unpublished Note by Lord Byron', *Byron Journal*, 16 (1988), 87.

30. This estimate as to the length of the prose note is based on Byron's instruction to Murray (*BLJ*, VIII, 61). The note would then begin with the paragraph opening: 'The great cause of the present deplorable state of English Poetry is to be attributed – to that absurd and systematic deprecation of Pope', and end with the sentence: 'But the term of his Ostracism – will expire' (Nicholson, pp. 104–18). A more concise version of the note is supplied by Moore in his 1832 edition of Byron's *Works* (*The Works of Lord Byron: With His Letters and Journals, and His Life*, 17 vols (London, 1832–3), IX, 81). This is given at line 473, on Wordsworth. Moore reproduces two portions of Byron's 'Some Observations upon an Article in *Blackwood's Edinburgh Magazine*' (1820; Nicholson, pp. 104, 106–7), but gives his source as '*B. Letters*, 1819'. Moore does not supply any note on Pope for l. 82, nor does he remove ll. 114a–b as Byron requested. His inclusion of the note to l. 473 and another of Byron's comments on Pope as an editorial note to l. 456 shows, however, that he was sensitive to Byron's emphasis in the later version of *Hints*.

31. These remarks are taken from the *Letter to John Murray Esqre* (1821), Nicholson, pp. 151, 133.

32. For a detailed discussion of the relationship between *Don Juan*, XI, 75–6, and Popean satire, see Bernard Beatty, 'Continuities and Discontinuities of Language and Voice in Dryden, Pope, and Byron', in *Byron: Augustan and Romantic*, edited by Andrew Rutherford (Basingstoke, 1990), pp. 125–7.

33. *The Romantics Reviewed: Contemporary Reviews of British Romantic Writers; Part B: Byron and Regency Society Poets*, edited by Donald H. Reiman, 5 vols (New York, 1972), III, 1182.

34. Letter of [26 January] 1819 from Naples; *The Complete Works of Percy Bysshe Shelley*, edited by Roger Ingpen and Walter E. Peck, 10 vols (London, 1965), X, 26.

Translators' Forum

Old English Poetry into Modern English Verse

M. J. Alexander

Over thirty-three years I have translated a good deal of Old English poetry into verse. Teachers of Old English sometimes feel unwanted, but the true Cinderella of English Studies is not Old English: it is translation. Although English was first written to translate the good news of Christianity to the Angles, English literary history has traditionally allowed translation only one moment of glory, with the Renaissance translators as supporters of the triumph of English, the language of a nation with its own 'authorized' Bible. Yet translation was a chief source of writing in English for a thousand years, a source which was not differentiated from what we now call original writing, and with the same prestige. Dr Johnson judged Pope's Homer 'a performance which no age or nation can pretend to equal'. He values it as a version of Homer but also as an achievement of English literature, the performance of an English author.

Yet Mr Pope had already been told by the great classical scholar Richard Bentley that though his *Iliad* was 'a very pretty poem', he 'must not call it Homer'. What hope, then, for Alexander's *Beowulf?*[1] Bentley's ruling limits the role of literary translation to prettiness, though the prettiness of poetry. With the rise of a more scientific philology, the standing of translation fell further, and it was at this very time that *Beowulf*, which did not have the prestige of a classical text, began to be translated: by Turner into English (1805), Gruntvig into Danish verse (1820), and Thorkelin into Latin (in the first edition of *Beowulf* in 1815; Klaeber's verdict on the translation is 'practically useless'). For scholars, originals became absolutely better than any translation, at the same time that for poets originality became absolutely better than skill. Some scholars since have regarded translation as an evil, except when done by their students, when it is merely bad. I know a scholar who calls courses in Classical Civilization 'Mickey Mouse courses' *because* they deal with texts in translation. He taught a course on 'Chaucer and his European Background' which required students to buy a Chaucer and two other texts: *The Consolation of Philosophy* and *Le Roman de la rose* in modern translations, practically useful rather than pretty. He felt no inconsistency, and indeed translations are often used as a matter of practical convenience, unreflectively. We rely on them more than we think. If poets are unacknowledged legislators, translators are invisible civil servants. Translation is not then a Mickey Mouse, pretty but useless, but a drudge, inferior but useful, to get at an idea in Plato or retrieve an image from the Bible.

I hear a dry voice say that if there has to be a translation of a classic text, let it be self-effacing, accurate, and useful, like the departmental secretary, so that no confusion can arise over which is the more important. An academic translator is to produce a crib, a companion, a foil. Indeed, Clark Hall is to *Beowulf* as Madge Alsop is to Dame Edna.[2] Replying on the side of the moderns against the ancients, Hugh Kenner has said that the classics only live in translation. In terms of literary culture as distinct from scholarship – if scholarship still overlaps with literary culture, if there is a literary culture which includes the best of the past – Kenner has a point. At which point, the distinction between original and translation becomes less important than whether there is a genuine transfer of cultural energy.

It was Ezra Pound's translation of *The Seafarer* which prompted me to translate other Old English poems into verse. When I asked Pound in 1961 if I could dedicate my book *The Earliest English Poems* to him, he replied: 'If you think . . . it can be done . . . without *irony*', a warning which I did not heed. Again, in 1968, when I was thinking of a university career, Professor Norman Davis warned me that my book was 'not an academic work'. Professor Eric Stanley later praised the introduction to my *Beowulf*, but scholars avoid comment on the translations themselves, perhaps out of politeness. If they see the point of verse translation, they may not know what criteria to apply. (I have been asked by scholars why I translated this word that way, the query of an examiner rather than a critic.)

I have written on Pound's *Seafarer*, and will only mention here F. C. Robinson's defence of its accuracy as a translation from an 1890s edition of Sweet's *Reader* which Pound used.[3] As an editor, Pound tells us that he omits what he calls the 'dignified but platitudinous address to the deity' at the end of the poem, relegated by Sweet to the back of the book and kept there by Dorothy Whitelock. Pound carried the analytic approach to the text to its conclusion by turning the angels back into Angles. As a translator, his aim was to re-create the impression the poem made upon him, using an archaic register and approximating to the verse-form of the original. My aims were similar, though humbler in intention and in the resources at my disposal. My general intention was life, not servile dependency.

Translating form as well as meaning involves the translator in shadowing the syntactic and stylistic conventions of Old English verse composition, such as the dense apposition of near-synonymous phrases known as variation. This is a style foreign to modern English, so that translators who aim at accuracy and a modern English prose cannot easily comb out these knots into a readable texture or create a consistent stylistic idiom. I except the prose *Beowulf* of G. N. Garmonsway, which is rich in vocabulary, dignified in rhetoric and cadence, and scrupulously attentive to stylistic as well as semantic nuance, a translation rather than a crib. The language the translator has to know is modern English. He must understand Old English but know how to use modern.

Anglo-Saxon audiences seem to have appreciated the formal properties of verse composition: traditional diction and phrase; variation; a riddling, teasing style in which straightforwardness may only be a form of variation. 'Thaet waes god cyning' did not simply inform the audience that Scyld was a good king. 'Thaet waes god cyning' is an understatement, a mild one by the standards of *Beowulf*. This style reflects a knowing, collusive relationship between poet and hearers. For listening to verse was a social experience, a dimension lost to the modern reader. The matter of Old English verse was originally collective, its occasion a communal meal. Social use is implicit in that verse, even in so anti-social a poem as *The Seafarer*, which insists on the soul's individual destiny over against the social virtues of the *comitatus*.

The archaic style and values of Anglo-Saxon poetry look archaeological and dead through the colourless medium of what E. V. Rieu called 'readable modern English prose' (the prose of the *New English Bible* has a comparable effect). The archaism of Old English verse, then, offers Pound a justification for bringing out the strangeness of *The Seafarer* in his version, a poem with a rhythmic life and psychic energy equivalent to that of the original; equivalent and not identical.

My own first versions, of *The Ruin* and *The Wanderer*, are Poundian. I responded to the existential impulse which had made Pound favour heathen over Christian renderings where there was a choice. In the first edition of *The Earliest English Poems*, I omitted the Christian endings of *The Seafarer* and *The Dream of the Rood* as later and inferior. Likewise, I chose to translate *gebideth*, at the end of the first line of *The Wanderer*, as 'longeth for [God's mercy]', though I knew that the consensus favoured 'experiences'. I felt that *The Wanderer* was about waiting for God's mercy, not experiencing it. Perhaps in 1961 I was waiting for God, something which in 1911 Pound was not doing. Subjective feelings are discounted by textual editors, who prefer dates. But even editors are subjects who live between dates.

To come to translating, *The Ruin* describes a ruined city, thought to be Roman as it has hot baths and is massively built in stone. I translated *burgsteall* (rendered as 'citadel' by Mackie) as 'acropolis', which suggests a Greek rather than Roman city.[4] Worse, in *The Wanderer* I translated *eardstapa* (usually rendered 'wanderer') as 'grasshopper', a rare but attested sense. These are unorthodox translations, taking risks with register, though defensibly so in terms of the dynamics of the whole – for it is as a whole that a translation is to be judged. These instances are far-fetched, but less ideological than Pound's bohemian Seafarer, who utters the line 'bides 'mid burghers some heavy business': these burghers are the Presbyterian bankers of Philadelphia, not dwellers in an Anglo-Saxon *burh*. My grasshopper and acropolis might be more puzzling to a scholar than to a modern reader, who might be more put off by the archaizing noticeable in my early versions. To take an extreme example:

> Snapped rooftrees, towers fallen,
> the work of the Giants, the stonesmiths,
> mouldereth
>   Rime scoureth gate-towers
>   rime on mortar.

Those who have heard Pound's recordings of his 'Usura' Canto, or his later Chinese translations, may find these lines from my version of *The Ruin* reminiscent in their liturgical cadence and in what I have recently learned to call their rhotacism. Pound can also be seen in the typographical layout of the lines. An archaism which calls attention to itself might work with a short, fragmentary, and indeed ruinous text like *The Ruin*. But translations from Old English cannot take too many thanes in dreary byrnies. Words such as 'mouldereth' remained at the bottom of my word-hoard.

The first two lines quoted above have a distribution of stresses acceptable in an Old English line but they lack alliteration. As I went on from elegies to translate the 325-line narrative poem *The Battle of Maldon*, I felt the need for a more connected syntax and a more regular verse than Pound had sought. All Old English poems are in the same metre, but different poems require different styles of translation, though this is not evident from all translations. Narrative needs a staple, unlike lyric. Pound's *Seafarer* mimics all Anglo-Saxon effects, not merely those produced by metre; indeed he ends the first line with a pun: *wrecan/* reckon. He does not in fact observe alliteration nor stress-pattern, though he sounds as if he does.

When I called on Ezra Pound in Rapallo, the lady who opened the door greeted me with the words 'Mister Beowulf, I presume.' She presumed wrong. If at that stage I had written a poem entitled 'On First Looking into Clark Hall's *Beowulf*', it would have begun 'Much had I travelled in the realms of lead.' But she was also a prophet. When eventually I succumbed, I knew more Old English, and worked for a more measured, connected, and reserved style. I tried to keep more strictly to the metre, alliteration, and even the sense. *Beowulf* has 3,182 lines, and I calculate that translating them took me an hour a line, a suitably monstrous length of time. I do not compare myself with Paul Valéry, but if I could not find the right word beginning with the right sound for the right position in the line, I had to recast the sentence altogether. As Ben Jonson says,

>   he
> Who casts to write a living line must sweat . . .
>   and strike the second heat
> Upon the muses' anvil; turn the same
> (And himself with it) that he thinks to frame;
> Or for the laurel he may gain a scorn.

A poetic translator is certainly made rather than born. As a poetic translator, I intend what I produce as a poem. *Ars est celare artem*, but this was like knitting a crossword. Like Beowulf contemplating the damage done by the dragon, I tried to think what law I had broken. Modern English has too many little words and too few endings to fit the rules for Old English verse, and sometimes the contrivance of a stress or an alliteration can be felt. And since I could not reproduce all the effects in the places where I saw them, I was prepared to redistribute effects, just as the most literal of translators redistributes words and phrases. At an extreme, my translation contains the words 'Night's table-laughter turned to morning's / Lamentation'; which render 'Tha waes after wiste wop up ahafen / Micel morgen-sweg' (128–9). I could not get the juxtaposition of 'wiste' and 'wop', and replaced it with an antithesis involving two features not in the original, a reference to a modern proverb (turning the tables) and a quiet play on the word 'morning'. Both seem appropriate and legitimate devices, paralleled elsewhere in the poem but not found at this point. But we do not judge a building from one brick. I did not in general try to improve on the original, but stayed as faithful to the sense as possible throughout the poem, so far as was compatible with producing a poem which reflected the formal qualities of the original. I stuck religiously, for example, to the laconic understatements which are commonly misunderstood at first by modern readers. Although Scyld was a very good king indeed, he remains in my version only a good one.

Some Old English verse deserves a classic status, but the Norman Conquest stifled its posterity. By the time scholars had sufficiently reopened the passage to Old English, translation was no longer a central poetic activity. Since Bentley and Johnson, there has been a widening of the gap between literature practised as an art and philology pursued as a science. Scholars began to translate into prose in the last century, and prose became the translator's norm. As for Old English, it became fully available to the English poetic tradition between Tennyson, who tried his hand at a few lines of *Beowulf* when he was an undergraduate and much later did a swinging *Brunanburh*, and Tolkien, who was a belated Victorian. This period, roughly contemporaneous with Queen Victoria but in Oxford continuing until about 1960, was the period of what may be called the romance of philology. In this period what we may call revived history was a main source of poetry. Before its first publication in 1815, *Beowulf* was antiquarian, and since the excavation of Sutton Hoo in 1939 it has shown signs of dying back into archaeology. For Tennyson, William Morris, and Ezra Pound, Old English could also be modern English, *tam antiqua tam nova*. For Eliot (in *Four Quartets*) and Auden, the *vetustas* of Old English is still part of its appeal, but they use Old English metre and effects in a more assimilated way. Assimilation has further advanced in the work of Hughes, Hill, Harrison, and Heaney ('Great British poets begin with H' – Peter Porter).

I referred to 'the romance of philology' and 'revived history' as Victorian phenomena. There may be a critical distance between the culture of an ancient text and the culture of a poetic translator – the distance at which translation becomes a need. In the Tennyson-to-Tolkien phase Old English was needed and was translated. Although the Anglo-Saxons and their language clearly stand at the beginning of the history of the English-speaking peoples, this ancestral relationship seems to have been felt with a special force during the period between Waterloo and *The Lord of the Rings*, and during this period Old English was translated into the bloodstream of literature in English.

University of St Andrews

NOTES

1. Penguin Classics (Harmondsworth, 1973). See also Alexander's *The Earliest English Poems* (Harmondsworth, 1966, 1977, 1991), and *Old English Riddles from the Exeter Book* (London, 1980, 1984).
2. John R. Clark Hall, *Beowulf and the Fight at Finnsburg* (London, 1901, 1911; revised edition by C. W. Wrenn, 1958).
3. My discussion of Pound's *Seafarer* is contained in Michael Alexander, *The*

Poetic Achievement of Ezra Pound (London, 1979), pp. 66–79. 'F. C. Robinson's apologia': Robinson, '"The Might of the North": Pound's Anglo-Saxon Studies and "The Seafarer"', *Yale Review*, 71 (1982), 199–224.

4. *The Exeter Book*, Part II, edited by W. S. Mackie (London, 1933), p. 158.

ACKNOWLEDGEMENT

This article was in an earlier form given at the Anglo-Saxon section of the ESSE Conference at Bordeaux, 4–8 September 1993.

Jean Paulhan's Allegories of Translation

Michael Syrotinski

Although it has become something of a commonplace in translation theory nowadays to dignify the activity of translation by defining it as an act of critical intervention upon a given text written in a source-language,[1] this analogy still remains to be 'translated' itself into academic practice. Translation is still all too often considered secondary or derivative with respect both to the creative originality of a given source text, and to so-called 'original' scholarship, and the emergence of Translation Studies as a valid autonomous field of teaching and research has, if anything, further contributed to the segregation, even ghettoization, of translation. There seems to be at work a subterranean, yet powerful, set of pressures forcing translation to the sidelines. Translators continue to be undervalued and underpaid, and usually misunderstood, but at the same time translation is something most of us involved in literary studies today do all the time to a lesser or greater extent, and which is often simply taken for granted. As someone who has published a number of translations, while also being engaged in scholarly research, I consider translation to be an integral part of my work, not only in that it is helping to make writers in whom I have a vested interest, such as Jean Paulhan, more accessible to a wider readership (though this would be reason enough), nor *a fortiori* because it is an activity that is so intimately bound up with the very creative processes involved in reading and writing. The problem of translation crops up continually within my own literary research, and it surfaces specifically within the texts of Paulhan at a number of significant moments. I would like in this article to look at a number of what I would call 'scenes' of translation, both from Paulhan's texts, and from a translation by Christine Laennec and myself of some of Paulhan's *récits*,[2] as a way of deliberately blurring a number of lines of demarcation that normally separate literary translation from literary criticism, and from translation as a mode of language teaching, so as to question certain presuppositions about the *place* of translation in literature and language studies, and to offer several suggestions about how these implications might be followed up in the teaching of literature and language.

First, a micro-example from one of the prose passages my students were asked to translate from English to French this year, from a newspaper article on the Channel Tunnel. The problem arose of how to translate 'go through the tunnel' into French. One *could* say 'traverser', and most French speakers would not think twice about doing so, but the more correct term would be 'passer par le tunnel'. The very same question comes up at the end of one of Paulhan's *récits*, *Le Pont Traversé* (*The Crossed Bridge*), which takes the form of a series of dreams that the narrator has in order to explain to himself a particularly difficult phase he's going through with a woman. The dreams, although extremely obscure and enigmatic, nevertheless provide a kind of answer to his doubts and questions, and allow him to be reconciled with the woman, this reconciliation giving the *récit* its title. In a note at the end, Paulhan (or the narrator) replies to an objection, based on Mme de Genlis's observation, that it is incorrect to say 'traverser un pont' (since *traverser* would strictly be used for crossing over an obstacle, and a bridge would be the means by which one crosses over the obstacle, the river). Here is the passage in question, followed (as with all subsequent quotations from Paulhan) by the Syrotinski–Laennec translation:

> L'on eût donc repoussé le mot s'il n'avait paru que son défaut même accusait plus nettement la sorte de confusion où l'on a reconnu le trait particulier des événements plus haut rapportés, et telle que les idées ou sentiments naturellement faits pour rapprocher, à leur tour devenaient une raison d'éloignement.[3]

> This word would therefore have been rejected if it hadn't seemed that its very flaw brought out all the more clearly the kind of confusion that could be seen as a particular feature of the events recounted above, and this confusion is such that the ideas or feelings naturally designed to bring us closer together, in their turn became a reason for moving further apart.

So it is precisely *because* of its imperfection, its *défaut*, that *traverser* is paradoxically the best word to express the combination of opacity and lucidity that characterizes the dreams, being both a means to an end and an obstacle to that end, the thing you cross over or through. Paulhan is continually attracted to these sorts of 'imperfections' of language, and indeed the word *défaut* itself is one that constantly recurs in Paulhan, and one for which it is often difficult to find an English equivalent. It means generally that 'something is wrong or missing', and in the *récits* we decided to use only two terms to translate it, 'flaw' and 'failing', so that its insistence would not be lost on the reader.

Paulhan is one of the neglected but central figures of twentieth-century French literature.[4] One might say that his career started out with translation. He spent the years 1908–10 in Madagascar, as the first teacher at the newly established *collège européen*. While there, he increasingly neglected his official duties, preferring to spend time with his Malagasy friends, and became fluent in Malagasy. He was fascinated in particular by proverbs, as they occurred in the traditional Malagasy poetry known as *hain-tenys*, and in the popular debate contests, as well as in ordinary conversation. Paulhan noticed how they stood out from ordinary language, and were invested with a mysterious authority, and the power literally to bring discussions to a halt, which was something he was at pains to account for. He translated a collection of *hain-tenys*, and wrote a number of essays narrating his attempts to learn to speak in proverbs.

These 'proverbs' are not what we might usually understand by the term, since they are by no means such determinate entities. Any saying could potentially become a proverb, and variations using a given fixed structure were common. As Paulhan notes, the social, even political importance of proverbs in Madagascar derives from the position they occupy at the juncture of the socially acceptable and the forbidden. The essay I will quote from, 'L'expérience du proverbe', is structured as a before–after narrative, in which the narrator's initial frustration in using proverbs is replaced, once he has learnt them, by a symmetrical frustration in not being able to understand *why* his proverbs are successful. One example early on in his text serves to illustrate just what is at stake for the narrator. It comes during a conversation with his friend Rajaona:

> *Rajaona*: Pour aller au marché, prenons donc un filanjana [type of chair carried by porters].
> *Moi*: Il n'y a qu'une heure de route, allons plutôt à pied. Le filanjana est bon pour les vieillards.
> *Rajaona*: Le respect s'achète. Si tu vas à pied au marché, l'on se moquera de toi.
>
> *Le respect s'achète* est un proverbe. Je ne m'en aperçois pas, nul mot ne m'en prévenait. Mais le tenant pour la simple suite de la phrase précédente, je réplique: J'aime mieux n'en faire qu'à mon aise, et que l'on me respecte un peu moins. D'ailleurs est-il sûr que
> . . .
>
> (*OC*, II, 110).

> *Rajaona*: Let's take a *filanjana* to go to market.

Me: It's only an hour's walk, let's go on foot. Only old people take *filanjanas*.

Rajaona: [lit.] You have to pay for respect. If you go to market on foot, people will make fun of you.

'*You have to pay for respect*' is a proverb. I don't notice it, no word warned me it was coming. But assuming it's just following on from the previous sentence, I reply:

I prefer to do as I please, and people can respect me a little less. Anyway, of course . . .

Since the narrator has not realized that it is a proverb, his two companions react as if he has said nothing at all, and continue the discussion, completely ignoring his intervention. As he goes on to understand, his mistake is in attributing *any* meaning to it at all, since the effectiveness of Malagasy proverbs depends not so much on their semantics as on a purely positional linguistic *force* that is akin to the syntax of a language. It is once he begins to forget about the meaning of what he is actually saying, and simply to repeat mechanically proverbs and phrases based on the syntactic structures of proverbial expressions, that he succeeds in impressing his friends in conversation, and in 'winning' discussions with proverbs. But he feels this to be something of a hollow victory, since at the same time he has the sense that he is not saying anything at all.

The difficulty Paulhan experiences with proverbs is indeed, as he himself notes on several occasions, a common problem of translation. Clichés in a foreign language always strike us as more colourful, more concrete, more imaginative and clever than corresponding terms in our own language, since what happens when we translate is that we often resurrect dead metaphors (or at least reawaken sleeping ones). What we take to be quaint and expressive is superficial and second-hand, 'just words', to the native speaker. And yet proverbs are also those parts of a language that are *most* language- or culture-specific (the French have a saying for it . . .). As Paulhan remarks, proverbs seem to be suspended between two mutually incompatible dimensions of language, which he defines as *sens* and *influence*, *phrase* and *fait*, *vouloir dire* and *dire*, and he is always on one or the other side of them, but cannot ever seem to 'take in' both sides at once. In translating proverbs, we necessarily run up against a more widespread linguistic tension, which contemporary literary theory has articulated variously as the tension between rhetoric and grammar, or constative and performative, or hermeneutics and poetics.[5]

Paulhan himself was well aware of this, and, in the theory of language and literature which he subsequently elaborated, proverbs and clichés become the prototype of a more pervasive 'mystery' at the heart of all literary expression. Yet it is not a mystery, or enigma, that he confines to literature. It involves a basic problem of expression, and one that he transfers to his analysis, for example, of aesthetics and politics. It's the latter I would like next to focus on.

After the Second World War Paulhan published a highly controversial text, *De la paille et du grain*,[6] condemning the *Comité national des écrivains* for conducting its own purge (épuration) of writers who were judged to have collaborated with the Nazis during the Occupation. This was all the more shocking to people at the time in that during the Occupation Paulhan himself had been one of the key figures of the literary Resistance, and his defence of collaborators seemed to be a betrayal of everything his fellow *Résistants* had fought for. As Paulhan saw it, however, the main crime that the collaborators were accused of, in a strictly legal sense, was antipatriotism, and one had to be very careful to distinguish between partisanship and patriotism, and to place patriotism in a wider historical perspective. Why, he asked, were the so-called antipatriots of 1939 any less tolerable than the antipatriots of 1914 or 1871 (he cites Louis Aragon and Arthur Rimbaud, two of the most anti-French of French writers)? If France was divided between Pétain and de Gaulle, or Fascism and Communism, then these could be seen as the two 'halves' of the *patrie*: physical and spiritual, sentimental and intellectual, outer form and inner essence. This Paulhan formulates in linguistic terms: 'For confusing the physical and the spiritual country to see in it only *one* "patrie", is not so different from taking words for ideas' (*OC*, V, 353). Any 'side' which claimed to be the unique representatives of the *patrie* would be indulging in partisanship, not patriotism: 'Du simple point de vue de la patrie, ils se valent: c'est blanc bonnet et bonnet blanc' (*OC*, V, 350; 'From the simple point of view of the *patrie*, they are equivalent: it's *blanc bonnet et bonnet blanc*'). It may be true that Paulhan, as many writers felt, was being politically disingenuous, but any reading of this essay has to take into account the sections which add to, and colour significantly, the explicit argument.[7] I want to look briefly at a couple of these moments, starting with the choice of the proverb that Paulhan uses ('*c'est blanc bonnet et bonnet blanc*') to summarize the various parallels he draws in his text. How could we translate it? What it *means* is something like 'It's six of one and half a dozen of the other', or 'It's swings and roundabouts', with the underlying notion of there being two equally acceptable ways of thinking of the same thing, and that the choice between the two makes no difference (why it works in French is, of course, that whether *blanc* precedes or follows the noun does not really affect the meaning). But any translation loses the symmetrical reversal of the syntax, which is itself an *example* of the reversibility that is one of the keys to understanding the argument of the essay. Any attempt to get across this idea of reversibility ('it's white bonnet and bonnet white') would completely lose the familiarity and the flavour of the proverb. It only works *within the context* of the essay, and it is in fact a pivotal moment in the text and in our understanding of it, since whether we take it seriously *as* a proverb determines the way in which we read the rest of the text, which contains a whole series of linguistic analogies or 'allegories'.

One such allegory is Paulhan's discussion of the recent refinements of the bidding system in the game of contract bridge, which he takes as a way of illustrating the disadvantages of a language which strives to become a perfect system of communication. The discussion is at the same time a critique of the ambitions of international languages such as Esperanto. While the tendency towards perfection of the bidding increases the efficiency of the game of bridge, it is in danger of becoming so automatic that one might as well play with one's cards on the table. The desire for absolute refinement is shown to be a vain ambition, since it is always open to an absolute misunderstanding of the kind that Paulhan constantly foregrounds, namely that while one person could intend a sign as an idea, another could take it as a word. Invented languages like Esperanto suffer from the same illusion, since they want a language that is unfailingly and universally comprehensible. Similarly – and this is where the allegory ties in with the 'main' argument of the text – the kind of purge of French literature proposed by the CNE is an attempt to perfect and purify the *patrie*, to separate the wheat from the chaff, and, in terms of language, to divide it into a part that is 'essential' and a part that is 'dispensable'. Paulhan goes very much against the grain of the predominant ideology of the time when he states that 'What attaches us to a language and makes us want to speak it is not that it is perfect' (*OC*, V, 324), and he argues passionately for a language that is rich with confusion, errors, and baroque turns of phrase. It is the flaws and defects of language that make it a language, just as antipatriots are the sign of a healthy *patrie*, and just as the impossibility of translation is that which makes translation possible, and necessary.

Paulhan's own theory of literary expression challenges assumptions about meaning-oriented theories of language, in a way which might appear naive to sophisticated late twentieth-century literary critics. Yet the peculiarity, and startling effectiveness, of his texts is that they themselves participate in, and become examples of, the phenomena he sets out to describe. Translating Paulhan thus poses an unusual challenge, since it involves renouncing the translator's supposed ideal of a fluent, seamless, target-language version of the original. A few examples from our own translation of Paulhan's *récits* will serve to indicate the precise nature of this difficulty. As we saw with the proverb '*c'est blanc bonnet et bonnet blanc*', the reversibility of which it is an example is absolutely untranslatable. Our desire to find an adequate equivalent is thwarted by the inherent 'asemantic' properties of the language itself, which we can do nothing about, but which Paulhan allows to take on the burden of proof. This is a characteristic of his writing in general. Paulhan's language is inhabited by awkwardness, but it is only very slightly off, and never radically disruptive, like his contemporaries at the time of the *récits*, the Surrealists, or the early Modernists. His`subtlety is very easy to overlook, which explains to some extent, I think, why he has been neglected. Readers of his texts feel this same impulse to make sense of them, to tidy them up and get rid of their strangeness. A recent new edition of Paulhan's *Pont Traversé*, for example, took the transitive verb *étranger* in the sentence 'Ce grincement me frappe et m'étrange . . . ' ('This squealing strikes me and stranges me . . . '), which is very unusual, but not the only instance of this usage in Paulhan's work, and turned it into *étrangler* ('Ce grincement me frappe et m'étrangle . . .')![18]

One of the most delicate problems in translating the *récits* was thus knowing just how far to go in keeping the awkwardness of style, and not making it sound like the result of 'bad translation'. An example of this kind of tic in Paulhan's French is the use of dislocated, isolated infinitives at the ends of sentences, such as 'Elle sort, revient sur le pré, faner' (*OC*, I, 44; 'She comes out, goes back into the meadow, to turn the hay' – the English works better, since one hears 'in order to', which isn't there in the French). Another example is 'Une petite bohémienne vient autour de nous, rôder' (*OC*, I, 51; literally, 'A small gipsy woman comes around us, to prowl' – here we opted for the present participle, 'prowling', so as to keep the verb adrift at the end of the sentence). Paulhan's syntax is quite elliptical, and there is often nothing more than the suggestion of a grammatical conjunction. In fact, connections between clauses and sentences are often made *disjunctively*; the narrative is left suspended somewhere between continuity and discontinuity, and the language of the *récits* never seems to 'get going' or to flow. One example comes in the *récit* titled *Progrès en amour assez lents* (*Progress in Love on the Slow Side*). It is a description of a storm:

> C'est un moment étrange, au début d'un orage, ce moment où la pluie, qui avait commencé par de lourdes gouttes, s'arrête tout à fait, pèse et semble hésiter. Mais le tonnerre se déchire encore: aussitôt la pièce d'à côté est pleine de bavardages: tout le monde est rentré.
>
> (*OC*, I, 80)

> It's a strange moment, at the beginning of a storm, that moment when the rain, which had begun with large drops, stops completely, hangs and seems to hesitate. But the thunder is still ripping the sky: the room next door is immediately filled with chatter: everyone has come back in.

The narrator starts out as if this were a general description of the moment of high tension just before a storm breaks, but in mid-sentence shifts to recounting the events of this *particular* thunderstorm. Like the moment of suspense before a storm, the narrative often 'hangs' in the air, an impression reinforced by the constant shift in tenses (here, a perpetual present exists almost simultaneously with a continuous present). So it was sometimes less the language itself that we were at pains to translate, as we tried to reproduce the exact measure of its nuances of meaning and tone, than the silences, the gaps, that are somewhere in the interstices of the language, there but not there, but which contribute very decisively to the peculiar quality, or 'lack of quality' (*défaut*) of the French. This raises an interesting general problem of translation, which is never addressed in translation theory: is silence the same in all languages?

And what of language which, more than being awkward, actually 'says nothing' ('ça ne me dit rien') to a French person, such as a proverb or a commonplace expression which is 'just words'? What is the difference between the 'nothing' of a proverb, which none the less exists as a kind of deictic, indicating simply that 'this is a proverb', and non-sense? We confronted this particular difficulty with one expression that we were unable to find an adequate translation for. At one point, one of the characters in *Progrès en amour assez lents* says out of the blue: 'Si quelque chose vous pèle, ce ne sera pas de cet oignon' (*OC*, I, 48), which translated literally means: 'If something peels you, it won't be (part of) this onion.' We asked several native French speakers, for whom it also 'said nothing'. Now it *sounds* as if it ought to be a saying of some kind, and maybe it is, although we are fairly certain it is not a well-known proverb. But even if we were to find out that it was a saying peculiar to some dialect or to a particular period in time, any attempt to translate it would lose the immediacy of its effect, especially if we attached some long explanatory footnote to it (like a joke whose punchline is laboriously explained).

One final example underlines the problematic nature of translation as Paulhan articulates it. It comes from near the end of *Le Pont Traversé*, in a dream that takes place in a strange country inhabited by people called the Nifis. The narrator of the dream seems to be in the same position as Paulhan was in Madagascar with respect to Malagasy proverbs. He describes two men talking together in the Nifi language:

L'un des hommes se plaignit: il souffrait de la tête. Son voisin se leva et s'allongeant à son côté lui pressa le front de ses mains: "Plus fort," dit l'autre. Ces mots me rappelèrent ma surprise.

Presque aussitôt j'en appris la raison. A la droite du malade étaient des joueurs de cartes. L'un deux reprenait son partenaire: 'Je ne t'avais pas dit de mettre la plus faible, eh tête! Ce sont des mots *nifis* simples.' Ils parlaient une langue étrangère.

Les mots sans doute m'auraient arrêté; j'avais dû saisir plus avant leur sens, dans l'instant juste où ils allaient se traduire en phrases – et comme en détournant une part pour moi.

(*OC*, I, 98)

One of the men complained: he had a headache. His neighbour arose and, lying down by his side, pressed his forehead with his hands: "Harder," said the other one. These words reminded me of my surprise.

Almost immediately I learned why. To the right of the sick man were some card players. One of them berated his partner: "I didn't tell you to put down the lowest one, did I? Those are just simple *nifi* words." They spoke a foreign language.

Those words would doubtless have given me pause; I must have grasped their meaning before, in the very instant when it was about to be translated into sentences – and as if diverting part of it for myself.

So although their language is unknown to the narrator, he is able to translate the *nifi* words through some mysterious process. He somehow catches the meaning precisely in the interval of its transformation from thoughts into words, but not without distorting it. It is as if he steals a bit of it away (diverts it from its proper course), and it never fully reaches its destination. The implication is that understanding is always at the expense of an incomplete translation; language never quite reaches its mark, but always falls short, or falls apart in some way.

Paulhan in fact ends up saying something very close to Walter Benjamin in 'The Task of the Translator', or at least what tends to be said in deconstructionist readings of this essay, which show Benjamin's concern to be less to situate the essence of translation in the transcendental 'intention' of a pure language, than to reveal a fissure, a radical disjunction, which is at the heart of all language.[9] Yet at the same time, translation participates in the afterlife of the original, assists in its becoming, and liberates it from the immobility to which it might be consigned through its canonization.

The difference between Paulhan and Benjamin is that while Benjamin is talking about the translation of Great Literature, as far as Paulhan is concerned there is fundamentally no difference between literature and everyday language, and his own writings (which borrow examples indiscriminately from the two) constantly serve to illustrate this confusion. Literature is simply, as he says at one point, 'du langage grossi' ('a fatter, or expanded language'). We have become accustomed to thinking of literature as the place where language can freely exercise its right to linguistic anarchy or innovation, to the point where it takes a lot to disturb and unsettle us any more. But what if, Paulhan asks, this unruliness, or what he often terms 'sickness', or *maladie* (and he does not use this term at all dismissively or contemptuously), what if it extends to all language? At one point in *Les Fleurs de Tarbes*, he says:

> J'ai dit, et chacun sait, que Sainte-Beuve entend Baudelaire de travers; mais il n'en est pas moins exact (bien qu'il soit moins connu) que mon voisin M. Bazot se trouve embarrassé pour parler à sa bonne et s'embrouille aux explications – un peu mystérieuses – de son jardinier. La maladie des Lettres serait, après tout, peu de chose, si elle ne révélait une maladie chronique de l'expression.
>
> (*OC*, III, 17)

> I have said, and everyone knows, that Sainte-Beuve misunderstands Baudelaire; but it is no less true (although it is less well-known) that my neighbor M. Bazot gets confused when talking to his maid, and is muddled by the – somewhat mysterious – explanations of his gardener. The sickness of Literature would, after all, be fairly insignificant if it didn't reveal a chronic sickness of expression.

Paulhan draws our attention to a widespread contamination, even epidemic, of language, which seems to have become infected with literature's 'disease'. But this is to imply that there was a time when language was somehow immune, or healthy. Such a utopian or prelapsarian view of language is, according to Paulhan, merely an illusion.

This has a number of important consequences for a re-evaluation of the relationship between the study of literature and the study of language. It challenges the traditional notion that 'poetics' is something confined to literature, or even one of its distinguishing traits. Paulhan is saying that every time we speak or write, and especially when we say things that 'mean nothing', such as clichés, commonplaces, and proverbs, we are being literary through and through. Translation (and this may be why it is often treated with such distrust) brings together the areas of language and literary criticism, and seems to assist this breakdown of the division traditionally separating them, because it highlights a radical failure at the heart of all language.

Central to the struggle to counter the devaluation of translation is the need to make it more *visible*. As Lawrence Venuti argues, the prevalent criterion of good translation as transparent or self-effacing itself contributes to translation's own invisibility within the academic world at large. As Venuti puts it, 'a fluent strategy aims to efface the translator's crucial intervention in the foreign text: he or she actively rewrites it in a different language to circulate in a different culture, but this very process results in a self-annihilation, ultimately contributing to the cultural marginality and economic exploitation which translators suffer today'.[10] Paulhan's texts, having themselves until recently suffered from an unwarranted marginalization, could be read as an attempt to reaffirm the visibility of translation, and the linguistic uncertainties it inevitably encounters. His writings also offer a subtle explanation of the mechanisms at work in keeping translation hidden, or stuck on the sidelines. It may be precisely because it poses so acutely the problem of 'originality' that translation is so troubling to 'original' scholarship. The undecidability that affects commonplace expressions (was it really meant, or was the person just saying that?) is infinitely extensible, encompassing both 'original' literature and 'original' scholarship on that literature, such that it forces us to ask: How original is anyone?

What standards, then, do we hold our students to, when such as Octavio Paz, Ortega y Gasset, and Walter Benjamin have all ended up saying that translation is to some extent impossible? In perpetuating the myth of a perfect language, are we not guilty of reducing the differences, covering over the flaws, the imperfections, as is the case, say, with Esperanto, or the *épuration*? Could we not use translation instead as a means of bringing to bear upon the study of language the same innovation and creative iconoclasm which (in collaboration with its more powerful partner, literary theory) it has applied to the study of literature? Recognizing the importance of translation goes hand-in-hand with a decanonization and desacralization of 'great literature', or of literature as such, but can be seen also as a means of safeguarding the life of literature, and of language, and of releasing it from its immobility.

Far from remaining confined to the more abstruse realms of theoretical debate, such a collusion would have a number of practical implications for the foreign language or literature classroom. By making students more aware of just what we are doing when we translate, we can release translation from the straitjacket which has constrained it for too long as the unhappy bedfellow of the grammar-translation method of language pedagogy. We ought to begin by drawing our students' attention to the destabilizing effect translation has on both the target and the source-languages. While aiming for a minimal level of correctness, by shifting the emphasis away from fluency and perfectibility as models to strive for, we can attempt to exploit the creative playfulness and the sheer enjoyment of language that is so crucial to its successful assimilation. If literary theory has taught us to become attentive not simply to the meaning of literary texts, but to the multiple ways in which they achieve that meaning, their rhetorical dimension, why can we not carry over this linguistic awareness to the study and teaching of language, and supplement grammatical accuracy with the playful energy of rhetorical effect?

What this ultimately involves is undoing the myth that one's relationship to one's native language is unproblematical, and somehow more natural than one's relationship to a foreign language. This, too, was one of Paulhan's early insights in Madagascar. When he tried to explain to the Malagasies what was happening in their own language when they spoke in proverbs, they became very uncomfortable, and clearly had a stake in hiding the discontinuities revealed by a closer inspection of the proverb. As Paulhan remarks: 'Il n'est pas besoin d'aller à Madagascar pour faire l'expérience du proverbe' ('You don't need to go to Madagascar to have the experience of the proverb'), since the 'experience of the proverb' is an experience of the strangeness of, the exile from, the language we all would like to call our 'own'. The potential of this insight, if exploited, becomes an invitation to renew the relationship to our own language, as well as to the target-language, with the same uncertainty, and exhilaration, which literature has always provoked, and which literary theory has helped to unlock.

University of Aberdeen

NOTES

1. The most influential study in this regard remains George Steiner's *After Babel: Aspects of Language and Translation* (Oxford, 1975; revised edition, 1992). See also Peter Newmark, *Approaches to Translation* (Oxford, 1981); Joseph F. Graham, *Difference in Translation* (Ithaca, 1985); and more recently Lawrence Venuti, *Rethinking Translation: Discourse, Subjectivity, Ideology* (London, 1992).
2. *Progress in Love on the Slow Side: Récits by Jean Paulhan, with an essay by Maurice Blanchot* (forthcoming, University of Nebraska Press, 1994).
3. Paulhan, *Oeuvres Complètes*, 5 vols (Paris, 1966–70; hereafter '*OC*'), I, 100.
4. Paulhan (1884–1968) was best known as the editor of the influential French journal *La Nouvelle Revue Française*, and is often referred to as the 'grey eminence' of French literature. He published many major French writers from

the 1920s to the 1960s, but tended to marginalize his own work. His best-known book is *Les Fleurs de Tarbes, ou la Terreur dans les lettres* (*The Flowers of Tarbes, or Terror in Literature*, forthcoming translation by Richard Howard, University of Nebraska Press). Some have seen him as a precursor of Jacques Derrida, Paul de Man, and Gérard Genette, in refocusing literary criticism on the rhetorical dimension of literary texts.

5. See, for example, Paul de Man's 'Semiology and Rhetoric', in his *Allegories of Reading* (New Haven, 1979), pp. 3–19.

6. This is usually translated as *Of the wheat and the chaff*, although I choose to translate it, for reasons which will become clearer, as *Some wheat and some chaff*.

7. For a more detailed discussion of Paulhan's essay in this light, see my 'Some Wheat and Some Chaff: Jean Paulhan and the Post-War Literary Purge in France', *Studies in Twentieth-Century Literature*, 16 (1992), 247–63.

8. *Le Pont Traversé* (Marseilles, 1986), p. 5.

9. Walter Benjamin, 'The Task of the Translator', in *Illuminations*, translated by Harry Zohn, edited by Hannah Arendt (New York, 1969). For deconstructionist readings, see Jacques Derrida, 'Des Tours de Babel', in Graham (n. 1), and Paul de Man, 'Conclusions: Walter Benjamin's "The Task of the Translator"', in his *The Resistance to Theory* (Manchester, 1986).

10. Venuti (n. 1), pp. 4–5.

Poetry in Translation

Latin Eating Poems

Alistair Elliot

PYTHAGORAS ON MEAT

     primusque animalia mensis
Arguit imponi; primus quoque talibus ora
Docta quidem soluit, sed non et credita, uerbis:
    'Parcite, mortales, dapibus temerare nefandis
Corpora. Sunt fruges, sunt deducentia ramos
Pondere poma suo tumidaeque in uitibus uuae;
Sunt herbae dulces, sunt quae mitescere flamma
Mollirique queant; nec uobis lacteus umor
Eripitur nec mella thymi redolentia florem;
Prodiga diuitias alimentaque mitia tellus
Suggerit atque epulas sine caede et sanguine praebet.
Carne ferae sedant ieiunia, nec tamen omnes;
Quippe equus et pecudes armentaque gramine uiuunt.
At quibis ingenium est immansuetumque ferumque,
Armeniae tigres iracundique leones
Cumque lupis ursi, dapibus cum sanguine gaudent.
Heu! quantum scelus est in uiscera uiscera condi
Congestoque auidum pinguescere corpore corpus
Alteriusque animantem animantis uiuere leto!
Scilicet in tantis opibus, quas optima matrum
Terra parit, nil te nisi tristia mandere saeuo
Vulnera dente iuuat ritusque referre Cyclopum?
Nec, nisi perdideris alium, placare uoracis
Et male morati poteris ieiunia uentris?
At uetus illa aetus, cui fecimus aurea nomen,
Fetibus arboreis et, quas humus educat, herbis
Fortunata fuit nec polluit ora cruore.
Tunc et aues tutae mouere per aera pennas
Et lepus impauidus mediis errauit in aruis;
Nec sua credulitas piscem suspenderat hamo;

Note: Alistair Elliot's *French Love Poems* (1991) and *Italian Landscape Poems* (1993) are both published by Bloodaxe, who will also probably be publishing his *Latin Eating Poems*. The fifth book of his own poems, *Turning the Stones*, also appeared in 1993 (Carcanet).

He was the first to call it an abuse
To put animals on tables, souls on menus;
This man of Samos was the first to say
Wise words like these, not followed to this day:
    "O creatures who can die, do not pollute
Your bodies, shrines you live in, with foul food.
There are still fields of grain, and trees whose boughs
Reach down with fruit; grapes swell towards your mouths;
There are sweet plants and some which can be made
Tender and sweet by fire; no one will raid
Your cellarful of milk; and it's no crime
To live on honey with a scent of thyme.
    This earth is lavish with metallic wealth;
And softer stuff as well, the means of health,
Is heaped for us, not killed, not oozing blood –
It is the beasts that live on slaughtered food,
And not all beasts: the sheep, cow, horse and ass
Settle their hunger with a meal of grass.
Just untamed animals of pride and violence,
Armenian tigers, irritable lions,
Or wolves and bears, prefer their banquets bloody.
Think what a crime, to bury a dead body
Inside another; to cram your greedy meat
With meat that fattens you who fattened it;
To live by swallowing someone else's life!
Of all the riches that our mother earth
Has borne us, do you only want to chew
Hacked muscle, like the giant with Odysseus' crew?
Or are the pangs and grumbles only stilled
In your ill-tempered tripes by something killed?
    In the olden days (or golden if you please)
Men were contented with the young of trees,
The fruit – or any plants the soil produces;
They never fouled their mouths with animal juices.
Then birds flew safely through the lower air
And in mid field you saw the fearless hare.
No fish, too trusting, hung themselves on hooks;

Cuncta sine insidiis nullamque timentia fraudem
Plenaque pacis erant. Postquam non utilis auctor
Victibus inuidit, quisquis fuit ille, leonum
Corporeasque dapes auidam demersit in aluum,
Fecit iter sceleri; primoque e caede ferarum
Incaluisse potest maculatum sanguine ferrum;
Idque satis fuerat nostrumque petentia letum
Corpora missa neci salua pietate fatemur;
Sed quam danda neci, tam non epulanda fuerunt.
Longius inde nefas abiit et prima putatur
Hostia sus meruisse mori, quia semina pando
Eruerit rostro spemque interceperit anni.
Vite caper morsa Bacchi mactatus ad aras
Dicitur ultoris; nocuit sua culpa duobus.
Quid meruistis oues, placidum pecus, inque tuendos
Natum homines, pleno quae fertis in ubere nectar,
Mollia quae nobis uestras uelamina lanas
Praebetis uitaque magis quam morte iuuatis?
Quid meruere boues, animal sine fraude dolisque,
Innocuum, simplex, natum tolerare labores?
Immemor est demum nec frugum munere dignus
Qui potuit curui dempto modo pondere aratri
Ruricolam mactare suum, qui trita labore
Illa, quibus totiens durum renouauerat aruum,
Tot dederat messes, percussit colla securi.
Nec satis est quod tale nefas committitur; ipsos
Inscripsere deos sceleri numenque supernum
Caede laboriferi credunt gaudere iuuenci.
Victima labe carens et praestantissima forma
(Nam placuisse nocet) uittis insignis et auro
Sistitur ante aras auditque ignara precantem

No hidden traps; no fear of tricks or crooks:
The world was full of peace. But then some bad
Inventor thought he'd eat what lions had –
Pure envy made him stuff his greedy skin
With flesh and blood – which blazed the way to sin.
    Probably it was first some predator
Whose death warmed steel and spotted it with gore.
That was all right: we say, the beast attacked,
So killing it left innocence intact.
We had to kill it – we had no such need
To feast on it. But that became the seed
Of crimes that followed: first perhaps a pig
Was sacrificed because it dared to dig
Broad-snouted lines through someone's new-sown field,
And so cut off the yearly hope of yield;
A goat that gnawed a vine, was slit at the altar –
Bacchus' revenge; both times, it was their fault.
Poor sheep, what harm did you do? Peaceful creature,
Seeming designed to comfort man by nature,
Bringing us nectar by the udderful
And soft warm coverings of your offered wool,
You are more use to us alive than dead!
What did that ox deserve? Did he defraud
Or trick a man? O harmless, artless stirk,
Born to endure the hardest kind of work!
But man is so ungrateful, so unworthy
Of what he's given, the nourishing crops of earth,
That when the plough's hung up, the heavy toil
All done, he kills the labourer of his soil –
That neck, so rubbed with effort which renewed
His stubborn field and made his harvests good,
He severs with an axe. And even that's
Not all his crime – he also implicates
The gods: he thinks the higher powers are pleased
To taste the death of his hard-working beast.
An offering without spot, a perfect form
(Here, to be judged a beauty does you harm),
Marked out with ribbons and gold leaf, he's led
Before the altar, hears some prayers said,

Imponique suae uidet inter cornua fronti,
Quas coluit, fruges percussaque sanguine cultros
Inficit in liquida praeuisos forsitan unda.
Protinus ereptas uiuenti pectore fibras
Inspiciunt mentesque deum scrutantur in illis.
Inde (fames homini uetitorum tanta ciborum est!)
Audetis uesci, genus o mortale. Quod, oro,
Ne facite et monitis animos aduertite nostris;
Cumque boum dabitis caesorum membra palato,
Mandere uos uestros scite et sentite colonos.'

Ovid, Metamorphoses, *XV, 72–142*

AN INVITATION

Cenabis bene, mi Fabulle, apud me
paucis, si tibi di fauent, diebus,
si tecum attuleris bonam atque magnam
cenam, non sine candida puella
et uino et sale et omnibus cachinnis.
haec si, inquam, attuleris, uenuste noster,
cenabis bene; nam tui Catulli
plenus sacculus est aranearum.
sed contra accipies meros amores
seu quid suauius elegantiusue est:
nam unguentum dabo, quod meae puellae
donarunt Veneres Cupidinesque,
quod tu cum olfacies, deos rogabis,
totum ut te faciant, Fabulle, nasum.

Catullus, XIII

Not understanding, rolls his eyes when corn
He helped to grow is poured between his horns
And on his brow, and then, stabbed, stains with gore
The knives seen glittering in clean bowls before.
Immediately from his living chest
They tear the organs and inspect the mess:
Here they can see the mind of god expressed.
And this you dare to feed on, mortal man,
So hungry for forbidden food! I ban
Such evil acts. Believe me, it is wrong:
And when you put these morsels on your tongue,
The limbs of cattle carved as butcher's meat,
Think: it's your fellow-farmer that you eat."

My dear Fabullus, in a few
Days, if the gods are kind to you,
You'll have a big and very good
Meal with me – if you bring the food,
Also the pretty girl, the wine,
The wit, the laughter. You shall dine,
I say, dear fellow, like a king,
Provided you bring everything.
The problem is, Catullus' purse
Is full of spiderwebs and fuzz.
And what will you get back? You'll get
Love in its undiluted state,
Or something sweeter and more suave:
I have an ointment you can have
Which Venus made and which her fair
Son Cupid gave my girl to wear.
Just smell it once, and you'll propose
The gods convert you all to nose.

THE FIRST ROMAN MEAL

Aeneas primique duces et pulcher Iulus
corpora sub ramis deponunt arboris altae,
instituuntque dapes et adorea liba per herbam
subiciunt epulis (sic Iuppiter ipse monebat)
et Cereale solum pomis agrestibus augent.
consumptis hic forte aliis, ut vertere morsus
exiguam in Cererem penuria adegit edendi,
et violare manu malisque audacibus orbem
fatalis crusti patulis nec parcere quadris:
'heus, etiam mensas consumimus' inquit Iulus,
nec plura, adludens. ea vox audita laborum
prima tulit finem, primamque loquentis ab ore
eripuit pater ac stupefactus numine pressit.
continuo 'salve fatis mihi debita tellus
vosque' ait 'o fidi Troiae salvete penates:
hic domus, haec patria est. genitor mihi talia namque
(nunc repeto) Anchises fatorum arcana reliquit:
"cum te, nate, fames ignota ad litora vectum
accisis coget dapibus consumere mensas,
tum sperare domos defessus, ibique memento
prima locare manu molirique aggere tecta."
haec erat illa fames, haec nos suprema manebat
exitiis positura modum.
quare agite et primo laeti cum lumine solis
quae loca, quive habeant homines, ubi moenia gentis,
vestigemus et a portu diversa petamus.

Aeneas, his captains and his handsome son
Lay on their elbows under the beams of a tree
And arranged a banquet: on the grass they laid
Some sacrificial cakes of coarse wheat bread
To use as plates (Zeus put this in their minds)
And offerings of wild fruit on this foundation
Of Ceres' grain. It happened that when the fruit
Was eaten, and poverty of food had forced them
To turn their teeth on Ceres' meagre portion,
Spoiling the fatal circles made of crust
With shameless force of hand and jaw, not sparing
Even these empty plates in quartered pieces,
"Look," said Iulus, "now we even eat tables" –
No more, one playful phrase. But that remark
Sank in, as the first sign of troubles ending.
Even as the word flew from Iulus' mouth
His father caught it: stunned with awe at feeling
Some god was there, he checked the boy; then cried,
"O country owed me by the word of Fate,
I greet you now; O loyal household gods
Of Troy, I greet you here: this is home now,
This is our fatherland.
     Now I recall
My father left me with a hint of this,
The sacred secret of our fate. He said,
'My son,
When hunger carries you to an unknown shore
And forces you when food is running short
Even to eat the tables, then – remember –
You can expect a home in your fatigue;
There you can mark a space for your first houses
And fortify them with a wall of earth.'
This was the hunger that he meant – our last,
For it will put an end to our distresses.

So come – and cheerfully at first light tomorrow
We must explore and see what place this is,
What sort of men live here, where are their towns.
We'll separate, going outwards from the harbour.

nunc pateras libate Iovi precibusque vocate
Anchisen genitorem, et vina reponite mensis.'

Virgil, Aeneid, *VII, 107–134*

WHAT A HOST!

Haec tibi, non alia, est ad cenam causa vocandi,
    versiculos recites ut, Ligurine, tuos.
deposui soleas, adfertur protinus ingens
    inter lactucas oxygarumque liber:
alter perlegitur, dum fercula prima morantur:
    tertius est, nec adhuc mensa secunda venit:
et quartum recitas et quintum denique librum.
    putidus est, totiens si mihi ponis aprum.
Quod si non scombris scelerata poemata donas,
    cenabis solus iam, Ligurine, domi.

Martial, III.50

A SORT OF INVITATION

Hesterna tibi nocte dixeramus,
quincunces puto post decem peractos,
cenares hodie, Procille, mecum.
tu factam tibi rem statim putasti
et non sobria verba subnotasti
exemplo nimium periculoso:
μισῶ μνάμονα συμπόταν, Procille.

Martial, I.27

TOASTS

Laevia sex cyathis, septum Iustina bibatur,
    quinque Lycas, Lyde quattuor, Ida tribus.
omnis ab infuso numeretur amica Falerno,
    et quia nulla venit, tu mihi, Somne, veni.

Martial, I.71

Now raise your cups, pour wine for Zeus, and name
My father in your prayer – Anchises! – Now
Put down your cups and serve the wine again."

You never have a reason to invite us
But this: your verses, that you must recite.
I've barely dropped my sandals: the first course is
Book One, with lettuce and vinegar-garum sauce.
The main dish waits while all Book Two is heard.
Before we get dessert we get the Third.
Then you read Four and Five. Brought on so often
Even wild boar would be a little off.
Look, Ligurinus, donate your noxious poems
To naked fish – or dine alone at home.

I must have said, the night before,
Somewhere around my fiftieth cup,
"Procillus, my dear chap, come up
And see me – it's the umpteenth floor."
You noted it, address and date,
Ignoring my unsober state.
That is a risky thing to do
When you go drinking avec moi:
I really hate celui qui boit
Et peut se souvenir de tout.

Let's drink to Laevia, counting up
The toasts until the sixth full cup,
Then to Justina, who gets more,
And Lycas (five) and Lyde (four).
And, by Falernian symmetry,
You'll guess we drink to Ida three.
But not a one's come round to keep
Me company; so you come, Sleep.

Dinner with the Poet Martial

Si tristi domicenio laboras,
Torani, potes esurire mecum.
non derunt tibi, si soles προπίνειν,
viles Cappadocae gravesque porri,
divisis cybium latebit ovis.
ponetur digitis tenendus ustis
nigra coliculus virens patella,
algentem modo qui reliquit hortum,
et pultem niveam premens botellus,
et pallens faba cum rubente lardo.
Mensae munera si voles secundae,
marcentes tibi porrigentur uvae
et nomen pira quae ferunt Syrorum,
et quas docta Neapolis creavit,
lento castaneae vapore tostae:
vinum tu facies bonum bibendo.
Post haec omnia forte si movebit
Bacchus quam solet esuritionem,
succurrent tibi nobiles olivae,
Piceni modo quas tulere rami,
et fervens cicer et tepens lupinus.
Parva est cenula,- quis potest negare? –
sed finges nihil audiesve fictum
et voltu placidus tuo recumbes;
nec crassum dominus leget volumen,
nec de Gadibus inprobis puellae
vibrabunt sine fine prurientes
lascivos docili tremore lumbos;
sed quod nec grave sit nec infacetum,
parvi tibia Condyli sonabit.
Haec est cenula. Claudiam sequeris.
Quam nobis cupis esse tu priorem?

Martial, V. 78

Toranius, don't eat gloomily
At home, come round and starve with me.
If you like starters with a drink,
There's lots of leeks (we'll bear their stink),
Lots of cheap Asian lettuces,
And under boiled eggs chopped to pieces
A slice of tunny lies in wait.
The main course next: a blackened plate
That burns your fingers with a head
Of bright green cabbage from its bed
In the freezing garden, and a sausage
Treading a shape of white pease-porridge,
Plus red-cheeked bacon with pale beans.
Then you will learn what "afters" means
Chez Martial: grapes about to rot,
Pears they call Syrian (which they're not),
And chestnuts grown in learned Naples
And roasted slowly for our tables.
The wine, when drunk by you, improves.
And after this, if Bacchus moves
The usual twinge of hunger in us,
There's reinforcements for our dinners:
Olives that hung last week in trees
Blown by an Adriatic breeze,
The pride of some Piceno farm,
And chick-peas (hot) and lupins (warm).
It's a small meal, I must admit.
But you shall hear no lies at it,
Nor have to lie; we can recline
At ease, with your own face, and mine.
Your modest host will not unroll
And read a fat poetic scroll;
Nor girls from impudent Cadiz
Vibrate their femininities,
Cranking around their well-trained bums
In ecstasy that never comes.
Instead, my little flautist slave
Will play us something not too grave,
Something to make the witty chuckle.
(His name is from his skill, The Knuckle.)
That's my small dinner. Will it do?
You'll sit by Claudia. But who
D'you want beside me, opposite you?

A PRESENT FOR PHYLLIS

Formonsa Phyllis nocte cum mihi tota
se praestitisset omnibus modis largam,
et cogitarem mane quod darem munus,
utrumne Cosmi, Nicerotis an libram,
an Baeticarum pondus acre lanarum,
an de moneta Caesaris decem flavos:
amplexa collum basioque tam longo
blandita quam sunt nuptiae columbarum,
rogare coepit Phyllis amphoram vini.

Martial, XII.65

TO JUVENAL AT SATURNALIA TIME

De nostro, facunde, tibi, Iuvenalis, agello
   Saturnalicias mittimus, ecce, nuces.
cetera lascivis donavit poma puellis
   mentula custodis luxuriosa dei.

Martial, VII.91

TABLE MANNERS FOR GIRLS

carpe cibos digitis (est quiddam gestus edendi),
   ora nec immunda tota perungue manu;
neue domi praesume dapes, sed desine citra
   quam capis: es paulo, quam potes esse, minus.
Priamides Helenen auide si spectet edentem,
   oderit et dicat 'stulta rapina mea est.'
aptius est deceatque magis potare puellas:
   cum Veneris puero non male, Bacche, facis.
hoc quoque, qua patiens caput est animusque pedesque
   constant, nec, quae sunt singula, bina uide.
turpe iacens mulier multo madefacta Lyaeo:
   digna est concubitus quoslibet illa pati.
nec somnis posita tutum succumbere mensa:
   per somnos fieri multa pudenda solent.

Ovid, Ars amatoria, *III, 755–68*

Beautiful Phyllis gave herself to me
All night, with every liberality,
And in the morning I'd just turned my mind
To how to thank her – scent? how much? what kind?
Some Spanish wool? or should I drop a hint
About some yellow sons of Caesar's mint? –
When suddenly she clasps me by the neck
And giving me a suffocating peck
Like a mating pigeon, in a cooing whine
She asks me for an amphora of wine.

O eloquent Juvenal! from my little acre
I send you nuts for Christmas – here they are.
Yes, there was other fruit, but the soft prick
Of my Priapus gave it all to girls . . .

Pick food like fruit. It matters: eat with grace
And fingertips, not hands that grease your face.
And don't dine first at home; just stop before
You're full – eat less than you can hold, not more:
If Paris had seen Helen eat with greed,
He'd have gone cold – 'That mouth I do not need' –
And told himself that sort of snatch was stupid.
But girls may drink: Bacchus goes well with Cupid,
Provided you've a head, and you're not troubled
In feet or wit, and you don't see things doubled.
But lying drunk brings shame: if wine's untied them,
Girls deserve anyone who lies beside them.
Nor is it safe to sleep at table: One
Easily does in sleep what is not done.

THE GOLDEN TOUCH

Hunc assueta cohors satyri bacchaeque frequentant,
At Silenus abest; titubantem annisque meroque
Ruricolae cepere Phryges uinctumque coronis
Ad regem duxere Midan, cui Thracius Orpheus
Orgia tradiderat cum Cecropio Eumolpo.
Qui simul agnouit socium comitemque sacrorum,
Hospitis aduentu festum genialiter egit
Per bis quinque dies et iunctas ordine noctes;
Et iam stellarum sublime coegerat agmen
Lucifer undecimus, Lydos cum laetus in agros
Rex uenit et iuueni Silenum reddit alumno.
Huic deus optandi gratum, sed inutile, fecit
Muneris arbitrium, gaudens altore recepto.
Ille, male usurus donis, ait: "Effice, quicquid
Corpore contigero, fuluum uertatur in aurum."
Annuit optatis nocituraque munera soluit
Liber et indoluit, quod non meliora petisset.
    Laetus abit gaudetque malo Berecyntius heros
Pollicitique fidem tangendo singula temptat;
Vixque sibi credens, non alta fronde uirentem
Ilice detraxit uirgam; uirga aurea facta est;
Tollit humo saxum; saxum quoque palluit auro;
Contigit et glaebam; contactu glaeba potenti
Massa fit; arentis Cereris decerpsit aristas;
Aurea messis erat; demptum tenet arbore pomum;
Hesperidas donasse putes; si postibus altis

The usual court of satyrs and Bacchantes
Surrounded Dionysus; they went on.
Silenus, tottering with years and wine,
Was left there, lost. Some Phrygian peasants caught him
And led him, chained in their lassoos of flowers,
To Midas, who was king and who had learned
The mysteries of Bacchus from the Thracian
Orpheus, and the Athenian Eumolpus.
Anyway, Midas recognised Silenus
As his old comrade in the sacred drinking,
And fêted his arrival with a party
That lasted for ten solid days and nights.
 On the eleventh morning Lucifer,
The day-star, had brought up the rear behind
The retreating constellations, when the king
Came out into the Lydian fields rejoicing
And gave Silenus back to the young god
Whom once he fostered. Bacchus was delighted
To get his foster-father back, and gave
Midas the choice of anything he wanted –
A pleasant favour leading to destruction,
For Midas would misuse the friendly offer:
He said, "Arrange it so that what my body
Touches, will turn to lion-coloured gold."
The god of drink and freedom nodded, keeping
The harmful bargain, with Olympian pain
That Midas had not asked for something better.
 But he goes happily away, rejoicing
At his own misfortune – this heroic son
Of the Great Mother of Mount Berecyntus.
He tests the present and the promise, touching
The things he passes, and can hardly trust
His own experience: pulling a low and leafy
Bough from an oak – the foliage crackles, golden;
Picking a stone up as it fades to gold;
Patting a lump of soil which is an ingot
On his dynamic contact. He breaks off
A few of Ceres' ripening stalks of corn –
The harvest's golden; when he plucks and holds
An apple from the tree, you'd rather think
It was a fruit that Hesperus' daughters gave him;

Admouit digitos, postes radiare uidentur;
Ille etiam liquidis palmas ubi lauerat undis,
Vnda fluens palmis Danaen eludere posset.
Vix spes ipse suas animo capit, aurea fingens
Omnia. Gaudenti mensas posuere ministri
Exstructas dapibus nec tostae frugis egentes;
Tum uero, siue ille sua Cerealia dextra
Munera contigerat, Cerealia dona rigebant;
Siue dapes auido conuellere dente parabat,
Lammina fulua dapes, admoto dente, premebat;
Miscuerat puris auctorem muneris undis;
Fusile per rictus aurum fluitare uideres.
Attonitus nouitate mali diuesque miserque
Effugere optat opes et, quae modo uouerat, odit.
Copia nulla famem releuat; sitis arida guttur
Vrit et inuiso meritus torquetur ab auro;
Ad caelumque manus et splendida bracchia tollens:
"Da ueniam, Lenaee pater, peccauimus;" inquit
"Sed miserere, precor, speciosoque eripe damno."
Mite deum numen; Bacchus peccasse fatentem
Restituit pactique fide data munera soluit;
"Neue mala optato maneas circumlitus auro,
Vade" ait "ad magnis uicinum Sardibus amnem
Perque iugum ripae labentibus obuius undis
Carpe uiam, donec uenias ad fluminis ortus;
Spumigeroque tuum fonti, qua plurimus exit,
Subde caput corpusque simul, simul elue crimen."
Rex iussae succedit aquae; uis aurea tinxit
Flumen et humano de corpore cessit in amnem;
Nunc quoque iam ueteris percepto semine uenae
Arua rigent auro madidis pallentia glaebis.

Ovid, Metamorphoses, *XI, 89–145*

His fingers graze a doorway of his palace,
And now it seems to glow; and when he rubs
His hands in perfect water as it's poured,
The shower of brilliant droplets might seduce
Another Danae. He can scarcely keep
His imagination still: it forms a world
Of gold. As he exults, the servants lay
The tables with a feast and heaps of bread.
But when he reaches out his hand and touches
The gift of Ceres, crust and crumb grow stiff;
And as his hungry tooth tears at the meat,
A tawny glaze of metal armours it.
He mixes wine, his benefactor's gift,
With water; you could see the liquid gold
Splash from his gagging mouth. So rich, so wretched,
Dazed by a horror new to everyone,
He longs to escape his wealth, and what he prayed for
Just hours ago, he loathes. All his possessions
Cannot relieve his hunger, and his throat
Burns with dry thirst: and this is what he earned,
To be tortured by the hateful touch of gold.

He lifts his hands to heaven, and his arms
Gilded and shining: "Forgive me, Father Bacchus,
Lord of the wine-press! I have sinned. But pity me:
Rescue me from my glittering reward."
Divine power can be gentle: Dionysus
Restored the sinner to his former self,
And took the favour back that he had promised:
"You mustn't linger with your body smeared
In ill-considered gold," he said to Midas;
"Go to great Sardis. There's a river there.
Along the path above the water, walk
To meet the descending stream, until you reach
The river's source. There in the foaming fountain
Where it most strongly rises, dip your head
And wash your body, wash away the fault."
The king went to the water and dived in
As he was told; the gold-producing power
Coloured the current; then it left his body
And passed into the body of the river.
And to this day the seed of that old vein
Is lodged there still: the fields go stiff with gold
And a sort of jaundice where the soil is damp.

Notes and Documents

Documents

Readers are invited to offer for publication in this section specimens of earlier writing on translation and associated subjects. Consideration will be given to any relevant work (or portion of a work) which is insufficiently known or to which access is difficult. Contributions should not normally exceed 3,500 words, should be in English (translated where necessary), and may carry whatever commentary seems appropriate.

A. W. Schlegel on the German Homer

Translated by Douglas Robinson

August Wilhelm von Schlegel (1767–1845), German scholar, critic, translator, and poet, was one of the most influential figures in the spread of German romanticism. He translated extensively from Shakespeare and from the Romance languages, including Calderón and Dante. Schlegel's views on translation were very much in the air in the last decade of the eighteenth and the first two decades of the nineteenth centuries. Himself heavily influenced by Herder, Schlegel would in turn influence Novalis, Goethe, Schleiermacher, and others, with the result that the period around the turn of the nineteenth century became in Germany one of the most striking confluences of translating activity in the history of the West.

The present translation is from 'Homers Werke von Johann Heinrich Voss' ('Voss's Homer', 1796).

Of all the languages into which prose and verse translations of Homer have been made, from the Syriac to the English, none can approach the original text with such happy fidelity as German. The very fact that the metrical art of the ancients, insofar as we know and can apply it, has found a secure foothold only in German gives it a distinct advantage over other languages, which may be more modern and even in part more elevated, but whose development has been less well-rounded. True enough, the Italians, the Spaniards, the French, and the English attempted to introduce Greek metres into their languages earlier than the Germans; but their attempts did not bear fruit – indeed, they are usually mentioned only as academic curiosities. Another prodigious advantage we have lies in our liberty to combine several primary concepts in a single word, a capacity that, like Latin itself, the Romance languages lack almost entirely.

There are, however, other reasons that make these latter languages unsuitable for translating Homer in particular, despite their classical appearance and their Greek background. As their simple beginnings were coarse and crude, so has their later cultivation been utterly erudite – a product of the schools, not a blossom of enhanced nature. Their poetic (especially their epic) forms bore the stamp of Alexandrian artistic diligence. Their heroic verse was too haughty to regress back to the unadorned yet golden modesty, the familiarity and innocent purity of the ancient singers. I am not concerned here with the phraseological exercises of the moderns; but had the ancient Latin work in this area survived, we might well find the *Odyssey* of Livius Andronicus,[1] in all its laborious fidelity, more Homeric than the polished imitations of the Augustan era.

These ruminations bring us to a concern that strikes more to the heart of the matter – indeed, on which everything else depends. There is in the spirit of our language, as in the character of our nation – if indeed the two are not one and the same thing – a most versatile flexibility. The German passion to know the foreign truly and deeply; the German willingness to enter into the most exotic thought-patterns and the most outlandish customs; the ardour with which Germans embrace authenticity of content, no matter how unusual the garb in which it appears – all this does often degenerate into a mania for imitation and a foolish predilection for the foreign, but it also always moves steadily towards a free appropriation of the best. By ruling out certain directions their national culture might have taken, our fellow-Europeans have rendered themselves incapable of entering deeply into a uniquely foreign mode of being; as a result, they are stuck with either domestic poverty or domestic wealth. The fact that they have among them so many supposed lovers of classical antiquity should not fool us; how many of them must first mentally dress a Greek or Roman up in some modish attire before they can find him attractive? Whereas the German inclination is unquestionably to read the ancients in their own sense, and the very fact that the mother tongue must act as go-between for every newly acquired image and mood is precisely what gives our language its advantage in translating them in their true spirit – necessarily in concert, though this is but a different aspect of the same flexibility.

This flexibility can in fact be used to derive standards for a German translation of Homer, standards that it would be silly to apply to a French or even an English translation – though this only makes the undertaking that much more difficult, and its successful completion that much more laudable. Language in itself is an inert tool: it waits upon the artist to unpack its potential with his deft touch. That this is not always an easy task is amply attested by the many miscarried attempts at a poetic translation of Homer, some of which were written by well-known authors like Bodmer, Stolberg, and Bürger (I mean his experiments with an iambic *Iliad*) just before or concurrently with the appearance of Voss's first *Odyssey*.[2] At first this latter met, deservedly, with the unanimous approval of the experts. But experts make up a small minority of the populace, and it was not to be expected either that this translation would be enthusiastically taken up by the masses, or that its translator would be adequately recompensed for it. Nevertheless, this foreseeable indifference failed to dampen Voss's noble ardour for his task, and twelve years later he enriched our literature for the second time with a completely revised *Odyssey* and a newly germanized *Iliad*. The human dedication, so rare in our day, and the scrupulous rigour with which this writer strove to attain that which he realized was perfection; the still more intimate acquaintance with the ancients and the broader sphere of learned expertise, of which he had by then given so much proof; the mature self-reliance of a poetic spirit who in his *Luise*[3] knew how to apply the manner of the Ionian singer to simple and natural descriptions that were picked up from everyday life but yet remained pure, delicate, and beautiful; the painstaking work on the German hexameter, in the construction of which, at least rhythmically, and perhaps expressively as well, he surpassed even Klopstock, the master of this art[4] – all this warranted the expectation that this new translation would leave scarcely anything to be desired, since its predecessor had already achieved so much. And if this expectation was not fully met, the fault probably lay more in the principles that guided Voss's work than in any deficiency in the way they were followed. Principles must be tested thoroughly; all that critics can do is object attentively to deviations, against which so many writers are protected by their careless haste.

As Wieland has so rightly noted (in the *Teutsche Merkur*, 1795, p. 12),[5] in a translation of Homer, fidelity, or rather, to get away from the notion of literal precision so commonly associated with fidelity, *truth* must be the translator's highest, indeed virtually his only, mandate. There are works whose re-creation allows artistic discretion as much free play as their original production did. Even very divergent copies of these may have merit if, independent of their originals, they give their readers pleasure. This approach becomes more hazardous, however, when the work's attractions arise partly out of its author's unique personality – when the author has unwittingly represented not only external objects but his inner subjectivity as well. Nothing is singly or separably present in a single being; its characteristics are all wrapped up in a coherent whole, so that one can distinctly feel it, indeed almost see it, when their steadfast inwardness does not permit conceptualization. As a result, even apparently minor alterations are enough to cast a false light over the whole work. In a word: individuality cannot be pieced out; it is an all-or-nothing affair. What we admire and love in the *Iliad* and the *Odyssey* is not the poet's person, which indeed is not to be found as a separate entity in heaven or on earth – which is to say, anywhere. The quest for his person has produced so many gloriously perverse interpretations of his poetry that one takes them for the felicitous effusions of an unusually gifted spirit, the wilful concoctions of a fine mind. What makes Homer famous, what maintains his fame among the entire human race in perpetuity, is not the man he was but the form of humanity he assumed, one of the greatest forms of its kind, impelled by a vast natural law. Homer is the spokesman of his age, and this lends him a greater distinction than his mere personality could ever attain. To clothe him in an alien form is thus to distort not an individual character, but a collective one. Distorted images of this most ancient of the ancients, the first Greek as it were, must inexorably lead to error regarding the entire course of Greek culture, for his childlike poetry fires and unfolds the germ of everything, the noblest and loveliest, to which this people has ever given rise. Nor may one believe that this entertaining poet will let himself be split off from the enlightening witness of antiquity; anyone who cannot understand this cannot enjoy him. We all know of beautiful souls who find in Homer a reflection of their own faces, and who labour to discover in him bedraggled beauties that simply are not there. Only a person of banal taste could fail to recognize the ghastly mismatch between form and content in, say, Pope's translation – or better, Pope's parody.

But who can discern Homer as he truly is? To this end, the worst approach is the philological one; with it even the countless writings to which learned Greeks devoted themselves would still leave much obscurity to spare – even if all of them had survived. But the double relationship of words, on the one hand outwardly to objects that we have never seen before, so that we have to come to know them through the words themselves, and on the other inwardly to a circle of images to which we have almost no hope of access, leaves us vulnerable to the most manifold deceptions. How easy it is to import later scientific developments back into a language that is entirely lacking in abstractions, or in precise concepts for anything dealing with the phenomenon or functioning of the inner person – a language that only distinguishes and combines fleeting sensory perceptions! The medium is all the more deceptive in that the forward march of culture has often taken the signified through a long series of shifts, while the signifer has remained the same. The poetic work's impact depends in the end only marginally on the meaning of words and phrases as conveyed by the understanding; it is rather the living breath of speech, a plenitude of animated sounds, that most fully sensitizes us to poetry – especially nature poetry, which always precedes the fine arts and the sciences. Our intuitive sense of these complexly intertwined stimuli, at once powerful and frail, is unfailing and unmediated only in our native language.

To a certain extent, that sense can be acquired in a foreign language, even a dead one; but only by comparing the different ways in which it is used in everyday life, in familiar or lofty prose styles, and in the various poetic genres. With Homer's poetry we are lacking in all such points of comparison, for, excepting the remnants of Hesiod, he stands alone in his era. We are completely in the dark as to the state of ordinary language in his time and region; and given the fact that his era still lacked a written prose literature, and as far as we know only possessed the one style of poetry, it is only through the relationship of Homer's poetic expression to this everyday usage that the achievement of his poetry can be determined with certainty. To be sure, we can surmise that the language of the Olympian Muse and her followers did not diverge greatly from that of the rest of humanity, just as in general in those days the mythical world, the most ancient source of poetry, still lay close to the real one; but in specific cases it is often difficult to tell ornamentation from necessity, lofty flights of fancy from the purely sensory perception of truth . . .

The detailed analysis of individual passages, which the diligence of the excellent translator obliges the critic to undertake, has brought us to an issue about which we have heretofore deliberately said nothing, so as not to confuse the various factors involved. We have been considering Voss's work purely as an interpretation of the Greek, not as its transposition into the German. The concept of translation contains both of these relationships. For a translation must enable a language to enter fully into the space of another, so as to follow not only its rules but also those conventions that cannot be determined by general prescriptions. Given the multiple and incommensurable divergences of languages, and the reliance of poetry not merely on overall meaning but on the subtlest nuances, all poetic translation must forever remain an imperfect approximation.

It goes without saying that every liberty allowed the original poet must be fully allowed the translator-poet as well, who is so greatly at a disadvantage. But it is equally obvious that every language has certain established bounds, primordial and deep-rooted limits, that cannot be overstepped without being quite rightly accused of being no true language at all, merely an argot of one's own concoction. No exigency is justification enough for taking the latter course. Were it truly impossible to give us an *Iliad* in pure German, unmarred by graecisms, it would be better to renounce all attempts to attain one.

A recent subject of debate has been the extent of the individual's right to contribute to the development of the language. That individual writers, especially poets, can have an enormous shaping influence on their language is well attested by the history of languages. And much that has been decried at first as a corrupting influence has later entered the language and undeniably ennobled it. We should not, therefore, reject without careful consideration proposals that an obvious gap in a language be filled with some new construction. Like all human devices, speech, too, that fair deed of our higher destiny, strives incessantly for improvement, and the individual performs a true service in becoming an instrument of this collective yearning. That individual's service has but a single indispensable proviso, that he not tear down while building up: the proposed innovation must not be at odds with what is already firmly established. If language were a mere hodgepodge of things similar and dissimilar, a formless mass, there would be no objection to one's changing or expanding it at will; every enrichment, without exception, would be an improvement. But this is not the case; it is a coherent totality, or at least professes to be progressively becoming one. Everything in it is attracted or repelled according to the laws of resemblance and kinship; collective forms flow through it, breathe life into its clay, and bring a binding force to bear on it. The simpler, the more inclusive and cohesive its laws are, the more perfect its organization will be; the greater the freedom that arises in line with these laws rather than in opposition to them, the better suited it will be to poetic use. Excessive positive legislation that leaves little or no space in which to develop original talents is a pernicious thing in language as in politics. If German is in truth as flexible as it is held up to be, this is not a problem for us, at least in comparison with some other languages. But that just makes us all the more cognizant of our obligation not to force anything upon it that is inimical to its nature, anything that it cannot melt down into homogeneous matter. The ability to re-create oneself in the image of a foreigner is only truly praiseworthy when one has autonomy to retain in the process, and does in fact retain it. Flexibility without one's own spirit – what would that be but a clarified nullity?

NOTES

1. Lucius Livius Andronicus (*c.* 284–204 B.C.), Roman poet whose *Odyssia* was probably used as a classroom crib for the original; only about fifty lines survive.
2. Johann Jakob Bodmer (1698–1783), Swiss historian, critic, and poet who translated Homer into hexameters. Friedrich Leopold, German poet who translated the *Iliad* in 1778. Gottfried August Bürger (1747–94), German poet. Johann Heinrich Voss (1751–1826) translated the *Odyssey* in 1781; his *Iliad* and a revised *Odyssey* appeared in 1793.
3. Voss's *Luise* (1795) was a naturalistic portrait of the life of a country pastor; it inspired Goethe's *Hermann und Dorothea*.
4. Friedrich Gottlieb Klopstock (1724–1803), German epic and lyric poet who anticipated the romantics. His most famous work, *Der Messias* (1749–73), was written in unrhymed hexameters.
5. Christoph Martin Wieland (1733–1813), German poet who founded the *Teutsche Merkur* (*German Mercury*) in 1773.

Review Essays

Textual Transmission and Translation in the Middle Ages

Roger Ellis

Apollonius of Tyre: Medieval and Renaissance Themes and Variations: Including the Text of Historia Apollonii Regis Tyri. By Elizabeth Archibald. Pp. 264. Woodbridge: D. S. Brewer, 1991. Hb. £35.

The Myths of Love: Classical Lovers in Medieval Literature. By Katherine Heinrichs. Pp. vii + 270. Pennsylvania and London: Pennsylvania State University Press, 1990. Hb. £27.

Chaucer and the Tradition of the 'Roman Antique'. By Barbara Nolan. Pp. 407 (Cambridge Studies in Medieval Literature, 15). Cambridge: Cambridge University Press, 1992. Hb. £45.

Chaucer's Dante: Allegory and Epic Theater in 'The Canterbury Tales'. By Richard Neuse. Pp. xi + 295. Berkeley, Los Angeles, and Oxford: University of California Press, 1991. Hb. £42.

Most – by some reckonings, all – medieval literature is a translation of one sort or another, and these four studies, if in very different ways, can be taken as confirmations of the truth of that proposition. Not that all of them address the question of translation head-on, or, for that matter, that all the texts studied are what we might wish to call translations. To take the most striking example, Archibald's exhaustive study of the medieval and Renaissance versions of the legend of Apollonius of Tyre (Appendix I lists forty-three Latin and vernacular versions of the story up to Shakespeare's *Pericles*) includes a number of instances of vernacular translation, but is really concerned with translation as a particular set of scribal practices involving the production of a new version of a work. Thus, both Latin and vernacular versions of the story can be placed on a sliding scale that goes from faithful copying to wholesale adaptation 'to suit changing literary tastes'. The line between translation and original work is thus more difficult to draw in medieval than in modern times. The distinction is, however, paradoxically affirmed by the notion of 'vernacularity' itself (to which Nolan's study makes regular and telling reference). Since translation in the Middle Ages is often understood in hierarchical terms, translation into or out of Latin (and, to a lesser extent, French) witnesses to the primacy of Latin at the same time as it seeks to carve out a space for the vernaculars into which, or out of which, texts are being translated.

We may need to qualify Archibald's implied view of translation as a mere set of scribal practices, not least because translation from a highly inflected language like Latin to a relatively uninflected one like Middle English involves the translator in a number of linguistic choices more complicated than any that a scribe makes when copying a Latin manuscript. Nevertheless, scribal practices do overlap significantly with translational practices, so the model is plausible and attractive. Consequently, adapting the famous account of literary composition by St Bonaventura, we can describe the translator as scribe, compiler, commentator, or even author.[1] Medieval translators regularly describe themselves as humble scribes: but their practice shows them just as often to be acting as compilers, commentators, and as what we would now think of as authors.

The idea of literal translation, which acknowledges the primacy of the source rather than of the cultural situation of the translator and his readers for the production of meaning, is rarely given house-room in these studies – or, indeed, in most other modern accounts of medieval translation. Neuse's view of Chaucer 'aspiring to carry on the epic tradition as redefined by Dante . . . and, at the same time, as befits a true continuator, detaching himself from some central aspects of Dantean epic' can be regarded as typical: a true continuator (read: translator) transforms (deforms) the tradition, even as he transmits it. Yet some notion of literal translation must underpin even the most exotic examples of literary transformation. Neuse can thus describe Chaucer's *Sir Thopas* as 'another parody version of [Dante's] *Comedy*' in part because the giant Olifaunt in the former recalls the giants seen by Dante in the latter: more to the point, because an offered comparison of Dante's giants to elephants ('elefanti') may have inspired Chaucer's choice of name for his giant by way of the Middle English word for elephant.

Translations which actively transform their originals present the modern student with formidable challenges of description and analysis. Yet even those medieval translations which take seriously the idea of literal translation – generally translations of religious works (above all the Bible) and philosophical classics (like the *De Consolatione Philosophiae*), sometimes perhaps translations of scientific works – are not without their difficulties. In the first place, before the advent of print technology and the possibility of standardized and authoritative/authorized versions of original works, translators were not usually well-placed to check the accuracy of the copy from which they were translating; popular texts like the *Historia Apollonii* survive in many different versions, and contamination of an original text by material from another tradition remains a regular possibility. A translator may thus have transmitted errors in good faith. Equally, he may not have understood terms in the original. (Thus, for example, Archibald shows that the Old English *Apollonius* translates "'ceroma", the waxy ointment used for massage', as 'some sort of game played with a spinning top'.) In any case, we generally do not know the precise manuscript copy of the original on which a translation was based, and are usually studying the original in a modern critical edition which will often discard those very errors which are of most interest to students of a translation in pursuit of its presumed authoritative original. Consequently, and given the overlap noted above between scribal and translational functions, we are very unlikely to be able to pronounce definitively about the good or bad faith of the translator in relation to specific details of the translation: error may reveal a translator who is faithfully copying a contaminated original as well as one who is operating as author. Hence this comment of Archibald's, which even now we do well to note: 'sometimes scholars working on a later version praise or blame the author for details or patterns which can in fact be traced back directly' to earlier versions of the story. In addition, a translator may be translating not from the original but from a translated version of it: or he may be using a translation alongside the original to supplement its readings and check his own. Such supplementary material can as easily complicate as explicate the meaning of the original: as, for example, the anonymous French version of Petrarch's version of the Griselde story did when Chaucer used it alongside the Petrarchan original to produce his translation, *The Clerk's Tale*.² The range of options available to a translator in such respects has been noted elsewhere with reference to Chaucer, who appears prominently in the studies of Heinrichs, Neuse, and Nolan, and glancingly in that of Archibald.

But there are other, more insidious ways in which the medieval translator acts, if not as author, certainly as something like the Bonaventuran commentator or compiler, and delivers readers a text other than what we would recognize as the original. In the Middle Ages, texts, especially patristic or classical ones, circulated in a form which made interpretive material available alongside the text itself, and many translators took up the option of incorporating this material, often silently, into their version. In some cases, this commentary material sought to reinforce the meaning of the text, for example by clarifying obscurity; in others, like the commentaries on the erotic poetry of Ovid, the meaning was not so much reinforced as reinvented, or overturned. Thus, writers who used material from the love poetry of Ovid had the option of presenting him, systematically or occasionally, through the moralizing filter of the commentary tradition.

Then – though the practice differs in degree rather than in kind from those previously noted – a writer could incorporate material into his translation from different originals which pulled in different directions. This comes to be almost a defining feature of the *romans antiques* at the centre of Nolan's study. As Nolan defines them, the *romans antiques* (translations of the stories of Troy and Thebes) can be most readily distinguished from contemporary chronicle literature, with which they have a number of features in common, in two ways. First, they include an active mediating narratorial presence, which marks the gap between past and present: in chronicle literature, by contrast, the relation of past to present is figured typically in terms of continuity 'from ancient Greece to contemporary France and England'. Second, the writers complicate their given historical narrative by the creation of love-stories, heavily influenced by Ovidian models (most notably, the *Heroides*), which threaten to take over as the centre of interest but are finally harmonized with the overarching historical material, typically by the portrayal of a marriage. This love material, usually read as the real centre of interest in the story, is, in Nolan's view, offered under judgement long before it is brought to heel at the end of the work: the judgement, quite simply, of the commentary tradition, with which clerkly writers must have been familiar, and which tended to speak with a moralizing voice when interpreting ' pagan' classical texts. In a similar way, Heinrichs sees the love poets she is studying as offering barely veiled criticisms of their foolishly lovestruck narrators, by means of extensive allusion to the same Ovidian and Virgilian models. An obvious instance is Chaucer's use of the philosophical frame of Boethius' *De Consolatione Philosophiae* to thicken the narrative textures and complicate the meaning of his principal source, Boccaccio's *Il Filostrato*, when producing his own translation, *Troilus and Criseyde*.

We may wish to distinguish formally the two practices noted in the previous paragraph. In the one case, translated works are complicated by the insertion of original material which is itself coloured by the commentary tradition's interpretations of Ovid; in the other, original love visions are complicated by translated material from Ovid and Virgil added in full knowledge of the prevailing medieval interpretations of that material. And there is a further formal distinction to be made, between the text as filtered through a commentary and the text as presented in relation to other original texts. The former shows us what St Bonaventura might have called the translator as commentator; the latter provides a clear instance of the translator as compiler. Yet beyond any such distinctions their two studies might yield, we find Heinrichs and Nolan in agreement on the usefulness of the commentary tradition as a frame for their own interpretations. Not surprisingly, in both, *fine amor* (*amour courtois*, 'courtly love') is judged unfavourably against love of God (so Heinrichs) and a 'legitimate [married] love' which integrates private and public interests (so Nolan).

The clerkly transformations of texts which the commentary tradition made possible did not take place in a vacuum, but were directed towards the situation and understandings of an actual readership. Even when not constrained directly by existing interpretations of an original text, therefore, a translator was likely to adapt his translation to the anticipated demands and expectations of his readers. Thus, for example, Nolan demonstrates that Boccaccio's *Teseida* complicates its presentation of the central figure Teseo by implied reference to the *Nicomachean Ethics*: this text was well known in the Neapolitan court circle in which Boccaccio was working, possibly for the King of Naples. In other words, Boccaccio is presenting an up-to-date version of the noble prince which he expects his immediate audience to recognize (and, perhaps, recognizing itself in the portrait, to reward him for his cleverness in presenting). This figure undergoes a change at the hands of Chaucer who, in his *Knight's Tale*, 'replaces Boccaccio's Aristotelian system with the less optimistic Ciceronian and Senecan system that had, until the mid-thirteenth century, typically informed medieval . . . guide-books for princes . . . deliberately replacing [Theseus'] Aristotelian virtues with the moral virtues outlined in Stoic and pseudo-Stoic treatises'. This time the changed emphasis may have to do with Chaucer's perception of and reaction to 'the many human inequalities in the "felaweship" . . . of the English court under Richard II'.[3]

It is at this point, when we seem to have travelled very far indeed from the idea of literal translation, and where translator and readers between them seem to be busy dividing up the dismembered carcass of an original text, that we come up against major difficulties of interpretation and evaluation. The question is simply put, but not easily answered. Given that Nolan and Heinrichs both identify as a central translational and compositional strategy the co-existence of what Heinrichs calls 'disparate elements', how should we relate those diversely interwoven elements to one another? Nolan and Heinrichs both look to the commentary tradition to provide the key. If a translated or original text includes material which is interpreted by medieval commentators, the latter can be used to interpret the former. This position inevitably involves reading texts on occasion against 'the grain of the letter', as Nolan inelegantly puts it. In

such cases the literal sense will typically express the restricted consciousness of a fictional narrator or character, which will be exposed as foolish
or immoral by the discovery of the higher sense(s); the latter, expressed
in direct or indirect recourse to the commentary tradition, as also in larger
features of the work like its narrative line, is the province of the author.
Where distinct, therefore, the two voices in the text, of narratorial
(in)experience and authorial wisdom, are presented in a clear hierarchical
relationship to each other. Thus, Nolan reads Boccaccio's *Filostrato* not
by way of the formal relation between fictional writer and reader initiated
in the prologue, or of the informal relation between narrator and
protagonist in the body of the text, but in the light of Boccaccio's clerkly
and 'moralizing commentary . . . of the kind one finds in medieval arts
of love [and] in glosses on Ovid's love poems'. Similarly, Heinrichs invites
us to read the *Roman de la rose* not in relation to its ending – a rose
deflowered – which, allied with other elements in the work, might appear
to endorse a kind of sexual *carpe diem*, but rather as an expression of 'the
impulse to examine and describe the dynamics of passionate love *even as
one criticizes it*' (my emphasis). Here, I regret to say, I ally myself with
those critics who, in the words of Heinrichs, 'object to applying the
traditional glosses on the myths to the interpretation of serious medieval
literature': not because I find the glosses, in Heinrichs's phrase, 'offensive
as criticism', but because, operating within 'the convention[s] of commentary, not of poetry', they seem to me as problematic a tool as the texts
which they are supposed to elucidate.

My difficulties with the approach suggested can best be demonstrated
by reference to the mythological glosses which Boccaccio produced for his
Teseida, in particular those for the temples of Mars and Venus in VII, 30
and VII, 50 respectively. These, one might think, would provide as
authoritative a key to the meaning of the work as one could wish to have,
not least because they are so much more substantial in scope than any of
Boccaccio's other glosses. Heinrichs and Nolan differ in the degree to
which they find explicit pointers to the work's meaning in the glosses
generally; but both agree that the glosses on the temples of Mars and
Venus (especially the latter) provide an interpretation of the work
consistent with what can be discovered from its narrative detail. Similarly,
Boccaccio's regular glossing of mythological detail elsewhere in the work
is susceptible of analysis by way of intepretations popularized by the
commentary tradition.

For both Heinrichs and Nolan, Boccaccio enters the work as glossator
because he fears that otherwise the moral of his work might pass by default.
Yet what is striking about the Mars and Venus glosses is less their size
than the fact that they are the only glosses in the whole work to offer an

explicitly moralizing commentary on its details, and then really only because the narrative has itself introduced a number of allegorical figures associated with the two gods. Elsewhere in the glosses, the gods are generally treated euhemeristically or as metaphors. In this respect, the glossator goes some way to reinforcing the main line of his narrative rather than resolving its inconsistencies. Gloss and text both present the gods as part of a complex cultural situation which scholarly enquiry must now recover. The Boccaccian glosses, therefore, in my view, reveal a glossator for the most part committed only to the explication of the story's surface detail: responding line by line and detail by detail to its local meanings, he makes the gloss almost into a parallel text, a medieval encyclopedia of classical mythology. This encyclopedia is not being read through any very obvious moral filter. The glossator's interest in the truth hidden under fiction ('la verità nascosta sotto la favola') generally has to do with recuperating not an abstract moral but a literal physical meaning; readers are then invited to compare and contrast the latter with their own situations. This preoccupation surfaces most obviously when the narrative offers mythological interpretations of events which may be described more simply – and the gloss will so describe them – as the effects of perfectly intelligible natural causes; it also appears when the gloss elucidates metaphoric utterances in the narrative. In other words, the gods and heroes of the past occur in Boccaccio as specific instances of the mental furniture which characters, writer, and readers alike use in an attempt to situate themselves relative to, so as to gain control over, the immediacy of experience. Rather than uncovering a single authoritative meaning, the glosses suggest the many different ways, none finally satisfactory, in which human beings have in the past attempted to rationalize and order experience.[4] We can, of course, read the glossator as another one of those pitifully deluded characters noted by Heinrichs (and the glossator is indeed a character in the fiction, though formally distinct from those whose actions he is annotating); but if we do, we have lost the firm ground on which we thought to take our stand. Alternatively, we could read the gloss, as Nolan does, as one among many signs that Boccaccio wants his book to look like an annotated classic: if so, we are attending more to the *idea of* the book than to the ideas *in* the book.

All this is by way of making the point that glosses are not self-evident proof-texts: everything depends upon the context in which they are being generated. Thus, for instance, the Latin glosses Chaucer and Hoccleve probably provided for some texts signify differently from Gower's in the *Confessio Amantis* and Boccaccio's in the *Teseida*, even though in each case the glosses are part of a campaign to claim for the writer the status of vernacular author. Chaucer and Hoccleve copy Latin originals into the gloss almost as a check on their new version, so that the Latin original remains the ultimate source of authority. By contrast, Gower uses the Latin for summaries of the individual stories, and to explain the work's overall structure. Here, the ultimate authority of the Latin language is acknowledged, but no particular Latin originals are credited with authority over the new version, which, by virtue of being a fuller version of what the Latin summary contains, is tacitly recognized as of primary authority. As for Boccaccio, his glosses cannot be read as if they were those provided by Dante for the *Convivio* or by Dino del Garbo for Cavalcanti's canzone 'Donna me prega', even though his citation of the latter (in the gloss to VII, 50) demonstrates clearly his awareness of, and determination to contribute to, a developing vernacular commentary tradition. Unlike Dante, Boccaccio seldom refers his readers to his sources, other than in the most general terms.[5] His own work is thus, like Gower's, the ultimate point of appeal, but, unlike Gower, his use of the vernacular for the gloss denies Latin even a toehold in the work, except as another element of a disappearing past. His assertion in the gloss to I, 2 that the Greek source has never been translated into Latin contrives to bypass the question of the relationship of the vernacular to Latin. One might even conclude that when Boccaccio took over the machinery of the commentary tradition, for the purposes of authorizing his own fiction, he was doing so as a complicated kind of in-joke, akin to what Eliot did when he provided notes for *The Waste Land*, or Coleridge when he annotated his *Ancient Mariner*. In any case, the kinds of reading that both Nolan and Heinrichs use the glosses to produce depend, as Nolan acknowledges, on the possibility of 'reflective rereading'. We can readily see that such 'reflective rereading' was available to readers of sacred texts from the story of Margery Kempe, who was read to over a period of seven or eight years out of spiritual classics which included 'the Bybyl wyth doctowrys ther-up-on', and from comments by the anonymous translator of the Brigittine Office, *The Myroure of oure Ladye*. But I do wonder about the audience for whom Boccaccio felt it necessary to provide that mythological information in the glosses, especially since so much of it merely elaborated what the text itself contained.

The difficulty can be focused in another way by referring again to the gloss to *Teseida* VII, 50, on the Temple of Venus. Heinrichs concludes, from the moralized account of Venus there given, that 'the classical lovers [depicted on the walls of the temple] are here intended to mean precisely what they mean in . . . the *De Claris Mulieribus*' (hereafter *DCM*): and, by clear implication, what they mean whenever they occur in mythographic writing. Yet, as Heinrichs notes, Boccaccio moralizes the lovers neither within the tale nor in his glosses. Moreover, the lovers are functioning to subtly different ends in the two works. Semiramis, for example, is credited with forcing her maids to wear trousers in both the gloss to the *Teseida* and the text of *DCM*: this action can be easily read as a condemnation of unwomanly behaviour, and prepares us equally easily for the condemnation of her incest with her son who was 'more fit for the affairs of Venus than for the government of a kingdom'. Indeed, in the *Teseida* gloss she forces all her maids into trousers to conceal the presence of the son among them. Yet, even here, she is credited with 'marvelous things in feats of arms' and with greatly extending the kingdom her husband left her on his death. In *DCM*, having first herself adopted trousers, she requires everyone to follow suit, but this time for a different reason: her son is too young to rule the country, and the army will not take direction from a woman. Since she looks and sounds like her son, she dresses up like him to make the army think he is leading them, and reveals her true identity only once she has proved her right to government. Boccaccio does not read this moment in the light of the incipient incest but, on the contrary, as an exemplum of the proposition that 'in order to govern it is not necessary to be a man, but to have courage': the kind of meaning one might have expected to find in a work on famous women. In other words, the literary figure takes its colour, and something of its meaning, from the immediate literary context in which it occurs, no less than from the all-embracing literary culture within which writers are working.

In their different ways, as I hope these remarks have shown, both Nolan and Heinrichs have made important contributions to the debate about the interpretation of medieval texts. In addition, Heinrichs's study contains an index which glosses all the mythological figures discussed, so that the work serves almost as a handbook of medieval mythography. Neuse wears his scholarship very differently, and to a very different end: the reinstatement of the literal sense, by means of which literature provides analogues or metaphors for the here-and-now of physical existence, at the expense of the preference of allegorists, modern no less than medieval, for abstract universals. In pursuit of this understanding, Neuse compares both the overarching structures and individual detail of Dante's *Divine Comedy* and Chaucer's *Canterbury Tales* to show in how many ways the former provided the latter with both model and point of departure. His clear respect for the 'integrity of the literal' leads him regularly to read the details of the texts as metaphors only of themselves, typically as psychological projections of the narrators, rather in the way that Boccaccio presented such details in his *Teseida* glosses. This also leads Neuse to a much more generous reading of the evidence than Nolan and Heinrichs provide of their material, and cheerfully to up-end orthodox views of the texts in ways that may mirror the perverse excesses of some of the more ingenious allegorists in the commentary tradition. Thus, in *The Monk's Tale*, 'the classical deities [in the story of Croesus] . . . serve a multiple purpose, one of them being to suggest that the Church's view of the Crucifixion as a definitive event is itself a subtle form of paganism'; in *The Canterbury Tales* as a whole 'the Wife of Bath's role . . . is more or less analogous to that of Beatrice in the *Comedy*'; the *envoy* of *The Clerk's Tale* signals 'the Clerk's embrace of a Dantean over against a Petrarchan perspective'. Some of these rewritings of the story seem to me merely to be pasting new labels on old wine bottles; others seem to fill the old bottles with such a heady modern brew as to risk cracking them. Nevertheless, I find myself in total sympathy with Neuse's general position, which paradoxically reinstates the idea of literality (in translation no less than in criticism) even as it appears to overturn it by its practice. It follows that I find myself in the ironic position, on the one hand, of preferring the scholarship of Heinrichs and Nolan, and, on the other, of much preferring Neuse's literary understandings. The latter presents allegory, for example, as the '"struggle", that is, the clash, without resolution, of different philosophical perspectives', or show how the mixed fictional audience of *The Canterbury Tales* 'makes impossible a "pure" poetry whose intelligibility depends on a knowledge of esoteric symbols or interpretive techniques' – those very symbols and techniques of interpretation which Nolan and Heinrichs have done so much to recuperate for us.

University of Wales College of Cardiff

NOTES

1. For a translation of the Bonaventura passage, see A. J. Minnis, *Medieval Theories of Authorship: Scholastic Literary Attitudes in the Middle Ages*, second edition (Aldershot, 1988), p. 94. The suggestive metaphor of translation and original work as a *(con)textus* and of the author/translator as a *contextor* is used by both Nolan and Neuse.

2. This feature is noted in Neuse's discussion of the tale; see also C. C. Morse, 'Critical Approaches to *The Clerk's Tale*', in *Chaucer's Religious Tales*, edited by C. D. Benson and E. Robertson (Cambridge, 1990), pp. 71–83.

3. A simpler explanation might be that Chaucer's audience was not as *au fait* with Aristotelian theories as they were with Stoic moralizings, and that Chaucer gave his audience what he knew they would recognize.

4. This view of Boccaccio can usefully be compared with that of Chaucer advanced by A. J. Minnis, *Chaucer and Pagan Antiquity* (Cambridge and Totowa, N.J., 1982), from which both Heinrichs and Nolan seek to distance themselves.

5. A notable exception, of course, is the citation of Virgil in the gloss to VI, 53, which I take as a sign that Boccaccio wants his readers to note a quotation they might otherwise miss.

Ancients and Moderns

Gordon Braden

Redeeming the Text: Latin Poetry and the Hermeneutics of Reception. By Charles Martindale. Pp. xvii+117 (Roman Literature and its Contexts). Cambridge: Cambridge University Press, 1993. Hb. £27.95, Pb. £8.95.

Horace Made New: Horatian Influences on British Writing from the Renaissance to the Twentieth Century. Edited by Charles Martindale and David Hopkins. Pp. xviii+330. Cambridge: Cambridge University Press, 1993. Hb. £37.50.

Shakespeare and Classical Tragedy: The Influence of Seneca. By Robert S. Miola. Pp. x+224. Oxford: Clarendon Press, 1992. Hb. £27.50.

Three books on the afterlife of classical Roman literature: one mainly programmatic, the other two attending to cases.

Redeeming the Text has, by Martindale's own account, a 'weak' thesis and a 'strong' thesis. 'The weak thesis is that numerous unexplored insights into ancient literature are locked up in imitations, translations and so forth'; Martindale adds, accurately, that 'this thesis may be uncontroversial, but it is more honoured in the breach than the observance'. Not the least reason for that breach, I would think, is that the work involved can be difficult and intimidating; it demands an assiduity of focus and imagination that does not obviously go with the rubric 'weak'. In this context, however, 'strong' refers to theoretical expansiveness:

> The 'strong' thesis is that our current interpretations of ancient texts, whether or not we are aware of it, are, in complex ways, constructed by the chain of receptions through which their continued readability has been effected. As a result we cannot get back to any originary meaning wholly free of subsequent accretions. Meaning is produced and exchanged socially and discursively.

This sort of thing is certainly not hard to write any more. The reader may well fast-forward, here and elsewhere in a notably short book, when

Martindale slips into a postmodern formalizing that for anyone who has been listening to literary criticism for the past couple of decades is pretty generic:

> instead of treating texts as having more or less fixed meanings located firmly within partly recoverable backgrounds, we could negotiate the possible connections which can be constructed between texts, yet with an awareness that this involves a constantly moving 'fusion of horizons'

– and so on. It is on his 'weak thesis' that Martindale is most likely to have something special to say (some of the illustrative examples are indeed excellent), while the 'strong thesis' hovers on the edge of white noise.

My reaction comes from the context of an American English department, and is not entirely fair. Martindale constantly reminds us that he writes from the much more straitened intellectual world of Classical Studies – still one of the tightest clubs in the business, where the larger positions he is taking are indeed not as easy to voice as they have become elsewhere. In one passage, he vigorously defends a younger critic in the field against the unattributed but, one gathers, not completely hypothetical scorn of his elders and betters ('this voice is adolescent, has never grown up'). An outsider can recognize and respect a different set of professional pressures. There is also an interesting, if still ultimately unsatisfying, agenda in Martindale's use of contemporary theory; for him as for Gadamer, an agnosticism about originary meaning actually intensifies the value of tradition, and some of the culminating statements are actually conservative:

> Something worth calling a 'meeting of minds' may in general be a rarer, and more precious, thing than we usually care to acknowledge, and could be seen, precisely, as *a simultaneity of communion and difference*. There are, perhaps, three discourses within which such matters have traditionally been discussed, the discourse of religion, the discourse of eros, and the discourse of art. All three have often been linked, and all three are, not infrequently, dismissed today, with some derision, as 'mystifications', by the radical and the sophisticated.

Martindale makes a point throughout of giving supporting citations from figures like C. S. Lewis and, especially, T. S. Eliot (I think Martindale has a real point to make here). He suggests things like 'The idea of Incarnation could be said to mediate between logocentricity . . . and non-logocentricity', and ends talking about 'the Love that moves the sun and the other stars'; the theological colours of the title are being proudly worn. I am sympathetic, but do not think for a minute that Martindale's strategy is going to inhibit the academic velociraptors that worry him (his own metaphor is 'angry Pharisaism'). Even a friendly reader might indeed conclude that Martindale has in effect shown – and I think this is probably the truth – that the theoretical principles he has taken up have no entailed consequences, but can be metabolized to suit the nutritional needs of any number of incompatible programmes.

Horace Made New has some theory garnish ('To talk of a textual Horace is not to deny that there was an individual Quintus Horatius Flaccus'), but is generally a meatier volume. Assembled on the successful model of Martindale's *Ovid Renewed* (1988), it gathers new essays by several hands to amount more or less to a history of Horace's fortunes among English poets from Wyatt to C. H. Sisson, who contributes a new imitation of Epode II:

> It's not too bad to dine off pheasant
> But home-grown olives do as well,
> And what he finds extremely pleasant
> Is chewing meadow-sweet and sorrel:
> Which one of course can supplement
> By hedgerow herbs that taste of tar,
> Or better, when such boons are sent
> A lamb run over by a car.

(Some future annotator may here cite a twentieth-century belief that it is usually the tastiest lambs that wander into traffic.) The not-quite-systematic nature of the book's coverage allows a good deal of local focus, and a satisfying amount of time is spent talking through particular poems; Cowley's version of *Sermones* II.6 and Dryden's of *Carmina* III.29 rate entire essays. Predictably, and properly, special attention is paid to the late seventeenth and early eighteenth centuries; there are two essays on Dryden, and Pope figures significantly in three. (In one of the former Paul Hammond retrieves a particularly delicious misquotation by Richard Flecknoe on the fate of a perforated woman when usefulness and sweetness get mixed.)

But perhaps the best surprises come later. Stephen Medcalf contributes a detailed account of, as he puts it, 'Horace's Kipling', which among other things gives apt context and commentary to 'A Translation', perhaps the most slyly literal attempt since Milton to do a Horatian ode directly in English ('There are whose study is of smells . . .'). Charles Tomlinson seems to defeat even his own expectations with how much he finds to say about Horace in the hands of twentieth-century poets – Pinsky, Frost, Bunting, Davie, Auden, Sisson, Pound – and also shares his and, it would seem, Davie's enthusiasm over J. V. Cunningham's simile for Horace's lyric transitions: 'He found that the progression from detail to detail was by a kind of imagic shift or transformation image which, like a train through a tunnel, brings one to a new prospect on the other side of the divide' – which is indeed the kind of trope that can make important sense to someone interested in going for the same effect, while simultaneously vaporizing long traditions of stolid perplexity. A brief 'Afterword' by Don Fowler on twentieth-century Horatian scholarship looks at the case of Eduard Fraenkel, and has some unusually lucid things to say both about the extra-professional interestedness that shaped his work and about the 'fractal' character of the narrative into which that work comes to fit: 'the English enthusiasm for Horace the public poet transforms itself into an ambiguous exaltation of the private voice, to be challenged by a German political refugee in the name of a historicism whose chief characteristic is a flight from history'.

The general quality of the contributions is fairly high, with intelligent local texture and little of the attitudinizing that this kind of topic can sometimes call forth. I think the only disappointing essay is Felicity Rosslyn's, which begins with the sort of fussing about reputations that her colleagues generally avoid: 'How can one praise Horace without employing terms that could as easily be used to bury him?' Taking a term from Rabelais, she argues that Horace's detractors are 'agelasts' (the current American term is 'humor-impaired'), and constructs a soft-focus bit of literary history in which rising agelasia in eighteenth-century England makes Gray less genuinely Horatian than Pope. She ends by arguing, accurately enough, that *Ode on the Death of a Favourite Cat* is not especially Horatian, but without having much of an argument as to why Horace is the relevant model to invoke here (the chain seems to be something like: Pope imitated Horace, Pope wrote mock-epics, Gray's poem is a kind of mock-epic). On the other hand, what seems to me the most memorable essay, A. D. Nuttall's *certamen* between Horace and Marvell, is ostensibly all about competitive praise: 'The secret and wholly impracticable purpose of the exercise is to see – as a child might put it – "which poet wins".' Actually, it turns out to be 'some sort of draw (Marvell ahead at first, Horace drawing level at the end)', a conclusion that Nuttall officially labels 'disappointing'; but it seems clear to me that the point is not in fact the verdict but the sharpness of attention to poetic effect with which the contest is conducted. Here is Nuttall explaining how *Carmina* IV.1 'can cause us to catch our breath, can shake us' in a way that *To His Coy Mistress* does not:

After the measured ironic scorn of the first part of the poem the tears are almost embarrassing – but that, indeed, is the point. *Facunda*, 'eloquent', is a stroke of genius. The Loeb translator unforgivably weakens the effect with 'once eloquent'. There is no word for 'once' in the Latin. Once again a deliberate collision is being loosened and rationalized by an explicator. Horace, here and now, is a good talker at dinner parties. That is why it is so shocking, so strange ('why, Ligurinus, why . . .?') that he should lose track of his sentence as the tears well in his eyes . . . The notion is applicable to a certain place in English poetry where Horace's lines are truly matched, to W. B. Yeats' 'Among School Children' . . . Yeats's stroke of genius is the word 'public'.

Comparison here is not scorekeeping but a way of finding out how to be clear; there is also a close juxtaposition of Horace and Anacreon, as well as the Kipling 'translation' that Medcalf discusses. The question of 'influence' is not really on the table, but I do not think it is missed. A seasoned reader is drawing unpredictably on what he knows in order to give specific recognition to poetry doing its job; a certain defensiveness on Nuttall's part (he writes of his 'entirely naive involvement in the whole exercise') is sad to notice, testimony to the oddness of our trade's marketplace. This kind of work can use all a literary critic's resources, and might reasonably be called the purpose of all that training; it is certainly one of the most (perhaps that should be 'few') obviously useful things that we do.

The third book takes up a topic that has generated intermittent controversy since F. W. Cunliffe's monograph of a century ago; Miola feels that the polemical case for the importance of Senecan tragedy to English Renaissance drama has been for the most part successfully made (by myself, among' others), but needs a systematic survey of the most important single corpus: 'knowledge of Seneca's contribution to Shakespeare resides largely in isolated studies of individual plays; there exists no integrated assessment'. Miola has some contributions to make to the 'positivistic' evidence here – he retrieves from archival obscurity a dissertation which claims to show that Shakespeare could not have acquired his overt Senecan quotations from any known *florilegia* – but he also wants to move beyond the traditional emphasis on verbal quotation or allusion ('the rigid columns of parallel passages') to 'more spacious perspectives': 'Sources manifest themselves in many forms, verbal and non-verbal – in transformed convention, rhetorical or structural format, scenic rhythm, ideational or imagistic concatenation, thematic articulation.' The connections he goes on to trace are indeed by a fair margin more complicated, more densely articulated, than anything that has been set out before. Miola has been very thorough in his canvass of secondary literature, and gives systematic development to the dispersed suggestions of others (perhaps most interestingly those of Harold Brooks on *Richard III* and *Midsummer Night's Dream*); he also has some new ideas of his own, some of them quite good. By the same token, though, he does not even seem interested in knowing when to stop, and to a greater degree even than is usual with such work his argument is apt to be subject to critical sorting out by others.

Here is a characteristic passage:

> *Troades* and *Titus Andronicus* open with ritualistic mourning scenes after a hard war; for both Seneca and Shakespeare Hecuba symbolizes grief, and Priam fallen Troy. More specifically, *Troades* and *Titus Andronicus* exhibit similar configurations of action, character, and design. Both plays feature a vanquished mother who struggles in vain to preserve the life of a son; both depict human sacrifice in honour of the valiant dead; and both make use of the tomb as a potent symbolic setting.

You do not have to be hostile to the enterprise to wonder if the parallels here are being generated largely by selective paraphrase. The Astyanax–Alarbus alignment requires some squinting. The famous poignancy of the killing of 'puer Astyanax' has to do with his being a mere child, while Shakespeare's Alarbus has to be of warrior age (he is elder brother to the murderous rapists of the next act); you find out that Miola also wants to link Astyanax with Mutius, whose mother is not around to struggle to preserve his life. Mutius (apparently unlike Astyanax) is eventually buried in the tomb in question, but no one in Shakespeare re-enacts or alludes to Andromache's concealing of her live son in the place of death. Miola is in fact on his way to a contrast of his own – 'Astyanax's brave death at least ratifies to some degree the heroic code that claims him. Alarbus merely dies a helpless victim' – but the ground of resemblance that would make such a contrast really significant has a gelatinous feel to it. Miola does review other possible sources – the *Titus* chapbook, Ovid's Procne story – to establish that Shakespeare did not get the tomb from them; and of course there is a strong general credibility in the association of any incident of murdered children with Seneca. I suppose in this case I would come out saying that the intertextual detailing is neither absurd nor compelling.

Sometimes it is easier to know what to think. When Miola tries to link the scenes between Hamlet and Horatio with that between Atreus and his *satelles*, his main example turns out to be the moment when Hamlet rouses himself for revenge and Horatio breathes scarcely a whiff of the 'loyal resistance' that Miola says he embodies; at such moments 'transformed convention' looks like an excuse for making things up. Elsewhere, however, Miola is luckier – in at least one case, I think, spectacularly so. The chapter 'Senecan *Furor*' is of course concerned with *Hercules furens*, and especially with the pattern of 'raging madness followed by a palliative sleep'; context here has proved easier to document than for other Senecan motifs, and much of Miola's discussion follows the footsteps of previous commentators. But his momentum leads him to be, as far as I know, the first critic to note in print the relevance of Hercules' waking scene (itself having moving precedent in Euripides) to the comparable scene in *King Lear*; this time he has the goods:

> The corresponding scene of *Leir* . . ., with its eating and ritualistic kneeling, and Leir's extended narrative, supplies no precedent for much of Shakespeare's action and rhetoric . . . Both Hercules and Lear fall into a deep restorative slumber in the presence of several sympathetic attendants, the chorus here replaced by the Doctor, Gentleman, and Cordelia. Upon waking, Hercules asks confused questions about his location . . . As we have seen, this interrogative awakening into painful self-consciousness was a topos variously employed on the Renaissance stage. La Taille uses the scene in *Saul Le Furieux* (1562) to depict Saul's recovery from madness . . . In *Richardus Tertius* (1580) Legge quotes the Senecan passage to suggest the confusion and fear of Henry Tudor, accidently separated from his army . . . ; in *Jack Drum's Entertainment* (1600) Marston uses these lines to mark the beginning, not the end of Pasquill's madness . . . ; and Fulke Greville adapts the passage extensively in *Alaham* (1600) to dramatize Hala's Herculean anagnorisis . . . Lear's version is spare and stark: 'Where have I been? Where am I? Fair daylight?' . . . Unlike Hercules (or Hala above), he finds his child miraculously alive.

Against what here are well-evidenced expectations, the *peripeteia* at the end comes across with full force. The Senecan universe in his head, Lear had every reason to think that he had destroyed this child; her living presence before him alters his whole sense of reality.

University of Virginia

Translation between Poetics and Ideology

Theo Hermans

Translation, Rewriting and the Manipulation of Literary Fame. By André Lefevere. Pp. viii+176. London and New York: Routledge, 1992. Pb. £11.99.

Translation/History/Culture: A Sourcebook. Edited by André Lefevere. Pp. xiv+182. London and New York: Routledge, 1992. Pb. £11.99.

Translating Literature: Practice and Theory in a Comparative Literature Context. By André Lefevere. Pp. vii+165. New York: Modern Language Association of America, 1992. $15.

Translation and Translation Theory in Seventeenth-Century Germany. Edited by James Hardin. Pp. 156. Amsterdam and Atlanta: Rodopi, 1992. Pb. Hfl.55.

André Lefevere's is a familiar name in Translation Studies. He has been around for some twenty years, publishing furiously and often provocatively. He has changed over the years, too, and his career mirrors some of the paradigmatic sea-changes in the field. His first book, *Translating Poetry: Seven Strategies and a Blueprint* (1975), still viewed literary translation as a loss-making business and tried to distil the optimum strategy from among a number of available options. He would soon shake off the normative touch, and in *Literary Knowledge* (1977), probably his least-known book, went in search of a new conceptual framework for the study of literature and translation. This was the time when the descriptive, target-oriented, polysystem-based approach was rearing its head, and Lefevere, together with scholars like Gideon Toury, Raymond van den Broeck, and José Lambert, proved one of its most polemical and effective voices. During these years he also brought out his best-known collection, *Translating Literature: The German Tradition* (1977), and collaborated with Van den Broeck on a Dutch-language *Invitation to Translation Studies* (1979). He went on to carve out his own niche, moving from the Low Countries to Austin, Texas, and gradually devising his own concepts and terminology for discussing translation. In the last ten years or so he has brought out a number of prose and verse translations, from a range of languages, but most of his critical work has been appearing in article form, and has not had the impact of the earlier books. He has come back now, with a vengeance: three books, all published within the space of a couple of months, two of them in the enterprising Routledge series 'Translation Studies' which Lefevere himself directs together with Susan Bassnett.

They are three very different books: a historical reader, a course-book, and a scholarly study. All three, however, are informed by the same approach to translation. The approach is set out in some detail and deployed in selected case-studies in *Translation, Rewriting and the Manipulation of Literary Fame*. It is summarized and illustrated with reference to many small-scale examples in the *Translating Literature* coursebook. And it is worked into the very structure of the 'sourcebook' *Translation/History/Culture*. Among the key elements in this approach is the view that translation is a form of 'rewriting'. There was a time when Lefevere spoke of translation as 'refraction', but that term appears to have been dropped; other forms of rewriting include not just the traditional ones, adaptation, summary, pastiche, and the like, but also editing, anthologizing, historiography, and criticism. They all constitute forms of mediation which manipulate and determine the 'image' of a literary work for a particular audience. For Lefevere, the most important factors in translation are, in descending order of importance: ideology, poetics, universe of discourse, and language. The study of translation, he argues, should recognize this hierarchy and its implications, and firmly locate the object of study in its socio-cultural, ideological, and poetological context.

The operative concepts which Lefevere derives from this position are set out in the opening chapters of *Translation, Rewriting and the Manipulation of Literary Fame*. The literary system, he explains, is controlled from within by professionals – critics, teachers, translators – who act as the guardians of the system's poetics and ideology, and from without by what he calls 'patronage', defined rather loosely as 'the powers (persons, institutions) that can further or hinder the reading, writing, and rewriting of literature'. Patronage, which may be differentiated or undifferentiated (roughly: totalitarian or decentralized), consists of three components, an ideological, an economic, and a status component. A poetics has two components: an inventory of devices, genres, motifs, etc., and a functional component, a concept of what the role of literature is, or should be, in a given society.

So far, so good. Neither the overall approach nor the methodological tools which Lefevere offers are strikingly new, even if his particular emphasis on terms like 'ideology', 'patronage', and 'poetics' probably is. Viewing the production and mediation of literature from this angle has the prime virtue of demystifying the object and directing the attention instead to the various conditioning factors, which ultimately involve questions of naked power. All this is refreshing and productive, and Lefevere argues his case with verve and humour. The trouble I have with it is that as a theoretical apparatus it remains far too rudimentary, that it is not consistently elaborated, and that some of the case-studies are treated in a reductive and ahistorical manner which is hard to justify in terms of the very approach they are meant to illustrate. I will try to substantiate these objections below, not in order to find fault with the detail of Lefevere's work for its own sake, but precisely because his work is of central importance to the discipline.

The first charge, that the theoretical apparatus is too rudimentary, is unfair, I know. Lefevere nowhere claims to be propounding a universal theory of literature. But he nowhere restricts the range of his theoretical concepts either. On the contrary, the general discussion refers freely to 'literature' and 'literatures' in the broadest sense, and the case-studies encompass Homer, Aristophanes, Catullus, Madame de Staël, Büchner, the Dutch writers Anne Frank and W. G. van Focquenbroch, the Arabic *qasidah*, and anthologies of African literature. That being the case, Lefevere's approach runs the same risk as, say, Itamar Even-Zohar's polysystem theory a decade or more ago. Its terms are too apodictic, too few, and therefore much too broad to be able to guide research in any meaningful way beyond a general orientation towards the social context of literature.

My second objection follows in part from the first. The fewer the terms of the theoretical apparatus, the heavier their load, and so Lefevere can be found speaking on one page of 'the inbuilt conservative weighting of institutions of patronage', only to observe on the next that 'change in a literary system is also closely connected with patronage'. His notion of . patronage, it transpires here, includes the reading public as well as individuals, groups, institutions, publishers, and 'the media, both news-papers and magazines and larger television corporations' (why the 'larger'?).

In other places, inconsistencies seem to creep in where they could have been avoided. Having distinguished between an inventory and a functional component of a poetics, and listed motifs, symbols, and prototypical characters and situations under the former, Lefevere appears to range themes under the functional component. Rather more disturbing is a muddled passage on prescriptive versus descriptive approaches to translation. What Lefevere intends to say here is clear enough, I think.

It is something like: most writing on translation has traditionally been prescriptive in nature, and this is why it has been so repetitive and unproductive; a descriptive approach to translation 'problems', which outlines various possible strategies, would be more productive. Such an approach, he adds a few pages later, should preferably refrain also from making evaluative statements, as these would only reveal the observer's prescriptive assumptions. His phrasing in the key passage, however, is in terms of a 'translation poetics' which is urged to abandon normativeness and embrace descriptivism. This cannot possibly be squared with the standard meaning of the term, or even with Lefevere's own definition of poetics as 'the dominant concept of what literature should (be allowed to) be', which both imply a normative element. The point, as I see it, is that the study of translation positions itself on a meta-level with regard to its object, and this meta-discourse is more likely to raise productive questions if it adopts a non-prescriptive stance and seeks to explain translation behaviour rather than to hand down rules or pass judgment on it. To make things worse, Lefevere goes on to produce a strongly normative – and uncharacteristically naive – statement to the effect that translators should know their languages and 'would be well advised to bow to the dictates of the dictionary' so as not to translate the Latin *passer* ('sparrow') by 'hippopotamus', for instance. Only a true believer can have this kind of faith in the ability of the dictionary to define what a word 'means' and what its 'equivalent' should be in another language. At the same time, the call to refrain from evaluative pronouncements, however sensible in itself, sounds somewhat hollow when confronted with Lefevere's casual remark that Catullus' sparrow poem 'could have been better written', or with the more substantial declaration about the 'metre and rhyme rule' of much traditional European verse translation which 'has been responsible for the failure of many a translation to carry its original across into the Western system'. I am not sure what exactly is meant here by an 'original' (with a certain essence?), by the notion of 'carrying across' (intact?), or that of 'failure' (what would have constituted 'success', and was it ever possible?), but the statement is nothing if not evaluative.

I do not want to labour the last objection listed above, that of the reductive and ahistorical procedure in some of the case-studies. Despite his disarmingly straightforward style, Lefevere covers an extremely wide range of material, and perhaps should not be criticized too harshly for occasionally slipping up. But an ineptly chosen example may unhinge an already uncertain theoretical point. Arguing, in a chapter on patronage, that educational institutions often leave a conservative imprint on the imagination of individual authors, and that as a consequence a writer's literary manifestoes may be innovative while his or her practice harks back to the canonized texts read at school, Lefevere invokes the case of Joachim du Bellay. Du Bellay issued a radical literary programme and went on to write French poems based on his own Latin poetry, and in so doing, Lefevere says, only rewrote his own rewritings of texts he had been exposed to as part of his education. The example does little more than betray a failure to appreciate the relation between Latin and vernacular culture in the Renaissance, and leaves one wondering about the (I think doubtful) validity of the broader claim.

I have focused on a number of points in *Translation, Rewriting and the Manipulation of Literary Fame*, which to my mind undermine the otherwise entirely sensible approach to translation which Lefevere advocates. There are more such points (for example, the claim that 'for readers who cannot check the translation against the original, the translation, quite simply, is the original' – I do not believe the matter is as simple as that), but, in fairness to Lefevere, there are also imaginative leaps, genuinely refreshing insights, and flashes of brilliance in what is essentially a very readable, even an engaging book. That is precisely what makes the lapses so infuriating.

The sourcebook *Translation/History/Culture*, a historical reader, is a very different work, but it has more in common with *Translation, Rewriting and the Manipulation of Literary Fame* than one might have expected. It too is important, refreshing, and infuriating. It is important for two reasons. First, it is an international reader, whereas most existing collections – and at least half-a-dozen have been published in recent years in German, French, Dutch, and Spanish alone – are monolingual. Lefevere has selected material written originally in Latin, French, German, and English, and provided new and eminently readable translations of all the foreign-language texts. Second, he has dug up a number of little-known texts on translation, mainly from the neo-Latin tradition. There are texts here by such figures as Leonardo Bruni, Juan Luis Vives, and Pierre Huet (Huetius) which hitherto were known only to specialists.

For all its philological spadework, however, this is by no means an innocent reader, and Lefevere is quite open about his intention. 'This collection is an attempt to influence the direction in which Translation Studies might most profitably develop', he writes, and in the very next sentence we are thrown the keywords 'power', 'patronage', 'ideology', 'poetics'. Accordingly, the book is put together along thematic rather than purely chronological lines. Each section contains a number of shorter extracts illustrating a particular aspect of translation. The sections cover: ideology; patronage; poetics; universe of discourse; the role of translation in language development and education; techniques and rules of translating; and 'images' of central texts. Between them these sections make up roughly the first half of the collection. The second half contains longer statements in which several of the factors just listed are dealt with in one way or another. Each section is preceded by a brief introduction and each author by a short explanatory note, but the documents themselves are presented without annotations.

There is an inherent risk in working with extracts. More than a decade ago Glyn Norton argued, entirely persuasively to my mind, that Étienne Dolet's celebrated *Manière de bien traduire d'une langue en aultre* of 1540 was not at all a set of rules and prescriptions for the practising translator, but a projection of the image of the ideal translator; and it takes the full text of Dolet's piece, and its context, to see Norton's point. Lefevere's extracts in the first part of his reader have as their only context the categories which he himself has provided – or imposed. Some of his extracts are so short as to be virtually meaningless. This is from Jean de Brèche, one of six texts quoted as illustrations of the power of patronage: 'The translator, a learned man and an expert in languages, has done his best to render into French the Aphorisms of Hippocrates . . . even though he foresees that his labor may incur the anger and mockery of many who seem to be eager to keep the sciences hidden from the people.' That's it. Since many of the extracts in this part of the book are less than a page in length, and deprived of any meaningful historical context, they can be made to say just about anything. Consequently, I do not believe for a moment that the collection has achieved what is claimed to be its central purpose, 'to reveal the basic categories that can be seen to have been the foundation of much thinking about the translation of literature', as Lefevere has it in the preface to the second part of the collection. All that the extracts reveal is the compiler's skill at selecting and cutting extracts to suit his purpose. The irony of it all is that in the very same paragraph Lefevere also – and quite rightly – insists 'that a productive study of the translation of literature can, for the most part, be only socio-historical in nature'. I would advise serious students of translation to rip out and throw away the first eighty pages of *Translation/ History/ Culture*. Not much would be lost anyhow, for, as we read in the bibliographical references, many of the shorter extracts are actually culled from existing and readily available collections.

The longer documents in the second part of the book are altogether more valuable. They redeem the book, so much so that we should probably take Lefevere's cavalier treatment of chronology in this section into the bargain. This is where we encounter Bruni, Huetius (translated here into English for the first time), Gaspard de Tende, Johann Jakob Bodmer, d'Alembert, and others. Although the absence of annotations will leave readers wondering where to trace the identity of Henricus Stephanus (Henri Estienne), Humfredus (Lawrence Humphrey?) or Italus Catena (?), the texts are sufficiently substantial and coherent in themselves to repay careful reading. Given the ever more widely recognized need for the primary documents concerning the history of translation and the history of thought about translation to be made available, this second part of Lefevere's sourcebook goes some way towards filling a huge gap.

In summing up his programme for the study of translation, Lefevere again stresses what to him – and to many others currently engaged in the descriptive study of translation history – appears to be the most productive line of enquiry:

> The most important thing is not how words are matched on the page, but why they are matched that way, what social, literary, ideological considerations led translators to translate as they did, what they hoped to achieve by translating as they did, whether they can be said to have achieved their goals or not, and why.

If, then, a large part of the third of Lefevere's new books, *Translating Literature: Practice and Theory in a Comparative Literature Context*, is still devoted to questions of linguistic form and literary usage, the reason is, clearly, that this is a coursebook, to be used in teaching or for self-study. The book positively bristles with witty, entertaining examples which any teacher worth his salt will want to appropriate. The exposition works its way up from the basic level – language – via the embedding of texts in literary and ideological contexts, to a consideration of the function of translation in a given culture. It takes a perhaps unexpected turn in Chapter 5, where Lefevere expresses the hope that 'the weakening of the disinclination for translation studies will also spell the end of the discrimination against translation as a scholarly activity'. The argument is for translations to be accepted as evidence of scholarly competence in awarding academic degrees. In Britain, I imagine it may be some time before this argument wins the day. In the meantime, we can draw inspiration from Lefevere's Chapter 6, 'Topics for Classroom Teaching and Research', a scintillating five-page list of questions about the nature and role of translation, good for several dozen student essays.

André Lefevere's views on the best way to study translation in general, and the history of literary translation in particular, are both challenging and important. They are not as new as he would have us believe, and they are not immune to criticism – and it is only proper that they should be kicked hard by one who essentially agrees with him. It is when turning from Lefevere's work to a collection like *Translation and Translation*

Theory in Seventeenth-Century Germany, edited by James Hardin, that one appreciates just how much Lefevere has to offer. The Hardin volume grew out of a meeting of the Society for German Renaissance and Baroque Literature held in Chicago in 1990. It contains essays focusing on translators (Harsdörffer, Opitz, Schaevius, Mencke, and Aegidius Albertinus), and on individual source-texts (Boethius' *Consolatio*, Amadis de Gaule, and a story by Cervantes). Much of it is sound philological work. Some of the more interesting pieces ask the kind of questions that can provide insight into the place and function of translation in seventeenth-century Germany. George Schoolfield on a rendering of a Propertius elegy, for example, questions why Opitz made the translation and why he published it when he did. But too many contributions are little more than desultory explorations without a sense of direction or of context, arguing about whether this or that text should be labelled translation or adaptation, 'mitdichtende Übertragung' or 'Umdichtung'. One essay begins by asking: 'Has the rewriting for the stage produced a literary transposition rather than just another translation?', to conclude entirely tautologically, eight pages later, that 'By transposing from one genre to another the effort of the dramatist has been elevated to the level of an original creation not just a translation.' The casual dismissal of texts as 'just translation' is almost touching in its innocence.

What the collection makes clear, though, is that there is a wealth of material to be discovered concerning the history of translation, and of thought about translation, as the discussions of the prefaces and other pronouncements by a Harsdörffer or a Johann Burckhardt Mencke amply show. At present, our knowledge of the history of translation theory is still too sketchy to read these pronouncements adequately and put them in context; in addition, we need to learn to ask productive questions of the material if we want to arrive at answers that might bring illumination. In both these areas, Lefevere is at least trying to create relevant openings.

University College London

Reviews

The Severed Word: Ovid's 'Heroides' and the Novela Sentimental. By Marina
Scordilis Brownlee. Princeton, N.J.: Princeton University Press, 1990. Pp.
ix+272. Hb. $37.50.

The initial point of reference for this survey of seven Spanish *novelas
sentimentales* is Ovid's *Heroides*, a text that Professor Brownlee believes
should earn for its creator the Foucaultian accolade of 'founder of
discursivity' as a result of the new attitude to language displayed in the
epistolary self-portraits that constitute the work. There is an account of
how Ovid's politically and discursively subversive text was totally misread
in the Middle Ages, as in the fragmentary treatment afforded it in Alfonso
X's universal history, which restores the legendary women to the heroic
world of male values from which the Latin poet had liberated them. But
with Juan Rodríguez del Padrón's fifteenth-century rewriting, the
Bursario (the earliest vernacular rendering of the entire Ovidian collection), we discover a restoration of Ovid's structure of consecutive letters.
And with his *Siervo libre de amor*, Juan Rodríguez would proceed to
juxtapose the novelistic discourse implicit in Ovid's text with that of
medieval romance.

Before examining the *Siervo libre* – the work that initiates the genre of
the sentimental romance – Brownlee turns her attention to two texts that
are regarded as predecessors of the pioneering Spanish work, and which
also depend on the same Ovidian model: Boccaccio's *Elegia di madonna
Fiammetta* and, a century later, Piccolomini's *Historia de duobus amantibus*.
Although there are similarities of plot – an adulterous wife seduced and
abandoned by her lover – the later work exploits epistolarity in such a way
as to highlight the problematic relationship of words and actions. Having
thus outlined what she terms the 'epistolary anatomy', the author moves
on to examine those works that reveal 'the allegorical paradox': the *Siervo
libre* and two texts not usually included in the canonical corpus of the
sentimental romance, Pedro de Portugal's *Sátira de felice e infelice vida* and
the anonymous *Triste deleytaçion*. She argues that all three challenge the
allegorical procedure, and establishes for each an intertextual pairing. The
Siervo libre utilizes thematic motifs and narrative ploys found in the *Vita
Nuova* and, to an extent, the *Commedia*, the effect of which is to suggest
the invalidity of courtly discourse. The *Sátira* points to the *Roman de la
rose*, but, unlike its subtext, separates myth and allegory. This is achieved
mainly by the intrusion of an exegetical apparatus that signals the
incorporation of 'an extratextual dimension in the courtly system that is
in its very nature necessarily intratextual, subjective, hermetic'. The lyric
structure is therefore supplanted by a novelistic one. Twelve *novelle* from
the *Decameron* are exploited in *Triste deleytaçion*. Once again, the courtly

ideal is undermined by the 'cynical empiricism' of *novella* discourse, while the allegorical conclusion, describing the protagonist's journey to the Otherworld, is a comical rewriting – and subverting – of Dante.

In the third and final section, entitled 'Linguistic Transgression', allegory is only a peripheral concern. It is semantic distortion that colours Diego de San Pedro's *Arnalte y Lucenda*, where the principle of metaphoric exchange is prominent: the characters engage in a discourse in which words, clothing, money, and sex are repeatedly transferred, and where terms such as 'honour', 'love', and 'friendship' are constantly misused and manipulated for selfish ends. For the same writer's *Cárcel de amor*, considered the epitome of the genre, Brownlee moves away from standard readings to focus on the level of the illocutionary act, where we encounter 'a relentless violation of the "appropriateness conditions"' of each of the genres present in the text. Words appear as 'sterile graphic markers' rather than as a vehicle for communication, most vividly demonstrated in Leriano's eating of the love-letters in a bizarre parody of the Eucharist.

The last two texts examined are Juan de Flores's *Grimalte y Gradissa* and *Grisel y Mirabella*. The former is an explicit continuation of Boccaccio's *Elegia*, albeit with an inverted focus, concentrating as it does on the consequences of action rather than speech. Moreover, Flores offers another option to his heroine – a movement out of the secrecy of her chamber to the outside world, an alternative enhanced by the incorporation of activity, contrasting with the 'paralytic inaction' of the Boccaccian subtext. And, as with other *novelas sentimentales*, linguistic alienation emerges as a major issue, notably in the way in which Flores makes Fiammetta suffer in actions the maledictions she had uttered in the *Elegia*. *Grisel* is, likewise, based on a rewriting of Boccaccio, the first tale in Day Four of the *Decameron*, and again the question of language and nominalism looms large. This is especially evident in the depiction of the king's incestuous inclination in terms of 'linguistic perversion' – a contamination that the linguistic integrity embodied in the words of Flores and his lady serves to highlight rather than to eradicate.

Finally, in a richly suggestive epilogue, Brownlee comments on other factors that lead to the breakdown of referentiality, particularly the incorporation of remote and savage landscapes that complement the lexical estrangement. And, as if by way of a last salvo, she indicates how the discursive originality commonly attributed to Celestina is discernible in the *novela sentimental*; how, for example, the *Cárcel de amor*, no less than Rojas's masterpiece, offered an 'encyclopaedia of discourses which undermined themselves'.

It will be evident from the above summary that this book represents a profound and detailed exploration of a largely neglected genre. Although the issues are complex, the argument is lucid and generally convincing, and only occasionally elliptical, as when a decisive contrast or conclusion is being sought. It can be commended both as a significant contribution to an understanding of the creative pressures and priorities at the heart of the sentimental romance, and, more broadly, as an intriguing insight into the embryonic European novel.

D. GARETH WALTERS
University of Glasgow

Upon the Dark Places: Anti-Semitism and Sexism in English Renaissance Bible Translation. By Ilona N. Rashkow. Pp. 180. Sheffield: Sheffield Academic Press, 1990. Hb. £30.

I normally associate books coming from the Sheffield Academic Press with interesting, often stimulating approaches to biblical topics. At the least, their authors are familiar with the most recent developments in biblical and literary scholarship. It is curious, therefore, to come across this dull, error-strewn account of 'Anti-Semitism and Sexism in English Renaissance Bible Translation'. In a sense, that sub-title says it all, for to write on sixteenth- and seventeenth-century Englishmen's misogyny and anti-semitism is rather like writing a book to argue that Frenchmen like good food. There might have been a point to the enterprise if Ilona Rashkow had attempted to show how Authorized Version renderings fed into the culture and, accordingly, helped set an agenda for vicious behaviour in later centuries. Something like Letty Russell's edition of essays on feminist responses to the Bible could have helped here, but Rashkow shows little sign of having done much reading in this area. Less ambitiously, she might have thought about the impact of the AV upon modern British and American Bible translations, and in doing so would have surprised herself by discovering that the Renaissance translators were actually less misogynistic than their modern counterparts: the rape of Tamar, one of the narratives which she treats, offers some very instructive contrasts. Also, consideration of the translators' anti-semitism would have benefited from being set within some appreciation of the English philo-semitic movement, charted by David Katz, which was developing around the time that the AV was translated.

Instead of attempting anything so interesting, the first quarter of this book is given over to a ridiculously uninformed account of the history of English Bible translation up to 1611. All of the work done in this field in the last forty years has passed her by – David Daiches's 1941 account of the AV seems to be her most recent authority – so that the mistakes are legion. On the first page of the actual study the Douai version is cited as an influence upon the AV (p. 13): the Rheims New Testament was, but the Douai Old Testament was not, so her constant citing of its notes is largely irrelevant. She rebukes Miles Coverdale for not mentioning the Hebrew text as one of his sources on his title page (p. 27) and writes later about his Hebrew knowledge (p. 59). Coverdale quite properly did not cite it because he did not use it, not knowing any Hebrew at all. The Geneva Bible, which appeared two years into Elizabeth's reign, is described as the only Bible printed when Mary was on the throne (p. 29), so Rashkow has clearly never read the preface to this version, with its impassioned call to Elizabeth to become a true Christian prince. Then, her claim that 'Hebrew could not easily be studied in Renaissance England' (p. 57) takes the breath away. In fact, Hebrew was on the curriculum of more than a few grammar schools, leave alone the universities.

All of this is poor scholarship. What follows is worse, as, working from simplistic ideas about translation, Rashkow pulls texts about to reveal their sexist and/or anti-semitic bias. To give one example: the AV translators are chastised for not consistently translating the Hebrew idiom *ish gibbor chayyil* with the same phrase wherever it occurs in the Old Testament, so that when the phrase is applied to Boaz we fail to realize how well suited he and Ruth are (p. 127). Never mind that this contradicts her earlier observation that the Old Testament texts span thousands of years, so such consistency would be completely misleading. More to the point is that this is a prescription which completely fails to consider that a translation is not something to be done to a formula. The AV translators said as much in their preface, pointing out that continual fixing upon word for word equivalents would 'savour of curiosity'. That is what this book does. It savours of curiosity, in the seventeenth-century sense of that word.

GERALD HAMMOND
University of Manchester

Volgarizzare e tradurre. By Gianfranco Folena. Turin: Einaudi, 1991. Pp. 105. Pb. Lit. 12,000.

Studi sulla traduzione nell'Inghilterra del seicento e del settecento. By Carmela Nocera Avila. Caltanissetta-Rome: Salvatore Sciascia Editore, 1990. Pp. 139. Lit. 20,000.

Translation Studies as a discipline is undergoing a phase of unprecedented development in the 1990s, and the state of the art in Italy is particularly healthy, as exemplified by the development of degree courses, new books and journals, and international conferences in the field. These two books represent different aspects of this development, though they are linked by a common interest in the history of translation theory and practice.

Gianfranco Folena's long essay, first published in a collection of essays on translation in 1973, has been reprinted as a booklet in its own right, with a short preface by the author in which he pays tribute to some of the more recent work that has appeared since his essay was written. Folena's study was ground-breaking in its day, and is still very relevant to work in Translation Studies, for he anticipated the Cultural Studies approach to translation that was to develop from the early work in polysystems theory pioneered by such scholars as Itamar Even-Zohar and Gideon Toury. Folena also recognized the need for a more systematic approach to the history of translation practice, and stresses the significance of history when he proposes that 'we cannot talk about "translation theory" except as part of general theories of literature, linguistics and hermeneutics'.

Folena is concerned with the role played by translation in the Middle Ages in the development of vernacular languages. He draws attention to the complexity of the processes of interlingual transfer, and locates translation in the tradition of medieval rhetoric. His concern with terminology is another indication of his insight into cultural history, and he is one of the first scholars to note, for example, that the term 'translation' in English is synonymous with the term 'compilation' in this period. Folena explores translation as a creative force in an age of transition, and I can recall reading his essay when it first came out with a sense of excitement that is still present rereading it twenty years later in the context of all that has happened in our field in the meantime.

Carmela Nocera Avila pays homage to Folena in her study of English translation practice in the fifteenth and sixteenth centuries. Where Folena recognizes the vital distinction between 'tradurre' and 'volgarizzare', Nocera Avila recognizes the significance of 'translating' and 'Englishing' in the period under consideration. Indeed, she starts with a citation from Folena, and uses his work to justify her demands for a historiography of translation. The difference between Folena and Nocera Avila lies precisely here: the one is a medievalist, who by a leap of consciousness was able to bridge disciplines and advance research in Translation Studies with a single bound; the other is an Anglicist, whose interest in the history of translation is filtered through her scholarship in the English Renaissance field, and who consequently applies the methodology of her predecessor to the period under consideration.

Folena and Nocera Avila represent two stages in Italian Translation Studies today, the precursor and the younger scholar whose thinking has been informed by the work of international figures such as Toury, Lambert, and Lefevere. Both these books have achieved some considerable success in the Italian context; it would be good to have them translated into other languages so that their insights could be transmitted to the wider, international public they deserve.

SUSAN BASSNETT
University of Warwick

The English Bible and the Seventeenth-Century Revolution. By Christopher Hill. Pp. xiii+466. London: Allen Lane, The Penguin Press, 1993. Hb. £25.

Tyndale's Old Testament: Being the Pentateuch of 1530, Joshua to 2 Chronicles of 1537, and Jonah. Edited by David Daniell. Pp. xxxvii+643. New Haven and London: Yale University Press, 1992. Pb. £22.50.

In the beginning of Christopher Hill's account of the biblical culture of mid-seventeenth-century England sit three introductory quotations, the first from the reformer William Tyndale, the second from the would-be poet Christopher Harvey, and the third from Shakespeare's *Richard III*, where the evil hunchback confesses to his use of a piece of Scripture to clothe his 'naked villainy'. To this third quotation Hill adds a footnote to the effect that 'similar examples of hypocritical use of the Bible abound in Marlowe's plays'; and he might well have added Iago's 'proofs of holy writ' to demonstrate how familiar stage villains were with the abuses of biblical citation. Already, then, on its opening page, Hill's book, by annotating a gloss, gestures towards the Geneva Bible, the translation which is the 'English Bible' of its title and which, in Hill's opinion, lies at the heart of the English Revolution. Although the Authorized Version was nearly thirty years old when the Civil War began, because it lacked any kind of interpretive annotation, it still could not compete with the much older Geneva version. Completed in 1560 and constantly reprinted through the next eighty years, this Bible offered its readers an exhaustive commentary squeezed into its margins, often to the point of overflowing, making it appear on the page an English equivalent to those rabbinical Bibles where the Hebrew text is surrounded by the Targum and by Rashi and other commentators, the commentary being in a minuscule print, as small words attending on the great Word which rules the world. James I hated these Geneva notes and ordered his 1611 translators to confine themselves to cross-references and alternative renderings.

Hill is surely right about the Geneva Bible, and literary scholars, particularly editors of Shakespeare, should take heed. Richard III's Bible would have been, anachronistically, like Caesar's clock, a Geneva version – and not, as many recent editors would have it, a Bishops' Bible. True, the latter was the most recent version, published in 1568, and was read from in many churches, but so inferior were its renderings, and so generally unpopular was it, that the Authorized Version translators based their work on the Geneva Bible, in spite of James's instruction to them to use the Bishops' text. Many of today's editors of Shakespeare assume that his Catholic background meant that he was not a Bible-reader, or, if he was, that he would not have read a Puritan version – hence their common citation of the Bishops' Bible as a source for the biblical echoes in the plays. Hill gets the balance much better: he has a lot to say about the Geneva Bible and gives the Bishops' Bible scarcely a mention.

What Hill does, triumphantly, is to restore the Geneva Bible to the centre of *seventeenth-century* life. He offers the most sustained and thought-provoking assessment of its marginal notes (and the ways in which they would have been interpreted) that has so far been attempted. Sometimes this comes in summary form – 'those sins which the marginal notes to the Geneva Bible especially emphasized were idolatry and persecution'; often specific examples are offered, as in the Geneva gloss on Jezebel's death, that it was 'a spectacle and example of God's judgments to all tyrants'. His point, too, is that the Geneva Bible, in spite of its name, was not a text which was read only, or even mainly, by Puritans, however loosely or precisely we define that term. It was owned and read by everyone (except for James I). So, when Christopher Harvey begins the poem which stands at the entrance to Hill's book with an incomparably awful invocation to the Bible –

> The Bible; that's the Book. The Book indeed,
>   The Book of Books,
>   On which who looks . . .

– the Bible which he is hailing is, despite the poem's date of publication

(1640), and despite the fact that Harvey was a devout Anglican, probably the Geneva Bible. One opportunity suggested by Hill's book to any bright young seventeenth-century scholar looking for a thesis topic would be to trace the actual influence of the Geneva Bible and of the Authorized Version upon poets and other writers, to find where and when the one took over from the other. In this respect Hill is deficient, missing evidence which could have strengthened his case. He does not, for example, cite Alan Rudrum's annotations to his edition of Henry Vaughan's poetry, where it becomes obvious that this anti-Puritan poet of the late 1640s and 1650s is constantly echoing the Geneva Bible, not the Authorized Version.

Vaughan could probably do this because, so far as the text is concerned, there was not much difference between the two Bibles. Although Hill is right to put the Geneva version at the heart of his study, he is wrong to let his wish to do so lead him to downgrade the Authorized Version. Early in the book, for instance, he sets Geneva texts against AV ones to show how the latter toe the establishment line, the idea emerging that there was an official version, offering the people anodyne translations of essentially subversive texts, and a popular, rebellious Bible which pointed the way towards the English Revolution. In fact, there are few texts which can be used in this way. The key one is I Peter 2.13, where the Geneva Bible has 'Submit your selves unto all manner ordinance of man . . . whether it be unto the King, as unto the superior', which the AV alters to '. . . to the King, as supreme'. And Hill, anyway, would argue that the real subversive potential comes in the marginal notes which every edition of the Geneva Bible contained and which were forbidden to the AV translators. It is odd, however, to see, a couple of pages later, Miles Smith's name crop up. Hill is explaining the idea that the Old Testament represents kings as, in essence, undesirable. He quotes Hugh Broughton, in his *Job. To the King* (1610), as stating baldly that 'the rulers that prosper are the wicked', adding that 'Broughton was one of the translators of the AV'. In fact, Broughton was certainly not one of the translators, to his famously high dudgeon. Immediately after making this error, Hill goes on to say that:

> Miles Smith, a learned bishop so puritanical that James I later appointed Laud his dean, observed that Hezekiah was called a rebel because he would not pay tribute to Sennacherib, King of Assyria. Daringly, he compared Elizabeth to Hezekiah: 'the Lord that fought for Hezekiah and Jerusalem will also fight for her Majesty and this realm against Sennacherib and the Spaniard'.

I wonder if he knows that Smith was a translator of the AV, and not only a translator but the man who took responsibility for the whole version, writing its well-known and long-loved Preface. It would not have hurt Hill's thesis, and it would have represented the English biblical tradition better, if he had acknowledged that the Authorized Version was not what James I wanted and intended it to be, but a consolidation of the Geneva Bible's renderings within the mainstream culture – a reason, perhaps, why there is no evidence of James ever actually authorizing it.

Opening with a quotation from Tyndale, followed by one from Harvey, sums up the effect of Hill's book, not only in its juxtaposition of Tyndale's powerful prose with Harvey's banalities – Tyndale is writing of prelates' complaints that knowledge of the Bible moves the people 'to rise against their princes, and to make all common, and to make havoc of other men's goods' – but in its time-span too. Tyndale, writing at the beginning of the Reformation, can present the Bible as a unified and unifying revelation. God's word, once translated and known by all, will create the true state, in men's hearts and in the commonwealth. By 1640, any idiot can burble on with the Bible to legitimate his nonsense. And from the realization of this comes the curious effect of this book, that, in imitation of its subject, it destroys itself. This happens around halfway through, when a book which seems to be concerned with demonstrating the absolute centrality of the Bible to all seventeenth-century life and thought then declares that the Bible was most definitely not central to seventeenth-century politics:

> Parliamentarian propagandists had no catch-all texts equivalent to 'the Lord's anointed', 'the powers that be', or 1 Peter II. 13–14, which told men to submit themselves 'unto the king, as unto the superior, or unto governors sent of him' . . . The Parliamentarians' popular slogans were drawn from the Norman Yoke, from the Anglo-Saxon constitution, from Good Queen Bess, rather than from the Bible . . . For royalists too the Bible, although useful for producing familiar popular slogans, was never of crucial importance: their serious claims were historical and constitutional.

The Bible, it soon turns out, was merely 'a rag-bag of quotations which could justify whatever a given individual or group wanted to do'. By page 232 Hill is sharing the Ranters' (alleged) enthusiasm for burning all of the Bibles, and thirty pages later is quoting mid-seventeenth-century claims that the Bible had become an idol, as evil to worship as any graven image. The turning-point was Charles I's execution, 'the high point of biblical influence on English politics', as if the people, when they saw what the Word could achieve, decided to have no more to do with it, so that by the end of the century any millenarian who used biblical texts to predict the end of the world was regarded 'as a medical case'.

All of this makes Hill's book a fascinating study of a culture in crisis because of its reliance upon a text. The fact that this was a translated text probably intensified the crisis, but not too much, for translation is only another form of interpretation. The American Constitution is written in fairly plain English, but it still needs translation by every succeeding generation, and the more the United States relies upon it the more troubled it becomes. What Hill shows up, most interestingly, and to his confessed surprise at the end of the book, is how reliant English culture was upon the Old Testament rather than the New. Like the American Constitution, or any other text, one effect of translation is to emphasize and prefer one part of the text over another. So, in seventeenth-century England, the Old Testament, with its narratives of tyrants destroyed by God and its prevailing idea of a chosen people, became the people's text to an almost astonishing degree. As Hill says, 'this book has turned out to be almost exclusively concerned with the Old Testament, apart from Revelation in the New Testament. This was not my intention when I started to think about the subject, but it is the way the material seemed to point.'

This makes David Daniell's edition of Tyndale's Old Testament translation all the more welcome, complementing, as it does, his edition of the revised New Testament which appeared a few years ago. Now, at last, for the first time since the sixteenth century, nearly all of Tyndale's Bible translation is in print, and we can see how our English Old Testament began. The first thing to say about this edition is how strikingly big it is. As Daniell explains in his introduction, Tyndale was executed before he could complete his translation of the Old Testament. He only published the Pentateuch and a translation of Jonah, but his translation of the historical books, from Joshua to II Chronicles, was published in the so-called Matthew's Bible, which appeared shortly after his death. Daniell reprints all of this Old Testament material, but this still means that all of the prophetic books, except for Jonah, and all of the poetic books, are missing: so there is no Isaiah, no Psalms, no Ecclesiastes, no Ezekiel. None the less, this edition is 643 pages long, where the New Testament ran to barely 400 pages. Here, then, is a further clue to the seventeenth-century English fascination with the Old Testament. As the most intense Bible readers in Europe, the Old Testament offered the English a virtual library in itself, a cornucopia of narrative, poetry, and wisdom literature compared with which the New Testament, with its one story – admittedly the greatest ever story – was thin stuff.

Not only in length, but also in effort, Tyndale's Old Testament translation outdid his work on the New, for to learn Hebrew sufficiently for him to challenge and improve on Luther's translation was a greater achievement even than was his mastering of New Testament Greek. It was not unprecedented for an Englishman to know biblical Hebrew in the 1520s – G. Lloyd Jones's recent edition of Robert Wakefield's *Oratio* illustrates his claims to priority – but Tyndale's achievement was still monumental. Many vernacular versions of the Old Testament appeared throughout Europe in the sixteenth century, but only Tyndale's, among the first wave of translators, showed any real scholarly independence from Luther, and only Tyndale's initiated a vernacular version which, as Hill's book amply demonstrates, had such a massive impact upon its own national culture. In those places where Tyndale did complete his translation, the Geneva Bible, like the Authorized Version after it, was largely reliant upon his work.

It would be wrong to exaggerate Tyndale's independence from Luther, whose German Bibles set the pattern for everything that happened up to January 1649 and beyond; but scholars ought to use Daniell's admirably presented modern-spelling text to try to assess how far Tyndale was developing as an independent translator of Hebrew. Most work which has so far been done in this area has been based on his 1530 Pentateuch and the brief Book of Jonah. This edition should encourage us to turn our attention to the post-Pentateuch translation of the historical books which was printed after Tyndale's death. That he was still working independently, not merely transcribing and adapting Luther, is borne out by the famous letter which he wrote during his final imprisonment, asking for warmer clothes and his Hebrew grammar. Now we may properly realize how much work on the Old Testament he was doing in his final months: Joshua to II Chronicles takes up more than half of this edition.

How then did Tyndale challenge and improve on Luther in these books? Here are a few examples from just one narrative, the story of Solomon's arbitration between the two mothers, told in I Kings 3 (III Kings 3 in Tyndale). For Luther's announcement that 'zwo huren' came to the king, Tyndale is more literal: 'Then came there two women that were harlots'. The one woman says, according to Tyndale, 'I was delivered of a child with her in the said house', which is close to, but not quite the same as Luther's 'und ich gelag bey yhr ym hause'. The other mother's child died, she claims, because, as Luther has it, 'sie hatte yhn ym schlaff erdruckt'; i.e. she lay on it in her sleep. But the Hebrew has only the verb and pronoun, hence Tyndale's tighter, and more brutal 'for she had overlaid it'. Then, in the narrative, Tyndale's rendering of the women's pleas differs in emphasis from Luther's. The German version has the one mother saying 'meyn son lebt und deyn son ist todt' and the other claiming that 'deyn son ist todt und meyn son lebt'. Tyndale's renderings put the focus more starkly upon the corpse and the living child: 'the living is my son and the dead thine . . . the dead is thy son, and the living mine'. Finally, and most characteristically, Luther slightly sentimentalizes the impulse which makes the right mother cry out, while Tyndale fixes on the source of her anguish: 'denn yhr mutterlich hertz erbebet uber yhren son': 'for her bowels yearned upon her son'.

To have one's bowels yearn for something is one example of a biblical idiom which has been overtaken by empirical science, a major theme of the second half of Christopher Hill's book, as he points to the Bible's sudden loss of power over the English people. But in the southern states of the USA, and in Northern Ireland, and any other place where the Word still has a fundamental power, it is not risible to talk about a people feeling something in their bowels: and for anyone who cares about the seventeenth century, the idiom possesses a wonderful force, reminding us of Cromwell's appeals to his adversaries and friends to consider whether 'in the bowels of Christ' they were doing what was right in the eyes of the Lord.

GERALD HAMMOND
University of Manchester

Parallel Lives: Spanish and English National Drama, 1580–1680. Edited by Louise and Peter Fothergill-Payne. London and Toronto: Associated University Presses, 1991. Pp. 329. Hb. £35.

This volume comprises a selection of the papers presented at an international conference held at the University of Calgary in 1991, the contributors being specialists in the fields of English and Spanish drama of the late Renaissance. The nineteen essays are grouped into four sections, each with a distinctive emphasis. Part 1, 'The Ideal Space', containing three articles, examines how the playhouses in Spain and England relate to a shared experience of performance and demand. The second part, 'The Common Ground', considers how a variety of playwrights present similar material in varying contexts and for different audiences. The third, 'The Great Divide', explores political and religious views in the two countries as manifested in drama. The brief final section, 'Unifying Myths', delves into Shakespeare's and Calderón's treatment of classical metamorphosis and cosmic transmutations.

Implicit in the title and explicit in the introduction is the claim that these contributions will collectively demonstrate a homogeneity of priority and outlook in the work of the two countries' dramatists. But this claim is not borne out. Articles such as Donald A. Beecher's examination of the medico-literary motif of lovesickness, or Frederick A. De Armas's exposition of the Senecan traits in Shakespeare's *Titus Andronicus* and Calderón's *La vida es sueño*, do, it is true, describe a parallel trend and an identity of coverage. But what we have here are topoi that belong to a wider realm, to the common traditions and heritage of medieval and Renaissance Europe. Leaving this aside, though, what will strike the reader of these essays is separateness, not convergence. Such is the effect of several of the essays contributed by the Hispanists represented in the collection. In his essay on the depiction of English characters on the Spanish stage and Spaniards on the English stage, Don W. Cruickshank exposes opposing approaches: 'English drama shows far more hostility to Spaniards than Spanish drama does towards the English', and whereas English playwrights caricature foreigners, their Spanish counterparts tend to reserve such treatment for their fellow-countrymen. A similar divergence of attitude also emerges in Teresa J. Kirscher's article 'The Mob in Shakespeare and Lope de Vega'. The English writer's contemptuous treatment – epitomized by the so-called 'stench motif' – contrasts sharply with Lope's, whose crowds 'are always consistent in their purpose and are presented as a political force to be reckoned with, a force that goes, depending on the play, sometimes for and sometimes against the national interest as perceived by the dramatist'. Indeed, the only section that amply fulfils the implications of the title is the first one on staging – a useful compendium, although some of the illustrations are not as clear as one would have expected in such an expensively priced book.

But this is only a minor quibble, more to do with the 'packaging' than the 'product'. My only reservation concerning the individual contributions is that a number of them have too much of the ephemeral feel of the conference paper. There are rough edges here and there, which for an oral presentation of an argument may be justifiable, even necessary, since in such circumstances we value the provocative as much as the authoritative. Thus Cynthia Rodriguez-Badendyck's engagingly iconoclastic comparison of Lope de Vega's *Castelvines y Monteses* and Shakespeare's *Romeo and Juliet* appears overstated: a piece of special pleading that would have benefited from a reconsideration of some of the sweeping judgements. (For example, the fact that the lovers struggle against 'various obstacles' in the English play while they are confronted by 'moral choices' in the Spanish work does not imply that the former is dramatically or, for that matter, aesthetically inferior.)

This volume, then, is best taken at face value, as a compilation of methodologically varied and consistently well-argued pieces: it is not a synthesis. But it is no less valuable for depending on its parts rather than on an editorially imposed coherence. I much enjoyed Dawn Smith's examination of the role of audience response in the Duchess of Malfi plays of Webster and Lope de Vega. Other readers, according to their critical tastes, will doubtless savour such items as Sharon Dahlgren Voros's semiotic study of revenge plays by Kyd and Calderón, or Henry W. Sullivan's Lacanian analysis of the incest motif in the drama of Tirso de Molina; while religious subjects are amply represented in the contributions of Kenneth Muir (secularity), Gregory Peter Andrachuk (the English schism), Donald T. Dietz (the Corpus Christi theatre), and José M. Ruano (hagiographical drama). Finally, the editors are to be congratulated for the despatch and thoroughness (I noted but a single misprint – p. 14, line 5) with which they have brought these essays into print.

D. GARETH WALTERS
University of Glasgow

Pope, Homer, and Manliness: Some Aspects of Eighteenth-Century Classical Learning. By Carolyn D. Williams. London and New York: Routledge, 1993. pp. xii+220. Hb. £37.50.

Dr Williams's book is an examination of notions of 'manliness' and 'manly learning' in eighteenth-century discussions and presentations of classical literature, particularly the Homeric translations of Alexander Pope. Three preliminary chapters (Part 1) survey a wide range of contemporary material, in an attempt to establish the range of meanings attached to the words 'manly' and 'manliness' (and their opposites) in Pope's day. 'Manliness', it is argued, was widely associated in the eighteenth century with rationality, property-owning responsibility, and the continuing health of the body politic. Classical education, in combating the dangers of 'effeminacy' – by removing the student from a female *milieu*, and developing his intellectual powers, physical stamina, and respect for moral virtue – was thought to be aptly described as 'manly learning'.

Part 2 of the book argues that Homer's epics were seen by Pope as the supreme example of male creativity, an encyclopedic source of moral wisdom which provided the supreme education in 'manly' virtue. In his translations, Williams claims, Pope systematically heightens Homer's stress on the 'masculine' virtues. Achilles' failings, for example, are seen not (as by some earlier commentators) as flaws to be shunned, but as 'manly excesses' to be condoned, even admired. The 'feminine' tendencies and personages in the poems, Williams maintains, are generally treated with sentimentality, coyness, cynicism, wariness, or condescension – or are subjected to moralizing, allegorical transformation. Thus, though Pope tempers the interpretative tradition which had seen the Trojans (and particularly Paris) as 'effeminate' 'Asiatics', he stresses the 'soft and effeminate' character of the Phaeacians, 'recasts' Briseis 'as a weeping Magdalen, or an accomplished actress in a lofty tragedy', sees the perfection of Andromache as lying in her (quintessentially feminine) 'fair defects, kind deceits, and amiable weaknesses', and treats even the virtuous Penelope as a figure from whom Telemachus must distance himself 'physically and emotionally' before he can achieve 'growth to heroic manliness'. Juno's infamous seduction of Jove (in *Iliad*, XIV), Williams suggests, is seen by Pope (as it had been by Addison) as an object-lesson for wives 'in keeping their husbands' affection'. Part 3 of the book serves as an appendix to the main argument, by considering, more cursorily, Pope's treatment of 'effeminacy' and 'heroism' in *The Rape of the Lock*, *The Dunciad*, and the (unrealized) plans for the epic *Brutus*.

This book addresses important issues, but the argument is, I believe, far too predictably conventional and partial (in both senses of the term) to be satisfactory. Williams makes full use, for example, of (often dubious) biographical anecdote to suggest Pope's sexual insecurities, and quotes copiously from the coy, condescending, cynical, or downright misogynistic remarks of Pope's contemporaries, and from those parts of Pope's (or his collaborators') prose writings which endorse (or seem at first sight to endorse) the conventionalities of his 'age'. But her book omits all mention of the intelligently sympathetic and conspicuously *un*condescending presentations of female principles, attributes, and personages to be found in Pope's poetry written before, or at the same time as, the *Homer*. Thus, for example, she nowhere notes the (one would have thought, in these circumstances, crucial) fact that the 'Nature' of whom Pope felt Homer the prime exponent and embodiment is presented in the *Essay on Criticism* as an emphatically *female* deity. Nor does the book contain any discussion of the triumphantly eloquent women protagonists of Pope's early Chaucer translations, of his passionately committed imagining of Eloisa's epistle to Abelard, or of the telling depiction of a woman's life lived according to oppressive male rules in the 'Epistle to Miss Blount, with the Works of Voiture'.

At no point, moreover, is any serious consideration ever given to the possibility (which I would maintain to be a fact) that Pope found the conventional assumptions of his 'age' radically challenged and extended, rather than merely confirmed, by his imaginative encounters with Homer. To take a key instance: Helen of Troy, Williams claims, is treated in Pope's *Iliad* 'with mingled sentimentality and cynicism'; she 'is always mistress of her fate, obeying Venus less from fear than vanity', and 'her attempt to blame divine agency for her misconduct is not taken seriously'. An inspection of the text and notes of Book III of Pope's poem, I believe, reveals precisely the opposite: that Pope has envisaged and portrayed

164 *Reviews*

Helen's tragic plight with an entirely uncondescending inwardness and delicacy, in which our consciousness of Helen's predicament – utterly dependent on Venus for the 'divine' beauty which she is simultaneously aware has been her undoing; profoundly repentant for the disloyalties and destruction of which she has been the cause; yet powerless to deny Venus' periodic 'invasion' of her mind and soul – is rendered all the more moving by the awe in which she is held by the Trojan elders, and by the compassion and humanity with which she is treated by Priam, the very person who has most cause to loathe her. In Pope's *Iliad*, I would maintain, Helen rises to a stature in which she becomes as moving and dignified an emblem of suffering humanity as any of the male heroes of the poem. In such a depiction Pope is, imaginatively, light-years away from the condescension to 'the fair sex' to be found in, for example, the pages of *The Spectator*, or any of the other 'contextual' material Williams adduces.

Pope's *Iliad* is, sadly, read by few people today. It would, I think, be extremely regrettable if any potential reader of this marvellously vivid, moving, and perpetually surprising poem (surely one of the most unjustly neglected masterpieces in the whole of English literature) were to be put off by the grudging and reductive accounts of the treatment of its women characters to be found in the pages of this book.

DAVID HOPKINS
University of Bristol

Over het Nut en de Wijze van Vertalen, Nederlandse Vertalreflectie (1750–1820) in een Westeuropees Kader. By L. G. Korpel. Amsterdam and Atlanta: Rodopi, 1992. Pp. 286. Hfl.45.

This study of translation discourse in the Netherlands between 1750 and 1820 is the very first of its kind, resulting from a new interest in the historical approach to Translation Studies, in which the traditional normative view has been replaced by a descriptive and interpretative one. Defended as a doctoral dissertation in November 1992, it aims to place the subject in a Western European context. It opens with an argued rejection of the modern polysystem theory, developed by Itamar Even-Zohar and others, as too rigid and dogmatic in its assumptions. In spite of her excessive use of the first-person pronoun in this chapter, the author's arguments have general validity here. However, one unfortunate consequence of her approach is that she has refrained from trying to account for the theories and opinions recorded, limiting herself to description only. For this purpose, she has adopted the historical methods suggested by the late Frederick Rener in his seminal study *Interpretatio:*

Language and Translation from Cicero to Tytler. Rener's argument is based on the strong relevance of the traditional humanistic teaching of grammar and rhetoric to the way translators rendered their source-texts and argued about their methods. In their turn, critics and theorists are also seen to think in these categories. On this basis, Korpel constructs a dichotomy between translation regarded as *interpretatio*, in which the translator seeks to copy the matter (*res*) of the original but is free to change the wording (*verba*), including any rhetorical devices, and on the other hand a method labelled *imitatio*, where the matter, too, is subject to alteration, adaptation, or improvement.

The difficulty with these categories is that, although they seem to be based on historical reality, they are hardly ever treated in such stark opposition in the discussions analysed. Nor are these two terms themselves used unequivocally in the texts in such a juxtaposition. It is more in accordance with the facts to suppose two sliding scales, side by side, one (from bondage to liberty) in matters of content, and one in questions of style. Translators and theorists must then be seen to perform various kinds of balancing acts in finding a viable stance. Moreover, the lack of an agreed terminology severely complicates the discussion, so that sometimes one man's 'fidelity' was another man's 'betrayal'. A popular term which allowed a translator a certain degree of freedom was 'navolging', but, if Korpel sees that as the Dutch equivalent of *imitatio*, the term by no means always implied what she takes the Latin word to mean, the freedom to alter content as well as form.

If there is no systematic analysis in this study of how the writers define their own terminology, or each other's, there is a section on the metaphors employed to describe the activity of translating, in the wake of earlier studies by others in this field, on other periods and languages. Perhaps the abundance of (related) clusters of metaphors precisely indicates the lack of exact definitions. Nor do changing trends in the usage of this imagery clearly indicate particular developments in thought.

The section just mentioned is one of five into which the author divides her analysis of translation discourse in Holland from 1750 to 1820. The other sections are: general characteristics of the discourse; the climate of opinion on translation; its legitimacy; and its definition. These sections constitute the central chapter of eighty-seven pages, in which an extensive corpus, painstakingly unearthed and diligently studied, is reduced to lucid order. A very conspicuous difference from the earlier part of the eighteenth century is the rise of the independent essay on translation, or devoting attention to it, in the newly developing periodical literature – such discussion had previously been carried on exclusively by translators themselves, in prefaces, dedications, and the like. Perhaps the most striking conclusion reached in this chapter is that the tone of the debate is generally strongly on the defensive, against a new but widespread contempt for translation in general. In contrast to what happens in Germany, developments towards a more source-language-oriented (or in the author's terminology 'retrospective') approach are hesitant and slow, with no clear breakthrough in that direction.

One complaint must be, however, that an important source of additional, and probably vital, information has been left untouched. This is the reviewing that went on in newspapers and, especially, in the rapidly increasing number of periodicals in the second half of the century. Their circulation was wide and their influence pervasive, so that the views expressed on particular translations must have had a considerable impact on the debate in general. It would also have been interesting to test the theory against the practice of translation in the same period. Of course, this would have required developing yet another methodology, since, again, there is nothing immediately available. It would also have resulted in an entirely different kind of study, taking in the history of translation itself. Even so, much information in this area can be gleaned from statistical data provided, from the bibliography of primary and secondary sources, and from discussion of these materials in other chapters. These other chapters seek to place the discussion of translation in a wider contemporary as well as historical context, by summarizing, from such secondary sources as are at present available, the material in Holland in the previous period and abroad in the same period. In addition, the author relates her own analysis to, and contrasts it with, previous studies responsible for the prevailing (unfavourable) picture of the state of translation in eighteenth-century Holland.

All in all, this is a wide-ranging study breaking a considerable amount of new ground, and a mine of information for those interested in the history of translation and translation theory. More than a third of it is, moreover, immediately accessible to the English reader through the long and excellent English summary and the bibliographical and statistical material provided.

C. W. SCHONEVELD
University of Leiden

Beppo: Histoire Vénitienne. Par George Gordon, Lord Byron. Traduit et présenté par Jean Malaplate. Pp. 77. Lausanne: Éditions L'Age d'Homme, 1988. Ffr.75.

In a witty appendix to this new bilingual edition of *Beppo*, Jean Malaplate recounts how, having finished his translation, he went to the Bibliothèque Nationale in search of previous attempts to render Byron's *ottava rima* tale in French verse. It was only then – with what surprise one can imagine – that he became aware of the peculiarity of the niche literary history had fashioned for him in the line of translators of *Beppo*. The two nineteenth-century predecessors he was able to find had contrived to make French *Beppo*s as singular in their way as the original by taking equal liberties with Byron's metrical scheme – but in opposite directions. S. Clogenson's rendering (1865) had expanded the Byronic *ottava rima* stanza of decasyllabic lines (ABABABCC) into a stanza of ten Alexandrines rhyming ABABCCBDDB; while Achille Morisseau's translation in a volume with *The Two Foscari* (1881) had reduced its original to eight octosyllabic lines per stanza (ABBACDDC varying to ABBACDCD). Curious to have a look at these oddities, which had had the effect of making Malaplate's own attempt at a metrically 'legitimate' reproduction of *Beppo*'s stanzaic form into a *via media*, I betook myself to the British Library, where I found them.

And entertaining reading they made. Clogenson's expanded and expansive *Beppo* has a relaxed chattiness, at times recalling Alfred de Musset's 'Mardoche', which is not inappropriate to the tone of Byron's Italianized narrator. If, as happens pretty frequently, the confidence arising from the extra elbow-room Clogenson accords himself carries him away from the original into small inventions, these are usually managed with tact. He might claim the authority of the poem's celebrated closing lines for the tendency of the medium to get the better of the artist:

> My pen is at the bottom of a page,
> Which being finished, here the story ends;
> 'Tis to be wished it had been sooner done,
> But stories somehow lengthen when begun.

Clogenson's version is characteristic:

> Mais ma plume est en bas d'une page, lecteur,
> Et je n'ai plus du tout d'encre en mon écritoire;
> C'est le cas ou jamais de finir cette histoire,
> Qui commençait, je crois, à tirer en longueur.

Running out of ink as the pen reaches the foot of the page might sound like making one excuse too many for the narrator's pose of desperate capriciousness, his last-ditch attempt to rein in a story bent on going its own way at any moment – just as the apologetic final line in French shifts the burden of guilt to the writer, rather than locating it in the act of telling that keeps defeating him. Perhaps we have here the translator's excuse for the laxative effects of his own metrical contrivance, which, it should be said, rarely tires the reader in itself – Clogenson versifies with ease and competence – but which can seem windy and schoolmasterly when one has Byron's text in the corner of one's eye, as is the case in this bilingual facing-page edition.

Clogenson's substantial and informative introduction indicates the cultivated readership he aimed at. Morisseau's brief preface frankly exposes his design to provide a digest of the Byronic *oeuvre* – emotional power in *The Two Foscari*, sparkling wit in *Beppo* – in the hope of catching the interest of readers with other claims on their time. He imagines them as part of a 'public affairé . . . sans loisirs pour l'étude . . . qui veut qu'on l'intruise sans l'arrêter, car il a pris le train rapide pour aller, brûlant les étapes, du plaisir à la peine, de la vie à la mort'. My rising alarm at the prospect of encountering a *Beppo* for the harassed railway commuter of the Third Republic in need of literary culture in small doses dissipated quickly as I read. Morisseau is rarely dull and never dilutes or hammers thin like Clogenson. His method is distillation. Stanza XXXVI in the original makes an exercise both typical and testing:

> Besides, within the Alps, to every woman
>   (Although, God knows, it is a grievous sin)
> 'Tis, I may say, permitted to have *two* men;
>   I can't tell who first brought the custom in,
> But 'Cavalier Serventes' are quite common,
>   And no one notices, nor cares a pin;
> And we may call this (not to say the worst)
> A *second* marriage which corrupts the *first*.

Morisseau translates:

> D'ailleurs l'usage a sa puissance,
> Et, s'il est un fait avéré,
> C'est qu'un amant est toléré
> Dans ces pays d'intolérance.
> Oui, la morale a beau crier,

> La chose est tournée en usage,
> C'est comme un second mariage
> Pour faire passer le premier.

It will be evident that these jaunty octosyllabics are, properly speaking, not a translation at all: they constitute an imitation, as Morisseau tells us in his preface he first thought of calling them. Other passages track the English text more closely, but his habitual method is to seize upon some striking feature of a stanza and build the new one round it, retaining such elements of the original as can be salvaged from an impulse to go his own way. Here, the characteristically Byronic opposition between public morality and worldly custom structures the opposed pairs that determine the progression of the stanza: la morale/l'usage, toléré/intolérance, second mariage/premier. The result is crisp and spirited, faithful, one might say, to the spirit of the original – provided one defines 'spirit' loosely. Therein lies part of the problem, obviously enough: the 'spirit' is notoriously volatile when released from the particulars in which it inheres. I would not wish to be severe on the quirky and occasionally beguiling Morisseau, much less prove to be one of those whom he addresses warily as 'ami ou plutôt ennemi lecteur'; but it is fair to say that to read him is to become vehemently engaged, *bon gré, mal gré*, in the process of weighing losses and gains that is the experience of judging translation comparatively, verse most of all. His happy rendering of the 'farthing candlelight' glow of the sun through London's smoke (stanza XLIII) as 'cet astre de Carême' marvellously plays with the Lenten theme of the poem while leaving out all reference to the English capital, that dour Lenten twin of Venice in Carnival.

Clogenson's version of the passage denies itself such licence:

> D'ailleurs, toute femme a le droit d'avoir deux hommes!
> – C'est peut-être un péché très-gros, mais c'est admis
> Partout au delà des Alpes, —— (Dieu! que nous sommes
> Donc en retard chez nous, où ce n'est point permis!)
> – Je ne sais pas trop bien comment en Italie
> Cette coutume a pu se trouver établie,
> Mais c'est une chose très-peu rare, qu'un cavalier
> Entre une femme et son mari, dans le ménage,
> Ait sa place, —— et c'est comme un second mariage,
> Par une adroite main greffé sur le premier.

The torpid additions in lines 3–4 ('Dieu . . . permis') and 8–9 ('Entre . . . place'), apart from making one wonder why a ten-line stanza should be necessary at all, focus the problem of voice in translating *Beppo*. The narrator's tone is an intimate function of the special circumstances of Byron's quasi-public exile from which he speaks (anonymously in the early editions) in an English larded with exotic words and phrases. These coordinates are exploited to create a fiction of Mediterranean liberation which allows Byron to maintain a finely balanced comic tension between the assumed roles of moralist and man of the world. It is a tension that leads to some of the poem's most celebrated effects – for example, to the explosion at the end of the stanza following this one:

> But Heaven preserve Old England from such courses!
> Or what becomes of damage and divorces?

Characteristically, both Clogenson and Morisseau shift the point of view from which the narrator speaks ('Dans ces pays d'intolérance'; 'au delà des Alpes', instead of the original's 'within the Alps'), a small signal among many larger ones of how they avoid fully taking on that duality of point of view that is at the heart of the narrating consciousness.

Compare Malaplate's translation of the same stanza:

> De ce côté des Alpes, même, il est permis
> (C'est un fort gros péché, Dieu le sait, qu'on tolère)
> Qu'une femme possède en somme deux maris.
> D'où l'usage est venu? C'est un profond mystère.
> Les cavaliers servants sont cependant admis
> Et nul ne s'en soucie ou n'en fait une affaire
> Au point qu'on peut parler, dans ce droit coutumier,
> De second mariage infirmant le premier.

'Infirmant' has a juridical sense which stretches the legal aspect of 'droit coutumier', itself an ironic exaggeration of 'l'usage', to a comic extreme. It departs somewhat from the more strictly moral-theological tone of the English, but this progression in which eros customary (so to speak) displaces the religious statute designed to curb and legitimize it justifies the departure; and the (almost) *rime riche* of the final couplet approximates a Byronic clinch. (The suggestion in the final couplet of Morisseau's version of a gastronomic metaphor, the second marriage helping one to digest the first, and the analogy of the horticultural graft in Clogenson's, both obscurely hint at their respective procedures as translators).

Poetic translation may be the closest literary equivalent to second marriage that regrets the first, and nowhere more so than in a bilingual facing-page edition where the virtues of the original spouse are perpetually on view. Byron's decasyllabics are at once more terse and less formally constrained than the French Alexandrine Malaplate chooses to render them. If the two syllables gained are considered fair compensation for the natural linguistic amplitude of French, as well as the traditionally severer conventions governing its rhyme and metre, we may think of the combat of translation as proceeding *à armes égales*. And indeed, reproducing the rhyme-pattern of Byron's stanza in Alexandrines poses no great obstacle to an adroit and fertile translator like Malaplate. What would have proved well-nigh impossible in the circumstances is any systematic attempt to imitate the off-rhymes, double rhymes and rhymes distorted for comic effect that speak to the habituated ear in *Beppo*. Malaplate is right to have renounced the effort as leading inevitably to pastiche, given his prior determination to be faithful to both poetic form and sense. Perhaps not entirely renounced; what Byron called the 'wicked necessity of rhyming' is really (as Byron knew) not just a matter of taking what the eye happens to light upon in *Walker's Lexicon* as a way out of a local difficulty. The work of translating multiplies creative frictions, and those occasions when poet and translator converge and nearly meet as rhymers were, for me, among the happiest of the enterprise. Byron's 'jealous – Othello's – fellows' (XVIII) is answered with 'le lot – Othello – conjungo', mimicking the imperfections as well as the sounds of its model, which is even on occasion outdone as if by way of compensation or homage: 'He [the devil] took them not; he very often waits, / And leaves old sinners to be young ones' baits' (LIV) prompts: 'Qui ne les prenait pas, car il préfère attendre / Avec les vieux pêcheurs appâtant l'âge tendre'.

Fine surprises like this one make savoury moments in a book which is consistently satisfying. By its format it addresses itself more particularly to those who know one of the languages involved and at least something of the other, and for these it holds sophisticated pleasures in plenty. *Beppo* might be said to define the qualities required of its translator in detailing the accomplishments of Laura's noble 'cavalier servente': 'and then he knew / Music and dancing, fiddling, French and Tuscan'. If, as Malaplate thinks, readers who appreciate these qualities when set in bilingual conversation are more numerous than is commonly imagined, this poised and articulate translation deserves to find them.

JACK DONOVAN
University of York

Cyrano de Bergerac. By Edmond Rostand. Translated by Edwin Morgan.
Pp. 144. Carcanet, 1992. Pb. £6.95.

Cyrano de Bergerac is a hero whose sole appetite is for talk – and then
more talk. He fasts poetically while all about him feast contentedly on
Ragueneau's pastries and Roxane's pumpkin-like carriage. Cyrano greedily translates everything into a succulent, racy tongue that now seems
guaranteed to have seduced a poet like Edwin Morgan, for whom the act
and idea of translation have always been central.

Cyrano's need to find a voice capable of interpreting for Roxane an
inner beauty betrayed by his physical imperfection is frustrated by the
obligation to translate Christian's Chippendale contours into their verbal
equivalent. As Morgan is careful to point out in his introduction, that
dilemma provides us with a 'heroic comedy'. It is articulated in a
mercurial, energetic spirit unafraid of mixing pathos and humour in a way
familiar to the poet of heroic elegies such as 'Cinquevalli', 'Che', and 'The
Death of Marilyn Monroe'. Morgan also draws attention to the 'many-
sidedness' of the real Cyrano, whom he describes as a 'poet, a Guards
officer, a dramatist, a musician, a writer of science-fiction, a student of
philosophy and physics, a freethinker, and gay', all activities and interests
which parallel exactly those of the Scots translator of Rostand's play. To
spectators of the first enjoyable production of this version by the
Communicado Theatre Company at the 1992 Edinburgh Festival, it
seemed that Rostand's interpretation of Cyrano's extravagance was the
natural meeting place for the authors of a 'Voyage to the Moon' and 'From
Glasgow to Saturn'.

Not that Morgan's understandable enthusiasm for Cyrano has encour-
aged him to take too many liberties with the text. He takes a nineteenth-
century version of a seventeenth-century story and uses a modern urban
Glaswegian Scots to present us with an exceptionally faithful translation,
in terms both of tone and lexis. Jacques Fallot gives way to Emilio Coia
as Cyrano's possible portraitist, and the journalist, Théophraste Renaudot,
becomes 'Murdoch Shturdoch'. In Act I, Rostand's 'Distributrice' hawks
'Oranges, lait, / Eau de framboise, aigre de cèdre' while Morgan, with
nostalgic generosity, gives his 'Usherette'

> Ices, ginger, tea,
> Raspberry yoghurt, Greek yoghurt, aw the yoghurts,
> Lovely Turkish delight, licorice awsorts,
> Popcoarn, hote chestnits, marshmallows,
> Chewin-gum, candyfloss . . .

But such amusing updatings, designed to pull in contemporary audiences, never distract from the characters and settings, all recognizably those of Rostand's play.

Occasional lines or single words added here and there unquestionably improve on the original. Cyrano, for example, is fond of Lignière

> Because this soak,
> This tun of muscat, this vodka-sozzled bloke
> Done somethin wance that shaws the best a folk:
> He saw his lady-love sip holy watter
> At the font eftir Mass, envied the blatter
> A the sweet draps, and like a fermer at a rowp
> Ran and slurped dry that non-alcoholic stowp!

Morgan's 'fermer at a rowp' is an invention, but one perhaps more faithful to Rostand's gauche 'fût de rossoli', and to the character of Cyrano's own comradely affection for him, than the French author's depiction of a gallant action. Similarly, Morgan's attention to 'the blatter / A the sweet draps' is an aural felicity missing from the original, in which the hero of the episode simply watches 'celle qu'il aimait prendre de l'eau bénite'.

Scene II.i ends with Ragueneau's agonized exclamations as his wife wraps up pastries in the pages of his friends' verses: 'Avec des vers, faire cela!' moans Ragueneau. Lise: 'Pas autre chose'. Ragueneau: 'Que faîtes-vous, alors madame, avec la prose?' Morgan adds one word to this and considerably heightens the comedy. Ragueneau: 'Hoo can ye make poetry intae *bags*?' Those *bags* are typical of the literal-minded genius that animates Glaswegian humour. Indeed, Morgan's Glaswegian frequently proves to be much more versatile a vehicle than standard English for translating Rostand's many neologisms and puns. When Cyrano warns Lise against cuckolding her husband, he says: 'Je defends que quelqu'un le ridicoculise.' In Scots, Cyrano declares he likes his friend: 'And so, Missus, ye're / Out of order if he's ridicuckoldous. Ye hear?' Other English versions I consulted merely yielded bland exhortations 'not to make a fool' of Ragueneau. Again, most English versions are quite foxed by the cadets' wordplay, which verges – but not entirely – on nonsense: 'Milledious! – Capdedious! – Mordious! – Pocapdedious!' Instead, Morgan, virtuoso of the 'Loch Ness Monster's Song', gives us 'Gawdsagawds! Gawdstoptop! – Gawdsdeddo! – Gawdspapawl!'

As Morgan points out in his introduction, however, Glaswegian Scots is also capable of the lyrical and the poetic, and he seizes all the opportunities to demonstrate this. Obvious examples abound, but this less obtrusive one is among the most telling, and a sure indication of the quality

of Morgan's intelligence as a translator. At the end of Act I, Cyrano hails
nocturnal Paris and describes the moon '[qui] coule aux pentes des toits
bleus'. One English translation shows us roofs 'like bright shields braving
the moon', but Morgan recognizes both the accuracy in the colour of those
roofs and the vivid poetic charge to be derived from so palpable a detail.
And so we get:

> Munelicht seepin doon blue roofs, a frame
> Ower fine fur scenes that huv nae hamely name.

A little later, Morgan's gift for mingling verse of comic and lyric panache
exactly matches that of Rostand in Cyrano's encounter with de Guiche in
Act III. Cyrano distracts de Guiche by pretending to be a drunken space-
traveller fallen from the moon, and the pleasure to be derived from lines
such as these – which are in many ways quintessential Morgan – is all the
greater for their precision as translation from the French:

> Paris – that's where I fell back!
> Last whirlwind express, better than Amtrak!
> Excuse me, Ah'll brush aff some ether. Yon wis a trip!
> Here's ma eyes hauf-closed wae stardust. The tip
> A ma spurs is clogged wae planet-fur.

All the famous set speeches – Cyrano on the merits of his nose, some of
the eloquent addresses to Roxane, the final death-scene – are rendered
here in a colourful, demotic tongue of great dexterity; but it may be worth
ending by drawing particular attention to Morgan's sympathetic realization of Rostand's merits as a verse *dramatist*. Morgan's own poetry is one
of many voices, and this play has given him his best opportunity yet to
demonstrate his inwardness with the way in which character depiction so
often shades into manipulation and advancement of plot. Here is a short
exchange between Roxane and the disguised and partially hidden Cyrano
from Act III. Roxane notes with unconscious irony that her lover's voice
sounds different:

> Cyrano: Aye, it's quite different. The night's ma gaird and grot.
> Here Ah kin daur tae be me, kin daur . . . But what –
> Ah don't know – aw this – forgie me – stealin
> Ower me, new and wunnerfu, the feelin . . .
> Roxane: It's new?
> Cyrano: It's new . . . totally . . . tae be sincere. . .
> Ma hert ay nippit . . . tae be laughed at . . . the fear . . .

This is Cyrano at his most touching and most atypical, catching himself off guard, shocked more by the novelty of sincerity than by the power of the love than inspires it. It is a reaction familiar to those who have been forced to suppress strong and unusual passion, and Morgan catches its poignancy exactly by giving the inarticulate slightly more room to breathe and more space to signify than Rostand does. He allows this by slowing down the pace of the exchange and by reducing the eloquence of Cyrano's remarks and pauses. In Rostand, one is sure that Cyrano's hesitation is that of a poet searching for the *mot juste*, and we expect him to find it. The Scots version, however, is – more movingly – less assured, the momentary stutter of a big bear of a Glaswegian gobsmacked by a sudden vision of the pitiful, wonderful irony of his situation. And in that exchange too – for those able to bear looking into the future – the next steps of the plot are foreshadowed. For we sense instinctively that Cyrano will not give up easily on such new-found riches.

Edwin Morgan's version is quite the funniest, most moving translation of *Cyrano* to date. Beyond its merits as a translation, it is another reminder of how powerful a medium Scots can be on the modern stage when used by someone sufficiently familiar with its various strengths. It is greatly to be hoped that Morgan will take a leaf from Cyrano's dramatic loquacity and turn his attention to other pieces from the European repertory. Failing that, he might even give us an original play of his own?

DAVID KINLOCH
University of Strathclyde

The Nouveau Roman: Fiction, Theory, and Politics. By Celia Britton. Macmillan, 1992. Pp. vi+231. Hb. £40.

The Politics of Style in the Fiction of Balzac, Beckett, and Cortazar. By M. R. Alexrod. Macmillan, 1992. Pp. xxi+128. Hb. £35.

It is interesting, reading Celia Britton's study on the *nouveau roman*, to ponder the great cultural divide between France and England after 1945, for it is increasingly obvious that the English tendency, postwar, is to repeat the construction of a cultural 'little England' harking back to insular and positivist traditions. France, on the other hand, begins a process of cultural renewal, one of whose major products – and, indeed, determinants – was the experimentalism of the *nouveau roman*. Of course, this renewal begins with Sartre's existentialism, itself influenced by an internationalist tradition in thinkers such as Husserl and Kierkegaard. If the aesthetic was national (the legacy of Balzac, Flaubert, Zola, Proust, and so on), the philosophy was more widely and heterogeneously continental.

Britton points out that the 'academic' or 'institutionalized' history of the *nouveau roman* is bracketed between two conferences: the Colloque de Cerisy of 1971, and the New York University conference of 1982. The first of these, in the French location, celebrates the marriage of theory with practice, of philosophy with fiction; the latter, in the anglophone world, repeatedly invokes the dogmatism of the absent Ricardou as grounds for their divorce. In both, the dominant names are those of Robbe-Grillet, Simon, Sarraute; Butor, Ricardou, and others hover at the margins of this *nouveau roman* 'tradition', many of whose greatest products date from the late 1950s.

Britton finds the source of the tradition in the reaction to Sartre, and specifically to the Sartrean demand for 'engagement'. She also hints pointedly at the significant philosophical problem of the ontology of the Object (a debate lingering into the current philosophies of Rosset or Baudrillard). It would have been instructive to have had more on the status of the Object, the Heideggerian 'thing', in postwar thinking. Such work might have taken the place of Britton's meditations on 'The Notion of Structure' and 'The Myth of Creation', which really re-chart an already familiar terrain.

One might have thought that the *nouveau roman* was an already well-chronicled phenomenon, and it occasions some surprise to see a new book appearing on it at this time. But this study does add quite significantly to the anglophone understanding of this school-which-never-was-a-school of fiction. Britton carefully and with due nicety traces the difficult relation of the *nouveau roman* to the dominant ideological concerns in French writing after 1945, and she is illuminating on its problematic relation to the journal *Tel Quel*, a journal whose concerns over the proper or adequate forms of revolutionary practices were broadly coterminous, for a while at least, with the texts of the *nouveau roman*. From this, Britton makes her most contemporary point: in the early stages of the *nouveau roman*, theory was itself a form of fiction, and *vice versa*. It is really between 1971 and 1982 that theory arduously wrenches itself free from aesthetic practice, leaving the *nouveau roman* and its practitioners to fend for themselves. A similar kind of argument, insisting on the intimate imbrication of theory with fiction, is to be found in Gerardine Meaney's recent *(Un)like Subjects*, which addresses French feminism in terms of various anglophone fictions. Both studies address the pressing contemporary point of the distance between theory and aesthetic practice.

The *nouveau roman* starts from the tendency to think theory in the form of fiction; and the real debt to Sartre is, I suspect, the debt to the philosophical novel. While the anglophone tradition writes its philosophical fiction in a safe, smug, positivist fashion (Iris Murdoch, say), the

French writers after Sartre attempted to implicate the reader directly – and as a function of the reading process itself – in the enactment of philosophical problems, such as the calling into question of subjectivity. It is here that the *nouveau roman* finds its proper mode of 'engagement'.

Britton's book seems slightly unsure of its intended audience, hovering at times between being a student primer (a function it carries out admirably) and being a more advanced attempt at the definitive history of its subject. Britton is well-placed, on the evidence of this study, to offer such a much-needed history in due course.

M. R. Axelrod closes *The Politics of Style* with a 'coda' in which he reveals that, in researching the volume, he 'came across a book titled *Reader-Response Criticism: From Formalism to Post-Structuralism*' (initially published in 1980), and he proceeds to offer an analysis of its cover. Given that much of the argument depends upon a (thoroughly untheorized and equally fully unrealized) sense of the culturally constructed audience for fictions of one type or another, it might properly have been expected that Alexrod would have come across Jane Tompkins's collection at an earlier moment. Further, the fact that the analysis is limited to a market-manager's image on the cover of the American edition of the book is indicative of the depth of scholarly analysis here. Alexrod's thesis is simple, even simplistic: books are commodities and figure significantly in a number of capitalist concerns; Scott and Balzac knew this, and also knew how to make (and squander) money from their writing; contemporary popular fiction – and some less populist academic fiction – shares the same fundamental structures as Scott and Balzac; texts which are experimental (such as Beckett's or Cortazar's) do not comfort their reader quite as much as those texts we used to call 'classic realist texts'. The discussion is written in a colloquial style, no doubt itself intended as a 'political' gesture. At one basic turn in the argument, Axelrod compares a passage from *Time Magazine* with passages from Breton's *Manifestes du surrealisme*, Marinetti's *Teoria e Invenzione Futurista*, Tzara's *Lampisteries*, and Artaud's *Ci-Gît*; and pronounces the somewhat prosaic passage from *Time* 'more acceptable, more preferable'. This is banal in the extreme; and wrong, to boot. Such value-judgements are never context-free. As with many would-be iconoclastic studies which take an overly simplified 'political' line, this one has to construct mythical objects of its criticism; a mythic mass culture, a mythic mass reader, a mythic Scottian structure for the novel, and so on. The thesis is simplistic and weakly constructed. The book serves no important intellectual function.

THOMAS DOCHERTY
Trinity College, Dublin

On the Motion and Immobility of Douve. By Yves Bonnefoy. Translated by Galway Kinnell, with an Introduction by Timothy Mathews. Pp. 160 (Bloodaxe Contemporary French Poets, 1). Newcastle-upon-Tyne: Bloodaxe, 1992. Pb. £7.95.

Translation, Poetics and The Stage: Six French Hamlets. By Romy Heylen. Pp. ix+170. London and New York: Routledge, 1993. Hb. £35.

Modern Poetry in Translation. New Series, No. 1 (Summer 1992) (Special Feature: Yves Bonnefoy, edited by Anthony Rudolf). Pp. 206. London: King's College, London, 1992. Pb. £9.

It was hardly reasonable for King Nebuchadnezzar to ask his wise men not only to interpret his dream for him but also to tell him what it was that he had dreamed. Yet he had a good reason for his request. He had forgotten the dream, but his dream had not 'forgotten' him. In his major essay 'Poetry and Truth', written in English and published in *Modern Poetry in Translation*, Bonnefoy ascribes to poetry the ungraspable insistence of this dream, 'both a need and a perpetual failure', and beautiful dream to which alone we cling for survival.

It is right and proper that the poetry, translations, and criticism of Yves Bonnefoy are becoming better known to English readers. As the successor to Roland Barthes at the Collège de France in Paris, his work stands alongside contemporary shifts in French critical theory, since, as Anthony Rudolf well puts it, he 'lives upon and writes the fault, the fissure, at the heart of knowledge . . . in Western culture, announced by Nietzsche, Kierkegaard, Dostoyevsky and Rimbaud'. The intensity of Bonnefoy's poetics of imperfection find their focus in a deeply responsible a/theology, still driven by his early reading of the Russian theologian Lev Shestov and his insistence on the God of Absence, that is, a theology not of proposition, but whose terms are recognized in the constant themes of the poetry – transcendence, hope, redemption, communion.

Bonnefoy's first book of poetry, *Du mouvement et de l'immobilité de Douve* (1953), is now translated a year after his most recent book, *Ce qui fut sans lumière* (1987). Already his themes and preoccupations are fixed: his use of the art of the Quattrocento, Poussin, Claude Lorraine, and Constable, the materiality and 'presence' of poetry, its incarnate reality, the responsibility of poetry to speak 'truth'. Galway Kinnell's translation is perhaps the most successful so far of a poet who, though himself fascinated by the art of translation, has categorically denied the possibility of translating a poem. His poetry continually strives to actualize his questioning of the primacy of mimetic realism in artistic and poetic representation, which, he insists, denies the world and excludes being.

Words carry the huge responsibility of simply being themselves, bearing the rhythms of the world and the 'world beyond'. In Kinnell's translation one realizes for the first time his closeness to Hopkins (and the radicality of the theological vision of the two poets). Comparing these translations with the earlier English versions of Rudolf, excellent though they are, one appreciates Kinnell's dry simplicity, his preference for the simple word, and his literal adherence to the fragmentariness and immediacy of the French: words as fragments of sound and vision. Bonnefoy should not be made lush, and never languorous, but clipped and sharp.

Such are the qualities which characterize his own translation into French of *Hamlet*, his fifth version of the play since 1957, analysed in detail in Romy Heylen's *Translation, Poetics and The Stage*. In this useful textbook, with its discussion of a 'cultural model of translation', we gain insight into Bonnefoy struggling with the impossibility of 'catching' Shakespeare in a language and culture which is historically resistant to his 'Englishness'. Bonnefoy has not only translated a great deal of Shakespeare, he has also written a great deal about the processes of such translation. Heylen is acute in drawing our attention to the similarity between the theory of Bonnefoy and the great essay of Walter Benjamin, 'The Task of the Translator'. Both focus on language rather than content and meaning, and both strive for an impossible Edenic speech – ultimately conceivable only in religious terms. Bonnefoy's translations of *Hamlet* become progressively more spare and straightforward, allowing Shakespeare to ride above the much denser, more abstract texts of the earlier French versions.

It is, I think, a pity that the otherwise excellent selection of writings edited by Anthony Rudolf in *Modern Poetry in Translation* contains none of Bonnefoy's translations from Shakespeare or Yeats, though there is a quite beautiful version of John Donne's 'A Hymne to Christ, at the author's last going into Germany'. It is good to see poems from John Naughton's translation of *Ce qui fut sans lumière* (here rendered as *What Was Without Light*, though Naughton's *In the Shadow's Light* is now more familiar and actually catches Bonnefoy's sense better), especially perhaps Bonnefoy's greatest poem 'Dedham, Seen from Langham'. One realizes, however, the importance of page-layout as the fragmentary poems are crushed four or five to a page, losing the sharp focus of Naughton's original Chicago volume. But the whole collection is worth having for Bonnefoy's essay 'Poetry and Truth' alone, recognizing as it does both Bonnefoy's debt to his predecessor Roland Barthes and his essential divergence from him. For Bonnefoy, poetry is a deeply serious matter, responsible to truth and moral integrity. He is still committed to the language of essence and ontology, yet at the same time one recognizes his closeness to the philosophy of Emmanuel Levinas and the critical thought of Paul Ricoeur in his sense of the turning towards the other which defines for him the act of poetry. Otherness, alterity, the responsibility for the other, lie at the heart of a poetic which roots transcendence in our world and deconstructs theology in order to make theology and religious thinking possible.

Bonnefoy's poetry and his acts of translation focus our attention wholly upon the word, the word *as* word, and not meaning or reference. And so the word becomes the thing itself, so that we behold its glory. In the struggle to present his work to English readers, we become even more conscious than before of his apprehension of presence in the word and at the same time his refusal to seek consolation, as Heylen puts it, 'by imposing some supreme conceptual order onto a poetry' he finally cannot contain. Bonnefoy needs to be taken more seriously by readers of French theory, and by theologians, as by readers and critics of poetry. The very impossibility of translating him makes translating him all the more necessary and important, as we seek to grasp with him the demands of the forgotten dream.

DAVID JASPER
University of Glasgow

Two Worlds, One Art: Literary Translation in Russia and America. By Lauren G. Leighton. Pp. xix+272. DeKalb: Northern Illinois University Press, 1991. Hb. £35.

Through the Russian Prism: Essays on Literature and Culture. By Joseph Frank. Pp. xii+237. Princeton, N.J.: Princeton University Press, 1990. Pb. £10.95.

Lauren G. Leighton's book is the first attempt at a comparative description of the role of translation and Translation Studies in the USA and the former USSR. Published before the collapse of the Soviet Union, it describes on the Soviet side a situation that is now merely historical. Intended primarily for the American reader and translator, her book's main concern is to inform about Russian translation theory and practice; and her perspective on this subject is a rosy one. She rightly emphasizes the continuous and systematic development of translation theory and practice in the former USSR, the universal respect for work in translation, the translator's independence of market conditions, of deadlines, and the like. She maintains the superior lot of Soviet translators and students of translation for their being able to rely on a systematically developed and shared terminology. Against this, translation theory was developed rather recently in the USA, and then not systematically. In Leighton's view, at least up until about twenty years ago, the lot of both the American translator and the American student of translation was a lonely search for solutions to fundamental and recurrent problems. This is the argument of the first of the book's five parts, a description broadly justified by the facts and by the considerable achievement of Soviet translators, particularly of poetry. But Leighton never mentions the morally countervailing fact that many poets in Soviet Russia turned to translation because it offered them their only way of earning a living with integrity. She is reluctant to admit the political pressures that the system applied.

However comfortable the lot of translators may have been in the Soviet Union, however lonely the lot of translators in America, the problems are, even in Leighton's view, ultimately the same. The second part of the book describes what amounts to a convergence of two distinct traditions as attention settles on problems such as the status of literal translation, the rendering of colloquialism, and the representation of foreign 'material culture'. The final part celebrates Soviet optimism in the face of these problems. The book's centre comprises a critical account of the practice of English-speaking and Russian-speaking translators: Rita Rait's Russian translations of Vonnegut, the English Solzhenitsyn, the Russian Mark Twain, the English Dostoyevsky and Chekhov, the Russian Whitman, and the English Pushkin.

This is a sound and useful book, but some shortcomings should be noted. Its uncritical attitude towards the achievements of Soviet translation and its focus on problems supposedly solved by Soviet translation theory is tied up with a certain neglect of historical circumstances. So, for example, though Leighton admits that the use of interlinear versions (always a common practice in Russia) suggests that 'language-acquisition is still a weak area of the Soviet school', she fails to point out the connection between their use and the Russian premiss that a translated poem should read like a Russian one, resulting in translations being composed by Russian poets from an intermediate Russian text rather than from the original. The special problems of drama translation are not mentioned. There are occasional errors of fact (for example, the different editions of Bely's *Petersburg* are confused: the Petrograd edition was published in 1916, not 1922, and the Berlin edition of 1922 was an abridged and revised edition of the Petrograd edition, not *vice versa*).

Joseph Frank is famous for his biography of Dostoyevsky, still in progress but with three volumes now complete. The volume under review contains material ancillary to this major work, and deals mainly, but not exclusively, with Dostoyevsky. It contains some twenty articles and reviews written between 1962 and 1986, most of them published previously, but now updated, arranged in four parts, and supplied with a useful index. The first part, 'Contemporaries', consists of four articles. In these, Frank deals with the response of critics in the West to the work of Jakobson and Bakhtin, with Nabokov's *Lectures on Russian Literature*, and with the novelist Ralph Ellis's debt to Dostoyevsky. The second part, 'Overviews', contains reviews of Western books on the development of nineteenth-century Russian socialist and radical thought. Part Three, 'Dostoyevsky', brings together essays on special problems of Dostoyevsky's biography and his literary and political works. The last part, 'The Dilemma of Radicalism', contains reviews of English books about radical thinkers such as Chernyshevsky and Bakunin. These articles promote no new vision, and they hardly constitute a new scholarly achievement; but most of them do illuminate aspects of nineteenth-century Russian literature. Those focused on matters of fact or of intellectual history are generally more valuable than those polemically engaged with contrary views.

This volume evidently has ambitions beyond the collection of the author's earlier work. Its rather misleading title calls for further comment. It suggests that Frank offers a treatment of Russian perpectives on literature and culture. But such treatment is hardly developed. By the author's own account, the title expresses the book's double intention 'to stress not only the fateful influence of Western ideas in Russia . . . but also the equally fateful . . . way, in which such ideas, in their Russian metamorphosis, have returned to affect their original progenitors'. This dual aim is hardly evident in the book itself. Most of the 'chapters' (they are really reviews) treat accounts, almost exclusively Western, of the various manifestations of nineteenth-century Russian ideology in anarchism, nihilism, and socialism, and their Western origins. Most of them repeat the argument that Western philosophical and social thought was received in Russia in an extremely simplified and distorted form, and that the origins not only of Soviet ideology, but also of the political fanaticism and inhumanity of later Bolshevist leaders, can be traced back to 'radical' critics like Chernyshevsky, Pisarev, and the like. These views are not baseless, but they are not critically discussed and developed here. They are instead simply repeated as an argument against the uncritical presentation of Russian thought. Most chapters centre not on Russian culture, but on the Russian distortion of Western culture. The book collects a Western critic's reviews on the work of Western scholars analysing the Russian reception of Western thought. It says more about the history of Western criticism than about Russian culture itself. 'Through the American Prism' might be a more appropriate title.

ULRIKE JEKUTSCH
University of Göttingen

Books Received

Alvarez, A., editor. *The Faber Book of Modern European Poetry*. Faber, 1992. Hb. £17.50. ISBN 0571143210.

Axelrod, M. R. *The Politics of Style in the Fiction of Balzac, Beckett, and Cortazar*. Macmillan, 1992. Hb. £35. ISBN 0333536487.

Barnstone, Willis. *The Poetics of Translation: History, Theory, Practice*. Yale University Press, 1993. Hb. £25. ISBN 0300051891.

Boccaccio, Giovanni. *The Decameron*, translated by Guido Waldman, with Introduction and Notes by Jonathan Usher. Oxford University Press, 1993. Pb. £7.99. ISBN 019282712X.

Bonnefoy, Yves. *On the Motion and Immobility of Douve/Du mouvement et de l'immobilité de Douve*, translated by Galway Kinnell. Bloodaxe, 1992. Pb. £7.95. ISBN 1852241322.

Büchner, Georg. *Complete Plays, Lenz, and Other Writings*, translated by John Reddick. Penguin, 1993. Pb. £6.99. ISBN 0140445862.

Byock, Jesse L., translator. *The Saga of the Volsungs: The Norse Epic of Sigurd the Dragon Slayer*. Hisarlik Press, 1992. Pb £7.95. ISBN 1874312036.

Cervantes, Miguel de. *Don Quixote*, translated by Charles Jarvis, edited by E. C. Riley. Oxford University Press, 1992. Pb. £6.99. ISBN 019282726X.

Char, René. *The Dawn Breakers/Les Matinaux*, edited and translated by Michael Worton. Bloodaxe, 1992. Pb. £7.95. ISBN 1852241330.

Cicero. *On Government*, translated by Michael Grant. Penguin, 1993. Pb. £7.99. ISBN 0140445951.

Clayton, Jay, and Eric Rothstein, editors. *Influence and Intertextuality in Literary History*. University of Wisconsin Press, 1991. Pb. £16.95. ISBN 0299130347.

Cranston, Maurice. *The Noble Savage: Jean-Jacques Rousseau, 1754–1762*. Penguin, 1993. Pb. £11.00. ISBN 0140139893.

Crossley-Holland, Kevin, translator. *The Exeter Book of Riddles*. Revised Edition. Penguin, 1993. Pb. £5.99. ISBN 0140433678.

Daniell, David, editor. *Tyndale's Old Testament: Being the Pentateuch of 1530, Joshua to 2 Chronicles of 1537, and Jonah*. Yale University Press, 1992. Pb. £22.50. ISBN 0300044194.

Dante. *The Divine Comedy*, translated by C. H. Sisson, with an Introduction by David H. Higgins. Oxford University Press, 1993. Pb. £8.99. ISBN 0192830732.

Dante. *Vita Nuova*, translated by Mark Musa. Oxford University Press, 1992. Pb. £4.99. ISBN 0192828770.

Dostoyevsky, Fyodor. *The Brothers Karamazov*, translated by David McDuff. Penguin, 1993. Pb. £6.99. ISBN 0140445277.

Dupin, Jacques. *Selected Poems*, translated by Paul Auster, Stephen Romer, and David Shapiro. Bloodaxe, 1992. Pb. £7.95. ISBN 1852242345.

Eliade, Mircea. *Bengal Nights*, translated [from the French edition] by Catherine Spencer. Carcanet, 1993. Hb. £14.95. ISBN 1857540026.

Erasmus. *Praise of Folly, and Letter to Maarten van Dorp*, 1515, translated by Betty Radice, with Introduction and Notes by A. H. T. Levi. Penguin, 1993. Pb. £6.99. ISBN 0140446087.

Fothergill-Payne, Louise and Peter, editors. *Parallel Lives: Spanish and English National Drama, 1580-1680*. Associated University Presses, 1991. Hb. £35. ISBN 0838751946.

Galdós, Benito Pérez. *Nazarín*, translated by Jo Labanyi. Oxford University Press, 1993. Pb. £5.99. ISBN 0192828789.

Gentzler, Edwin. *Contemporary Translation Theories*. Routledge, 1993. Pb. £10.99. ISBN 0415091721.

Gervais, David. *Literary Englands: Versions of 'Englishness' in Modern Writing*. Cambridge University Press, 1993. Hb. £30. ISBN 0521443385.

Grimmelshausen, Johann. *The Adventures of Simplicius Simplicissimus*, translated by George Schulz-Behrend. Second Edition. Camden House, 1993. Hb. $47. ISBN 1879751372.

Gutt, Ernst-August. *Translation and Relevance: Cognition and Context*. Blackwell, 1991. Hb. £30. ISBN 0631178570.

Hardin, James, editor. *Translation and Translation Theory in Seventeenth-Century Germany*. Rodopi, 1992. Pb. Hfl.55. ISBN 9051834144.

Harrison, Anthony. *Victorian Poets and Romantic Poems*. University of Virginia Press, 1992. Pb. £11.95. ISBN 0813912640.

Heine, Heinrich. *Selected Prose*, translated by Ritchie Robertson. Penguin, 1993. Pb. £7.99. ISBN 0140445552.

Henderson, Helena, translator. *The Maiden who Rose from the Sea and other Finnish Folktales*. Hisarlik Press, 1992. Hb. £14.95. ISBN 187431201X.

Heylen, Romy. *Translation, Poetics and the Stage: Six French Hamlets*. Routledge, 1993. Hb. £35. ISBN 0415076897.

Hill, Christopher. *The English Bible and the Seventeenth-Century Revolution*. Allen Lane/Penguin, 1993. Hb. £25. ISBN 0713990783.

Hirata, Hosea. *The Poetry and Poetics of Nishiwaki Junzaburo: Modernism in Translation*. Princeton University Press, 1993. Hb. £32.50. ISBN 0691069816.

Hugo, Victor. *Notre Dame de Paris*, translated by Alban Krailsheimer. Oxford University Press, 1993. Pb. £6.99. ISBN 0192829114.

Jasper, David, editor. *Translating Religious Texts: Translation, Transgression and Interpretation.* Macmillan, 1993. Hb. £35. ISBN 0333570065.

Kharms, Daniil. *Incidences*, edited and translated by Neil Cornwell. Serpent's Tail, 1993. Pb. £9.99. ISBN 1852423064.

Korpel, L. G. *Over het Nut en de Wijze der Vertalingen: Nederlandse Vertalreflectie (1750–1820) in een Westeuropees Kader.* Rodopi, 1992. Pb. Hfl.45. ISBN 905183411X.

Kranz, Gisbert. *Niederwald und andere Gedichte.* Michael Claren, 1984. Pb. ISBN 3922549101.

Kranz, Gisbert, editor and translator. *Gedichte auf Bilder: Anthologie und Galerie.* Deutscher Taschenbuch Verlag, 1976. Pb. DM 8.80. ISBN 342301086X.

Lafayette, Madame de. *The Princesse de Clèves*, translated by Terence Cave. Oxford University Press, 1992. Pb. £4.99. ISBN 0192826875.

Larsen, Shirley, editor. *Translation: A Means to an End (The Dolphin*, 18). Aarhus University Press, 1990. Pb. DKr.148. ISSN 0164487.

Lefevere, André. *Translation, Rewriting and the Manipulation of Literary Fame.* Routledge, 1992. Pb. £11.99. ISBN 0415077001.

Lefevere, André. *Translation/History/Culture: A Sourcebook.* Routledge, 1992. Pb. £11.99. ISBN 0415076986.

Leighton, Lauren G. *Two Worlds, One Art: Literary Translation in Russia and America.* Northern Illinois University Press, 1991. Hb. $35. ISBN 0875801609.

Livingstone, Dinah. *Poetry Handbook: For Readers and Writers.* Macmillan, 1992. Pb. 8.99. ISBN 033354207X.

Mann, Thomas. *Selected Stories.* Translated by David Luke. Penguin, 1993. Pb. £6.99. ISBN 0140186786.

Martindale, Charles. *Redeeming the Text: Latin Poetry and the Hemeneutics of Reception.* Cambridge University Press, 1993. Pb. £8.95. ISBN 0521427193.

Matarasso, Pauline. *The Cistercian World: Monastic Writings of the Twelfth Century.* Penguin, 1993. Pb. £6.99. ISBN 0140433562.

Michaux, Henri. *Spaced, Displaced/Déplacements, Dégagements*, translated by David and Helen Constantine. Bloodaxe, 1992. Pb. £7.95. ISBN 1852241357.

Milosz, Czelaw. *Provinces: Poems 1987–1991*, translated by the author and Robert Hass. Carcanet, 1993. Pb. £6.95. ISBN 1857540018.

Miner, Earl, and Jennifer Brady, editors. *Literary Transmission and Authority: Dryden and Other Writers.* Cambridge University Press, 1993. Hb. £30. ISBN 0521441110.

Miola, Robert S. *Shakespeare and Classical Tragedy: The Influence of Seneca.* Clarendon Press, 1992. Hb. £27.50. ISBN 0198112646.

Montaigne, Michel de. *The Complete Essays*, translated by M. A. Screech. Penguin, 1993. Pb. £9.99. ISBN 0140446044.

Montaigne, Michel de. *The Essays: A Selection*, translated by M. A. Screech. Penguin, 1993. Pb. £6.99. ISBN 0140446028.

Morgan, Edwin, translator. *Edmond Rostand's Cyrano de Bergerac*. Carcanet, 1992. Pb. £6.95. ISBN 185754028X.

Newlyn, Lucy. *Paradise Lost and the Romantic Reader*. Clarendon Press, 1993. Hb. £35. ISBN 0198112777.

Nocera Avila, C., N. Pantelo, and D. Pezzini. *Early Modern English: Trends, Forms, and Texts*. Schena, 1992. ISBN 8875146144.

Nolan, Barbara. *Chaucer and the Tradition of the 'Roman Antique'*. Cambridge University Press, 1992. Hb. £45. ISBN 0521391695.

Norton, David. *The History of the Bible as Literature. Volume 1: From Antiquity to 1700*. Cambridge University Press, 1993. Hb. £50. ISBN 051333989.

Norton, David. *The History of the Bible as Literature. Volume 2: From 1700 to the Present Day*. Cambridge University Press, 1993. Hb. £50. ISBN 051333987.

Offord, Derek. *Modern Russian: An Advanced Grammar Course*. Bristol Classical Press, 1993. Pb. £14.99. ISBN 1853993611.

Ornston, Darius Gray, Jr. *Translating Freud*. Yale University Press, 1993. Pb. £17.95. ISBN 0300054548.

Ovid's Heroines: A Verse Translation of the Heroides, by Daryl Hine. Yale University Press, 1993. Pb. £8.95. ISBN 0300050941.

Plato. *The Last Days of Socrates: Euthyphro, Apology, Crito, Phaedo*, translated by Hugh Tredennick and Harold Tarrant. Penguin, 1993. Pb. £5.99. ISBN 014044582X.

Pym, Anthony. *Epistemological Problems in Translation and its Reaching: A Seminar for Thinking Students*. Ediciones Caminade, 1993. Pb. $19.50.

Queiros, Jose Maria Eça de. *The Maias*, translated by Patricia McGowan Pinheiro and Ann Stevens. Carcanet, 1993. Hb. £14.95. ISBN 1857540336.

Queiros, Jose Maria Eça de. *The Yellow Sofa and Three Portraits*, translated by John Vetch, Richard Franko Goldman, and Luis Marques. Carcanet, 1993. Hb. £14.95. ISBN 1857540344.

Rashkow, Ilona. *Upon the Dark Places: Anti-Semitism and Sexism in English Renaissance Biblical Translation*. Sheffield Academic Press, 1990. Hb. £30. ISBN 1850752516.

Rilke, Rainer Maria. *The Duino Elegies*, translated by Leslie Norris and Alan Keele. Camden House, 1993. Hb. $49. ISBN 1879751011.

Ritsos, Giannes. *The Fourth Dimension*, translated by Peter Green and Beverly Bardsley. Anvil Press, 1993. Pb. £14.95. ISBN 0856462527.

Round, Nicholas G., editor. *Libro Llamado 'Fedron': Plato's 'Phaedo', translated by Pero Diaz de Toledo (MS Madrid, Biblioteca Nacional Vitr 17,4)*. Tamesis Books, 1993. Hb. £35. ISBN 1855660245.

Saslow, James M., translator. *The Poetry of Michelangelo: An Annotated Translation*. Yale University Press, 1993. Pb. £14.95. ISBN 0300055099.

Singer, Isaac Bashevis. *The Death of Methuselah and Other Stories*. Penguin, 1990. Pb. £6.99. ISBN 0140186980.

Steiner, George. *After Babel: Aspects of Language and Translation*. Second Edition. Oxford University Press, 1992. Pb. £9.99. ISBN 0192828746.

Stone, Brian, translator. *The Owl and the Nightingale, Cleanness, St Erkenwald*. Penguin, 1988. Pb. £6.99. ISBN 0140442456.

Thornhill, Arthur H., III. *Six Circles, One Dewdrop: The Religio-Aestheic World of Komparu Zenchiku*. Princeton University Press, 1993. Hb. £30. ISBN 069107352X.

Vallejo, Cesar. *Trilce*, translated by Rebecca Seiferle. Sheep Meadow Press, 1992. Pb. $12.95. ISBN 1878818120.

Will, Frederic. *Translation Theory and Practice: Reassembling the Tower*. Edwin Mellen Press, 1993. Hb. £39.95. ISBN 0773492348.

Williams, Carolyn D. *Pope, Homer, and Manliness: Some Aspects of Eighteenth-Century Classical Learning*. Routledge, 1993. Hb. £37.50. ISBN 0415056004.

Zlateva, Palma, editor and translator. *Translation as Social Action: Russian and Bulgarian Perspectives*. Routledge, 1993. Pb. £14.99. ISBN 041507696X.

Zola, Émile. *Germinal*, translated by Peter Collier. Penguin, 1993. Pb. £5.99. ISBN 0192827014.

JOURNALS RECEIVED

TTR: Traduction, Terminologie, Redaction, Vol 6, no 1: *L'Histoire en Traduction*, edited by Paul St-Pierre. Concordia University (Montreal), 1993. ISBN 2980332909.

Announcements

The British Comparative Literature Association's Triennial International Conference will be held in Edinburgh, Scotland, from 12–15 July 1995. The Conference title will be 'Cities, Gardens, Wildernesses'; papers and participants are warmly invited. Contact:

Dr Howard Gaskill,
Secretary, BCLA,
Dept of German,
University of Edinburgh,
George Square,
Edinburgh EH8 9JX, UK
Tel: +44 31 650 3627; Fax: +44 31 650 6536;
E-Mail: Howard.Gaskill@ed.ac.uk

The Fourth Conference of the International Society for the Study of European Ideas will be held at Karl-Franzens-Universität, Graz, Austria, from 22–27 August 1994. The Conference title will be: 'The European Legacy: Towards New Paradigms', and participants from a wide range of Humanities disciplines are welcome. Prospective participants should contact either/or:

Prof. Ezra Talmor,
Dept of Philosophy,
Haifa University,
Mount Carmel,
Haifa 31999, Israel
Tel: +972 3 938 645; Fax: +972 3 938 6500

Prof. Walter Hölbling,
Institut f. Amerikanistik,
Karl-Franzens-Universität,
Körblergasse 20/I,
A-8010 Graz, Austria
Tel: +43 316 380 2466; Fax: +43 316 384898;
E-Mail bitnet: hoelbling-@edvz.uni-graz.ada.at

The University of Glasgow Centre for European Romanticism announces a conference on 'Romantic Geographies', an 'attempt to renew thinking on Romantics' concepts of geography'. The conference will take place at Glasgow University, 27–29 September 1994. Contact:

Prof. Colin Smethurst,
Centre for European Romanticism,
Dept of French,
University of Glasgow,
Glasgow G12 8QQ, UK
Tel: +44 41 339 8855

Notes for Intending Contributors

Translation and Literature will publish articles, notes, and reviews on literary translation of all periods, focusing on English literature in its foreign relations. It will also publish work on other forms of commerce between writers which involve the use of the past and of the foreign, including those processes described by such terms as 'imitation', 'influence', and 'allusion'. The serial's scope will extend to the activity of 'translation' between literary and non-literary forms.

The Editors invite contributions in the above areas, up to 10,000 words for articles; 3,500 for notes (which should concentrate on factual matters); and 5,000 for Translators' Forum. Contributions (one copy) should be sent to the General Editor or the American Editor, as appropriate. Contributions should conform to MHRA Style; a Style Sheet is available from the General Editor. All contributions will be refereed by at least two scholars, usually including at least one member of the Editorial or Advisory Boards. The editors are sympathetic to a broad range of critical and theoretical approaches.

Contributors of articles will receive one copy of the volume and ten copies of their article. Contributors of other material will receive ten copies of their contribution. Typescripts not accepted for publication will not be returned unless expressly requested.

Books for review are accepted on the understanding that a review cannot be guaranteed, and that books not reviewed are not returnable. A list of books received will, however, appear in each issue of *Translation and Literature*. Books for review should be forwarded to the Review Editor.

TRANSLATION
& LITERATURE

Articles, notes and reviews on literary translation of all kinds and periods, focusing on English literature in its foreign relations. Contributors are drawn from a variety of specialisms and issues discussed are relevant to scholars in English, European and American literature.

Subscription Rates

ISSN 0968-1361
Published annually

Institutional rates		*Postage*
UK and EEC	£21.50	Surface postage is included in the subscription.
Overseas	£21.50	Please add £7.50 for airmail delivery.

Order Form
To subscribe to the next issue of **Translation & Literature**, complete the form below and return to:

Subscriptions
Edinburgh University Press Ltd
22 George Square
Edinburgh
EH8 9LF
UK

Please enter my subscription to **Translation & Literature**, Volume 4, 1995

☐ I enclose the correct remittance (please make cheques payable to Edinburgh University Press Ltd).

☐ Please debit my VISA/Mastercard account number

_____

Expiry date
_____

Name _____

Address _____

_____

_____ Post Code _____